RENEWING
ADMINISTRATION

RENEWING

ADMINISTRATION

Preparing Colleges and Universities for the 21st Century

DIANA G. OBLINGER
Global Education Industry, IBM

RICHARD N. KATZ
EDUCAUSE

EDITORS

Sponsored by EDUCAUSE and IBM

ANKER PUBLISHING COMPANY, INC.
Bolton, Massachusetts

RENEWING ADMINISTRATION
Preparing Colleges and Universities for the 21st Century

ISBN 1-882982-27-4

Composition by Keller and Keller *Designs in Print*
Cover design by Delaney Design

Anker Publishing Company, Inc.
176 Ballville Road
P. O. Box 249
Bolton, MA 01740-0249

www.ankerpub.com

ABOUT THE AUTHORS

WENDELL C. BRASE is vice chancellor for administrative and business services at the University of California, Irvine (UCI). With 20 years of experience in the UC system (13 years at UC Santa Cruz, seven years at UCI), he is responsible for UC Irvine's administrative, financial, and business services. UCI's administrative and business services have received six national awards for process improvement, innovation, and administrative streamlining, including first prize in NACUBO's Higher Education Awards Program (1996); Best Practices Award from CAUSE (1997); and the RIT/USA Today Quality Cup Award (1998). Earlier in his career, Mr. Brase was associate director of the laboratory for laser energetics at the University of Rochester, a laser-fusion project, and assistant director of the Eastman School of Music. He has published several articles in *Planning for Higher Education,* has been a director of the Society for College and University Planning (SCUP), is active in the National Association of College and University Business Officers (NACUBO), and holds two degrees from the Sloan School of Management, Massachusetts Institute of Technology.

MARTIN C. CLAGUE led IBM's initiative to provide a broad range of products and services to businesses that are eager to improve their competitiveness with leading-edge technologies, such as enterprise e-mail, messaging and collaboration, web application servers, and e-business solutions. A former member of IBM's Internet executive council, Mr. Clague was also responsible for a worldwide network of network computing centers providing a focal point for mapping complex network computing and e-business solutions. Mr. Clague's 32-year IBM career included senior management positions in marketing, sales, services, and product development in the United States and Europe. Mr. Clague holds a BA in mathematics from Hiram College. He recently retired from IBM.

THOMAS R. CONNOLLY is an executive consultant in IBM's Higher Education Consulting Group. He is an employee relations expert with significant experience in human resource reengineering, policy, and organizational development. He was the project manager for IBM's human resource reengineering efforts and codeveloped IBM's organization change methodology. Prior to his consulting career, Mr. Connolly was human resources manager at IBM's technology packaging facility in Endicott, New York, during which time he helped introduce programs such as benefits cost sharing and a new performance measurement system. Mr. Connolly attended Northeastern University and received an MA in organization development and human resources from Manhattanville College.

SISTER JANET EISNER, SND, has since 1979 served as president of Emmanuel College where she was previously acting president, member of the faculty, director of admissions, and chair of the English department. She received a BA degree from Emmanuel College, an MA from Boston College, and a PhD in English language and literature from the University of Michigan. She is a graduate of the Harvard University postdoctoral Institute for Educational Management. Northeastern University recognized her with an honorary doctorate of humane letters in 1984. President Eisner is a Sister of Notre Dame de Namur. She serves on numerous boards and commissions, and her prior service includes positions such as being on the executive committee of the Medical, Academic, and Scientific Community Organization, Inc. (MASCO); a member of the American Council on Education's Commission on Credit and Credentials, and a member of the Massachusetts Board of Regents of Higher Education.

MICHAEL FINLAYSON has served as the vice president for administration and human resources at the University of Toronto since 1994, with responsibilities that include administrative management systems. He was appointed vice president for human resources of the University of Toronto in 1991. Finlayson received an MA in history from the University of Melbourne and a PhD from the University of Toronto, where he joined the faculty as a lecturer in the department of history. He was awarded tenure in the department in 1974, became its chair in 1987, and continues to hold an appointment and teach a graduate seminar in 17th-century English history.

WILLIAM J. FLEMING received a PhD in Latin American history from Indiana University. Mr. Fleming served on the faculties of Indiana University–Purdue University, Indianapolis (1976–80) and the University of Texas, Pan American (1980–89). In 1989, he joined the office of information technology (OIT) at Boston College as director, information processing support. In that position he has helped to guide several strategic changes for the OIT, including new support strategies, the development of campus technology standards, and a comprehensive approach to university-wide technology resource management.

BERNARD W. GLEASON was the recipient of the 1992 CAUSE Elite Award in recognition of his career achievements. He has also received the Carnegie-Mellon/American Management Systems Award for achievement in managing information technology. In 1990, Mr. Gleason authored the CAUSE professional paper, "Open Access: A User Information System." This paper has served as a blueprint for colleges and universities in planning the implementation of enterprise-wide, self-service administrative information systems. Mr. Gleason received a BS from Boston College and an MBA from Babson College.

KRISTINE A. HAFNER coordinates the strategic planning and performance measurement initiatives for the nine-campus University of California system. Prior to joining the University of California, she managed a business transformation consulting practice where she assisted a wide range of higher education clients in their efforts to improve the delivery of services and to build institutional performance management systems. Ms. Hafner has contributed to books on leading-edge practices in higher education administration and has spoken on institutional performance measurement at numerous conferences. She holds a BA in modern languages and an MA and PhD in French from the University of Wisconsin. She also studied business administration at the University of Pennsylvania Wharton Graduate School of Business and at IBM's Advanced Business Institute/Harvard Business School seminars.

MICHAEL N. HANDBERG is director of web development at the University of Minnesota, where he is leading a team to develop a web site that integrates all student and human resource services using a customer-focused approach. Mr. Handberg is also working on a web-based project that integrates career, occupational, and educational information from the department of economic security, children, family, and learning and all educational institutions in the state of Minnesota. In addition, he works on Minnesota's virtual university and I-SEEK, a statewide system designed to provide career and education planning. He graduated from the University of Minnesota with a BA in political science and a minor in Chinese. Upon graduation, he worked in the registrar's office as the senior editor of the *Course Guide*, a publication he started as a student. With the emergence of the web, he worked to publish the *Course Guide* on the web, a project that grew to include all of the services and publications in the registrar's office.

JOHN C. HENDERSON is chair of the management information systems department and director of the systems research center at Boston University's school of management. He received a PhD from the University of Texas, Austin. He is a noted researcher, consultant, and executive educator with published papers appearing in journals such as *Management Science, Sloan Management Review, MIS Quarterly, IBM Systems Journal, European Management Journal,* and many others. Currently, his research focuses on three main areas: managing strategic partnerships, aligning business and IT strategies, and knowledge management. Mr. Henderson has served on the editorial boards of *Journal of Management Information Systems, Decision Sciences, and Management Science* where he was the departmental editor. Prior to joining Boston University, Mr. Henderson served on the faculty at the MIT Sloan School of Management.

RICHARD N. KATZ is vice president of EDUCAUSE, where he is responsible for developing and delivering the association's educational program through a variety of publications, international conferences, workshops, seminars, and management institutes. Mr. Katz is also responsible for member and corporate relations, research and development, and outreach. Prior to joining the association, Mr. Katz held a variety of management and executive positions spanning 14 years at the University of California (UC) system. In 1994, he staffed the system's nine-campus improved management initiatives. This initiative defined UC's directions in human resources, capital programs, and institutional accountability. As executive director of business planning and practices, he was responsible for guiding or implementing many strategic management initiatives. At UC, Katz was awarded the Gurevich Prize and the Olsten Award, and he was the second recipient of the university's Innovative Management and Leadership Award. Katz is a well-known conference keynote speaker and presenter. He is the author, coauthor, or editor of more than two dozen books, monographs, and articles on a variety of higher education, management, and technology topics. He received a BA from the University of Pittsburgh and an MBA from UCLA.

SHARON L. KISER serves the University of North Carolina, Charlotte as the sponsored programs financial manager. The position includes financial responsibilities from contracts and grants, gifts, endowments, and affiliated foundations. Her experience is a culmination of 25 years of work in various areas of business administration within the university. She earned a BS in accounting from UNC, Charlotte and continues her education through active participation in professional organizations, including the Society of Research Administrators (SRA) and the National Council of University Research Administrators (NCURA).

ROBERT B. KVAVIK is professor of political science and associate vice president and executive officer at the University of Minnesota. He is the project director of the university's $42 million Enterprise Project which installs new computer and software systems for student services, human resources, web-based systems, and infrastructure. Kvavik joined the faculty in 1968 as a specialist on comparative politics. He now serves as executive officer and chief of staff for the office of the executive vice president and provost and is the university's chief planning officer. He has served as vice provost, assistant vice president for international education, director for research development, director of the center for European studies, and director of graduate studies and associate chair of the political science department. He has extensive experience as a consultant to universities in Europe, Latin America, and Asia in the areas of program assessment, planning, and development.

RUSS LEA received a PhD from the State University of New York College of Environmental Science and Forestry. He began his career at North Carolina State University (NCSU) in the College of Forest Resources as a post-doctoral fellow and was promoted to full professor in 1989. In 1996, he was appointed associate vice chancellor for research, overseeing the office of research administration at NCSU. In this role, Mr. Lea represents the university to external research sponsors, aids the faculty in their search for new funding opportunities, provides planning to increase external funding through new partnerships, and searches for ways to use university research resources to aid the economic development of North Carolina. Also under Mr. Lea's direction is the sponsored programs office, which processed 2,030 proposals in the 1997–98 academic year and received 2,119 awards, with grants valued in excess of $128 million.

TERESA W. LOCKARD is the director of computing support services at the University of Virginia. She holds a BA in government and foreign affairs and an MA in public administration, both from the University of Virginia. After working for the city of Charlottesville, Lockard returned to the university as an employee. She served as director of the budget prior to joining the department of information technology and communications. In addition to leading the departmental computing support program, Lockard's current job responsibilities include training, instructional technology, customer communications and publications, research support, the help desk, and student services.

POLLEY ANN MCCLURE is vice president, chief information officer, and professor of environment science at the University of Virginia. She also has served as dean for academic computing at Indiana University and as executive director of university computing services. Ms. McClure speaks, publishes, and consults extensively on the subjects of information technology management and instructional technologies. In 1993, she won the CAUSE/EFFECT Contributor of the Year Award for her collaborative paper, "Administrative Workstation Project at Indiana University." She also serves on several boards and committees that advance the mission of higher education nationally, including the board of directors of EDUCAUSE.

JAMES P. MCKEE leads a specialized consulting practice within IBM's Education Consulting Group, helping clients transform research administration organizations and processes. He focuses on process improvements that are enabled by emerging electronic research administration initiatives and systems. Over the past five years, Mr. McKee has also worked closely with a consortium of universities to create Grant Application and Management System (GAMS), a comprehensive research administration system. He has facilitated collaborative efforts between this consortium of universities and the electronic commerce initiatives taking place at the federal level. Since joining IBM in 1983, Mr. McKee has worked with federal government and higher education clients to implement projects in such diverse areas as atmospheric modeling, scientific visualization, parallel computing, geographic information systems, statistical modeling, and multimedia instructional computing. He has a BS in mechanical engineering from Virginia Polytechnic Institute.

D. QUINN MILLS is at the Harvard Business School, where he teaches about leadership, strategy, organizations, and human resources; he also advises major corporations and consulting companies. Previously, 1968–75, he taught at MIT's Sloan School of Management. From 1967–74 he had overall responsibility for the American government for wages, prices, and production in the capital goods industries, constituting some 18% of America's gross domestic product. A prolific author, Mr. Mills has written books on business strategy, network organizations, demographics and marketing, empowerment, and union relations. He has won awards for his teaching and is a fellow of the National Academy of Human Resources. Mills earned MA and PhD degrees in economics from Harvard University. He received a BA from Ohio Wesleyan University.

DIANA G. OBLINGER is the academic programs and strategy executive for the IBM Global Education Industry. She is known for her leadership in academic technology, student mobile computing, and distributed learning. Prior to joining IBM, Oblinger was responsible for the academic programs of 17 departments with 250 faculty and over 2,000 students at the University of Missouri, Columbia. She also spent several years on the faculty at the University of Missouri and at Michigan State University in teaching, advising, and research. Ms. Oblinger is the coauthor of *What Business Wants from Higher Education*, the coeditor of *The Learning Revolution: The Challenge of Information Technology in the Academy* and *The Future Compatible Campus: Planning, Designing, and Implementing Information Technology in the Academy*, and the author of numerous papers on enhancing instruction with technology. She has received three outstanding teaching awards, an outstanding research award, and was named Young Alumnus of the Year by Iowa State University. Oblinger holds BS, MS, and PhD degrees from Iowa State University. She has received several awards since joining IBM.

GINGER PINHOLSTER is a science writer who handles national media relations for the University of Delaware's office of public relations. Originally a newspaper reporter, she received a first-place Associated Press Award in 1988, then held media relations positions with the Georgia Institute of Technology Research Institute and the National Academy of Sciences before joining the University of Delaware in 1996. In 1998, she received a silver medal for research, medicine, and science news writing in a national competition of the Council for the Advancement and Support of Science.

JANET M. PUMO is the principal of transformation consulting for higher education with IBM's Global Education Industry. She specializes in strategic planning and organizational effectiveness, using her background to assist institutions in aligning their information technology investments with their strategic priorities. Ms. Pumo has 14 years of experience working with clients in higher education, financial services, manufacturing, and the utilities industries. She has coauthored a case study on business transformation that was published by the Harvard Business School Press. Ms. Pumo graduated from Northwestern University with a BS in psychology and business management. She has continued her professional education with over 600 hours of related coursework in leadership effectiveness.

DAVID P. ROSELLE is the 25th president of the University of Delaware, a position he has held since 1990. He is a graduate of West Chester

University and Duke University and holds a PhD in mathematics. Formerly on the faculties of the University of Maryland and Louisiana State University, he joined the faculty of Virginia Polytechnic Institute and State University in 1974 as professor of mathematics. At Virginia Tech, he was appointed dean of the graduate school in 1979, dean of research and graduate studies in 1981, and provost in 1983, a position he held until assuming the presidency at the University of Kentucky in July 1987. Roselle is the editor of three books and the author of numerous research articles. He also serves as a trustee or board member for several organizations, including the National Science Foundation Directorate for Education and Human Resources Advisory Committee. Among his many awards and recognitions is the CAUSE Recognition Award for Institutional Leadership.

JOHN W. SMITH is a technology planning associate at the University of Virginia. Mr. Smith has served in academic departments as well as in computing support and has managed entrepreneurial start-up projects. Smith's technology career began at Indiana University where he served as the first manager of the small computer support group and helped shape the institution's vision of computing as technical advisor to the dean for academic computing. He later served as facilities director of the computer science department where he led the department's transition from a time-shared UNIX environment to a more flexible, distributed environment.

MANI R. SUBRAMANI is assistant professor of information and decision sciences in the Carlson School of Management at the University of Minnesota, Minneapolis. Mr. Subramani has more than seven years of management experience in the sales, support, and product management functions in the information technology industry. His current area of focus is to help managers make strategic decisions related to the deployment and management of information technologies. His research is directed toward the relationships between information systems providers in organizations and their clients. Mr. Subramani holds a BE (Honors) in electrical and electronics engineering, Birla Institute of Technology and Science, Pilani, India, a PGDM from the Indian Institute of Management, Bangalore, India, and a DBA in information systems from Boston University.

CONTENTS

About the Authors   v
Foreword   xvii
Preface   xxi
Acknowledgments   xxvi

PART I: ADMINISTRATION

1 Capturing the First Keystrokes: A Technological
Transformation at the University of Delaware   3
David P. Roselle and Ginger Pinholster

2 Rethinking "Rethinking Administration":
A Cautionary Tale   20
Michael Finlayson

PART II: EMERGING ADMINISTRATIVE STRATEGIES

3 Understanding e-Business   45
Martin C. Clague

4 Distributed Computing Support   62
Polley Ann McClure, John W. Smith, and Teresa W. Lockard

5 The Shifting Ground Between Markets and Hierarchy:
Managing a Portfolio of Relationships   99
John C. Henderson and Mani R. Subramani

6 The Colleges of the Fenway   126
Sister Janet Eisner, SND

7 Transforming Student Services   139
       Robert B. Kvavik and Michael N. Handberg

8 Transforming Research Administration   155
       James P. McKee, Sharon L. Kiser, and Russ Lea

9 Transforming Human Resources in Higher Education   191
       Thomas R. Connolly

10 Agora: Building the Campus of the Future—Today   218
       Bernard W. Gleason and William J. Fleming

PART III: SUSTAINING CHANGE

11 Partnership for Performance: The Balanced Scorecard Put to
       the Test at the University of California   245
       Kristine A. Hafner

12 Why Some Enterprise Improvement Models Have More
       Lasting Effects Than Others   265
       Wendell C. Brase

13 Managing Change in Higher Education: A Leader's
       Guide   288
       D. Quinn Mills and Janet M. Pumo

14 Renewal as an Institutional Imperative   302
       Richard N. Katz and Diana G. Oblinger

References   315
Index   323

FOREWORD

This volume includes a collection of useful and important chapters describing how various institutions have begun to transform their administrative services. Dealing effectively with the needed transformation within our colleges and universities is one of the greatest challenges facing higher education. As I have written elsewhere,

> Continuing incremental changes to an entrenched conservative tradition have perhaps created an illusion of receptivity in academe to new circumstances. But with the rise of a society based on the knowledge worker, we are now experiencing a different kind of change. It is no longer incremental. It is discontinuous and transformational. Transformational change occurs when something comes about that is so radical it alters the basic performance of daily activities. When simple change becomes transforming change, the desire for continuity becomes a dysfunctional mirage (Battin & Hawkins, 1998).

The contributors to *Renewing Administration* have dismissed this mirage and tried to identify some of the necessary transformational changes that may be required. They raise some alternatives that are useful for all of us in higher education to consider. But beyond these chapters, it is important to recognize the enormous challenge before us, to understand what has led to this need for transformation, and why our institutions are so loathe to move more aggressively in these directions. It seems that a brief examination of the history of administrative computing may shed some light on these dilemmas.

Administrative computing has been a reasonably low priority on most campuses over the last few decades. While there have been exceptions, investments in administrative applications have been made in order to keep the business running, to adapt to new government regulations, or to meet some fairly immediate external pressures. Unlike commercial enterprises, information systems have not been seen as strategic in understanding the "business" of higher education, in developing new markets, or in providing data for in-depth analyses of the cost of production. Instead, for most campuses, the emphasis on maintaining a reliable set of transaction processing systems has been the primary focus. Many of our administrative systems have had a command-and-control focus, driven partially by the technology of the time, but also reinforced by administrative cultures within the business affairs, human resources, and student services units on our campuses. While there may have been the best of intentions in providing better service to the various customers of these systems, the technology did not easily lend itself to such efforts, and funding for such ventures was difficult, if not impossible, given the competing academic and other priorities on most campuses.

In the late 1980s and early 1990s, campuses began, perhaps for the first time in the history of the academy, to experience serious market pressures and unparalleled pressure from a variety of sources to become more accountable. During this period, many institutions of higher education seemed to simultaneously "invent" strategic planning on their campuses, drawing upon the activities, the fads, the practices, and the theories in vogue in the private sector. A large number of campuses began to implement programs of Total Quality Management (TQM), business process reengineering, customer service and satisfaction programs, etc. Many of these efforts were driven by a need for campuses to reduce costs, to streamline, and to become far more efficient. There was great disparity in the success of many of these efforts because of the traditional and fairly conservative nature of our campus cultures. The change process, as described in many of the chapters in this volume, was often a far bigger challenge than the creation of the necessary computer code. Part of the problem in obtaining the necessary "buy in" had to do with convincing various on-campus constituencies that there was a need to change—that there were real threats to our institutions—and that this need called for new and renewed efforts. It shouldn't escape the reader's attention that during this period, networks were still relatively new innovations on most campuses and the World Wide Web didn't even exist.

A second phase of reengineering began in the latter half of the decade, drawing upon the enhanced capabilities of the technology (the ubiquitous nature of hardware, the increasing robustness of the network, the advent of the web for an enormous segment of the society, the emergence of electronic commerce, etc.). However, our campuses were also provided with an unprecedented motivation to draw upon these technological opportunities as they faced the potential collapse of their systems because of the "Year 2000" (Y2K) problem, the technological threat to our ability to continue to use the systems which perform the necessary daily transactions. The Y2K issue has caused a significant increase in funding for administrative operations, but there appears to be a concomitant expectation that new functionality, more "friendly" user interfaces, and possibly radically different services will emanate from these investments—expectations far beyond just correcting the software errors associated with the millennium.

The point of this historical perspective is to point out how episodic the attention to the administration of our institutions has been. Today, there is an important and radically increased level of interaction between technology, organizational structures, business functions, and the new demands of our customers. This new synergy gives us the opportunity to rethink how our institutions of higher education operate and serve various constituencies. The challenge to all of us is to determine whether or not we have the collective will to continue to enhance services and renew the way in which our campuses are administered and managed when there isn't an ominous crisis such as Y2K looming. The need for constant renewal is critical, as emphasized by John Gardner, in his classic book, *Self-Renewal: The Individual and the Innovative Society.* In it he states:

> When organizations and societies are young, they are flexible, fluid, not yet paralyzed by rigid specialization, and willing to try anything once. As the organization or society ages, vitality diminishes, flexibility gives way to rigidity, creativity fades, and there is a loss of capacity to meet challenges from unexpected directions. Call to mind the adaptability of youth and the way in which that adaptability diminishes over the years. Call to mind the vigor and recklessness of some new organizations and societies—our own frontier settlements, for example—and reflect on how frequently these qualities are buried under the weight of tradition and history (Gardner, 1963).

The chapters that follow in this book illustrate a number of efforts to reclaim some of the vitality and adaptability that Gardner described and that is so badly needed in higher education today. The authors illuminate technological applications and practices that make institutions both more effective and more efficient. However, in order to really transform and renew our institutions, certain questions need to be addressed and incorporated into the way in which we approach administrative issues on campus. These include:

- Can we define the desirable outcomes we are seeking?
- Can we define processes that allow our institutions to more readily accept change?
- Can these efforts really contribute to transforming our campus infrastructures, not just enhance our current processes incrementally?
- Can creative electronic commerce solutions be designed that serve students as well as generate income?

These chapters provide us specific information, but also increase our insight into these larger issues. They help us not only think about how we do our business, but also what business we are in.

I hope you, too, will find these viewpoints provocative and useful as you attempt to meet these challenges on your own campus.

Brian L. Hawkins
President
EDUCAUSE

REFERENCES

Battin, P., & Hawkins, B. L. (1998). *The mirage of continuity: Reconfiguring academic information resources in the 21st century.* Washington, DC: Council on Library and Information Resources and the Association of American Universities.

Gardner, J. W. (1963). *Self-renewal: The individual and the innovative society.* New York, NY: Harper & Row.

PREFACE

Many institutions are working to renew administration. They are eliminating unnecessary work, dismantling unproductive policies, and reengineering processes to achieve efficiencies and create a more learner-centered environment. Much of the renewal flows from a change in how we view the work of the organization. For administrative functions—student services, research administration, human resources, and so on—our view is shifting from one that was focused on regulation and compliance to one of customer service, flexibility, and adaptability.

This volume deals expressly with the administrative dimension of the higher education enterprise: the environment, processes, and tools that make it possible for educators to deliver instruction, for students to learn, and for researchers to produce meaningful scholarship. The insights reflected by this volume's contributors suggest both a legacy of and need for change in a number of arenas.

The opening chapter describes a series of transformations made at the University of Delaware, many of which were stimulated by the philosophy of "capturing keystrokes rather than reams of paper." Roselle and Pinholster describe the changes made at Delaware including one-stop shopping to improve student services, creating a better living and learning environment, and transforming learning. Information technology (IT) was used to improve administrative efficiency and reduce the cost of administration; however, using IT was not a goal in itself.

Finlayson uses reengineering at the University of Toronto as the basis of his "cautionary tale" in Chapter 2. Prompted by six years of massive budget reductions, too many confusing rules/procedures, multiple hand-offs, as well as unfriendly and inconsistent systems, he traces the university's process of rethinking administration. He describes reengineering successes (purchasing cards, improved turn-around time for reports, etc.) yet details some of the human costs (loss of jobs, fear). We are cautioned that linking reengineering and systems renewal with downsizing was not wise.

One of the trends predicted to change how business is conducted is e-commerce. In Chapter 3, Clague describes e-business, a broader concept than e-commerce. E-business is much more than buying and selling goods and services over the web. Although e-business sounds like it would have limited applicability to higher education, many concepts apply. Discussions encompass providing service, promoting brand awareness, extending market reach, distributing information, delivering distance learning, managing business partners, and web-based transactions.

How to provide support for IT is a persistent issue, particularly since IT is distributed across campus. McClure, Smith, and Lockard describe models of distributed computing support in Chapter 4. The architecture of distributed computing support will vary, however, based on academic culture, governance, etc. Support topologies are detailed along with definitions of responsibility and authority. Four examples of distributed support programs illustrate how the principles can be adapted to yield success in very different environments.

In Chapter 5, Henderson and Subramani explore the concept of partnerships. Many higher education institutions are turning more and more to partnerships or strategic alliances to enhance instruction, research, and institutional support. The relationships described range from those that are similar to a market exchange to ones that are so seamlessly integrated that it would be difficult to differentiate between the partners. The authors develop a taxonomy of four different types of relationships. Each carries implications about the level of trust, governance system, organizational structure, and the use of information technology.

In Chapter 6, Sister Janet Eisner describes the shared services model developed by five small colleges in Boston: the Colleges of the Fenway. They developed a series of collaborative principles that have enabled them to work together. In many respects, they leverage their collective strengths (and purchasing power) so that they can remain viable as independent, small colleges. Among the programs instituted, to date, are cross-registration, specific academic initiatives, and cost savings through joint purchasing (e.g., insurance). College and university leaders of the future will need to do much more connecting and combining rather than dividing and conquering.

"Transforming Student Services" (Chapter 7) details the context for change in student services at the University of Minnesota and the emergence of a different vision where student transactions will be completed automatically and be self-initiated. Kvavik and Handberg describe the need for change in business practices and culture, in addition to the technical changes required. The move from a silo-based to a one-stop shopping approach is detailed. Beyond the technical and conceptual frameworks required, much of the ultimate success of the transformation rests on the new professional roles that are required for staff as well as for users.

Transformation of the research enterprise is described in Chapter 8. The changes in research administration range from a larger role in economic development to creating hybrid organizations that can deal with multidisciplinary problems. According to McKee, Kiser, and Lea, many of the changes revolve around moving from a compliance-based philosophy to one of service. Implications for reengineering, new professional roles, and information technology are detailed.

In "Transforming Human Resources" (Chapter 9), Connolly describes the changes occurring in college and university human resources programs. His focus is on 1) what works well in HR, 2) best practices, 3) a vision for how HR should operate, and 4) how to change the processes and ensure buy-in. Today HR is being called on to do more than transaction processing: It is being asked to take a stronger leadership role and deliver better service. This chapter's appendix contains an extensive list of best practices for various HR segments (e.g., employee relations, selection and hiring, performance assessment, etc.).

Gleason and Fleming describe the creation of Project Agora and its highly intuitive, customer friendly intranet (Chapter 10). The philosophies guiding Project Agora are described (e.g., "customer neighborhoods," just-in-time information delivery, do-it-yourself, one-stop shopping, etc.). Also, a series of intranet principles are defined followed by the details of specific features. The system presents users with a series of options that save time and eliminate guesswork using various workflow engines. Applications range from the generation of class lists to recording grades for faculty or establishing email accounts or ordering tickets for students.

In Chapter 11, Hafner describes the balanced scorecard and its application to the University of California system. The balanced scorecard framework provides a way to look at performance from multiple perspectives (financial, internal business measures, customer perspective, as well as innovation and learning perspectives). The original methodology of Kaplan and Norton was adapted to the vision and goals of the University of California system. Hafner describes the development of a performance measurement culture as well as the use of the balanced scorecard as a planning tool. The final section deals with lessons learned.

In a chapter that deals with enterprise improvement models, Brase describes the UC Irvine change management model (Chapter 12). The model is based on 1) teamwork principles, 2) simplification of goals and principles, and 3) effectiveness principles, such as accountability and performance. He describes how these elements were incorporated into the performance evaluation process, organizational goals, reward systems, and recognition programs. His analysis of the data shows that management qualities provide the foundation for workplace respect. This is the precursor to workplace cooperation, which, in turn, leads to unit performance. A critical conclusion is that supervisors' behaviors must support the change management model if there is to be sustainable change.

Pumo and Mills describe the philosophies of change management and apply them to higher education in Chapter 13. The chapter advocates that leaders keep in mind Kotter's principles of change management in order to integrate as much change as possible into the organization. The principles discussed include 1) establish a sense of urgency, 2) form a powerful coalition, 3) create a vision, 4) communicate the vision, 5) empower others to act on the vision, 6) consolidate improvements and produce more change, and 7) institutionalize new approaches.

The final chapter (Chapter 14) brings the various themes of the volume together. In "Renewal as an Institutional Imperative," colleges and universities are challenged to renew themselves with rapid, concerted, and planned action along many fronts. These areas include institutional leadership and governance; culture, organization, and human resources; and information technology, resources, and services. The ability of colleges and universities to seize the opportunity to retain preeminence in preparing individuals for citizenship and economic prosperity in the Knowledge Age will depend on those institutions' abilities to renew themselves.

We believe that colleges and universities are remarkable and unusual organizations. Their durability and sustainability derives, in part, from the ability to adapt to changing conditions. We hope this volume will provide our colleagues in higher education with the philosophies, concepts, and examples that will enable them to create stronger and more vibrant institutions.

Diana G. Oblinger

Richard N. Katz

ACKNOWLEDGMENTS

We would like to thank our colleagues who have shared their renewing administration efforts with us. We hope that this collection of insights will help others as they seek to rethink, renew, and revitalize higher education administration.

—*Diana G. Oblinger and Richard N. Katz*

I would like to thank my colleagues in business and academia for challenging us with new ideas and presenting opportunities to continually grow. I owe much to my parents for their support and all they have taught me. And, I am indebted to my family for their encouragement and devotion.

—*Diana G. Oblinger*

I would like to thank my many friends in higher education whose innovations provide a constant source of inspiration. I would also like to thank my mother, whose courage is a source of strength. Most of all, I thank Peggy and Tony. Their love is my source of renewal.

—*Richard N. Katz*

PART I

Administration

1

Capturing the First Keystrokes: A Technological Transformation at the University of Delaware

David P. Roselle and Ginger Pinholster

INTRODUCTION

The University of Delaware (UD) has undergone a technological transformation that will continue well into the 21st century. The uses of technology to improve administrative efficiency and reduce the cost of administration and the uses of technology to enhance learning experiences were not themselves goals. Instead, these were tactical decisions to reallocate funds in support of increases in faculty and staff compensation, increases in student scholarships, and improved facilities and access to the most modern equipment.

Much credit is due to the many associates who have so willingly, enthusiastically, and intelligently participated in the university's transformation. Their stories, told here, illuminate the transformation of the University of Delaware.

TRANSFORMATIONS

Bright green, yellow, and purple objects dance across a World Wide Web screen, bringing to life the inner workings of a modern photo-copier. As a long, purple wire rolls from right to left, the flat, green photoconducting plate suddenly turns red, illustrating a positive charge. Seconds later, a blue light flashes, illuminating an original document, and the copy plate is bombarded by black specks of nega-tively charged toner fluid, hitchhiking on larger carrier particles.

Though it resembles a cartoon, this simple animation helps non-science majors at the University of Delaware master the complex mechanics of photoconductivity. Similarly, undergraduates enrolled in associate professor George H. Watson's introductory physics courses can explore the principles governing motor rotations—with-out getting their hands dirty. Watson still brings mechanical devices into the classroom, but he also creates computerized lessons to sup-plement hands-on teaching and reinforce important concepts.

From web-connected residence hall rooms, classrooms, and com-puting sites campus-wide, Watson says students can replay the ani-mations "to their hearts' content." The goal of enhanced student understanding is more readily attained because of the self-paced nature of this form of instruction.

During classes in Gore Hall, Watson explores his web-based lessons on a wall-sized screen, using a touch-controlled master panel to manipulate the sound volume and image quality. Students log onto laptops, or swivel in theater-style chairs to form small groups. In this way, the classic Georgian architecture of the university's new 65,000-square-foot classroom facility works in tandem with instructional technologies to help students become lifelong and active learners—a key institutional goal. With guidance from Watson, who works closely with a UD team of nationally recognized pioneers in problem-based learning, undergraduates are becoming critical thinkers, particularly through research experiences in web-connected classrooms.

Web lessons help UD undergraduates learn to appreciate the sci-entific process and the world around them, regardless of whether they plan to pursue technical careers. Watson's approach to classroom learning and his innovative use of technology exemplifies the univer-sity's dual focus on undergraduate discovery and computing power.

His initiatives, together with similar efforts by faculty colleagues, have launched UD into the elite ranks of 10 US institutions that in 1997 the National Science Foundation said were demonstrating "bold leadership" in classrooms. The university's strength in information technologies also earned a CAUSE Award for Excellence in Campus Networking in 1994, when UD was described as a model for other institutions of higher learning across the country. In 1995, UD earned another CAUSE award for best practices in service. And, in 1998, UD was ranked 11th in the nation—fourth among state-assisted institutions—by *Yahoo! Internet Life* magazine, in its "Most Wired" campus listing.

This metamorphosis of UD's computing resources didn't happen overnight. Creating an environment capable of producing two Rhodes scholars within the past several years—including 1998 winner Douglas Mauro de Lorenzo—required reengineering every office, every laboratory, every library, and every student space on five different campuses, from the university's tree-lined central mall in Newark to the Hugh R. Sharp campus off Roosevelt Inlet in Lewes. The attitude is that network access should be viewed as we view electricity: everywhere available and free to the end user.

The university's investment in information technologies has not been trivial. But the return on that expenditure has surpassed even the most optimistic predictions in terms of recruitment and retention of faculty, staff, and students; enhanced services and resources for faculty, staff, and students; increased institutional efficiency; the ability to decrease or reallocate personnel; reduced paper costs; and other benefits.

BEGINNING WITH BURROUGHS

It was not until 1984 that the university began to move away from an outdated processing system produced by Burroughs (a company that later became part of Unisys) toward an online, IBM-based central computing facility. Executive vice president David E. Hollowell, who came to the University of Delaware in 1988, noted that computing-wise the university was in the dark ages and had administrative systems and procedures that dated back to the days when UD was a much smaller institution. The Burroughs equipment dated from the mid-1970s, according to Daniel J. Grim, executive director of Network and Systems Services at UD. Those administrative offices connected to Burroughs did so through dumb terminals, and a few faculty were connected to Arpanet, an early 1980s predecessor to the Internet.

A fledgling campus network, including three nodes at key sites, was installed by the late 1980s. Then, in 1990, a new UD administration announced a series of sweeping network improvements which were implemented under the direction of Hollowell and Susan J. Foster. Soon thereafter, Foster was promoted to vice president for information technologies, and in 1997, Foster was elected to serve as chair of the board of directors for CAUSE.

In 1998, those efforts resulted in a campus-wide network with a backbone bandwidth capable of processing more than one billion bits of information per second (bps), delivering 10 million bps to desktops and residence hall rooms. Such progress is a far cry from the computing power available to UD students in the late 1980s when the university's system delivered ". . . somewhere in the neighborhood of 700 packets of information per second," Grim says.

To make the leap from 700 packets to 10 million bps per second, UD first had to install a 700-mile-long network and replace virtually all existing hardware and software. The early days of that monumental effort were "like a roller coaster ride," Grim recalls. By 1993, he adds, "We had accomplished things I never would have imagined could happen." Every student's residence room had been hard-wired to the Ethernet, an "on-ramp" to the Internet. Every classroom and faculty office had been hard-wired by the following summer, and by 1995, the entire campus was equipped with outlets providing direct access to the rapidly expanding information superhighway.

Throughout this process, information technologies at UD were purchased, customized, and installed to enrich the academic experience for each student—specifically by capturing keystrokes, or ideas, rather than reams of paper. When a user's first keystrokes are captured electronically, they can be harnessed to achieve savings of time, paper, and money. Faculty members and support staff who have been freed from tedious exercises, such as typing and retyping manuscripts and administrative forms, can focus instead on more elevated responsibilities. Likewise, administrators provide faster, less expensive service to students and faculty when they have been freed from mountains of repetitive paperwork. Finally, the educational experience becomes more pleasant and rewarding and the students who, for example, drop and add courses simply via phone or computer are actually participants in a process that has been reengineered to be more accurate, provide better service, and require far less staff support.

From the outset of UD's technological transformation, administrators concluded that information technologies should support key institutional goals. Throughout the 1990s, several goals have been emphasized.

◆ UD should be a student-friendly institution.

◆ Compensation levels for UD faculty and staff should be competitive.

◆ Financial aid and scholarships for students should increase.

◆ The living and learning environments should be excellent.

Technology was not installed haphazardly, or simply for its own sake, but as a tool for broadening educational opportunities while also supporting a leaner, more efficient university administration. In all cases, Hollowell says, "UD strives to integrate cutting-edge technologies into the whole fabric of the institution, from student life to instruction, from administration to resources."

PURSUING THE PAPERLESS CAMPUS

In February 1998, there were 1,250 UD employees who made 5,323 purchases using a new electronic accounting system that was established in 1997. Those transactions represented $1.7 million worth of purchases, an average purchase amount of $321.

Before 1997, many of these purchases would have required preparing and processing multiple copies of paper forms. A "Purchase Order with Check" (POWC) program accounted for roughly 30,000 transactions, totaling $4 million worth of business, reports George S. Walueff, assistant director of UD's office of purchasing.

Under the new program, each UD unit issues a purchasing card to designated employees, allowing them to complete day-to-day transactions in real-time. Vendors receive immediate payment from the credit card company, which then routes a single invoice to UD. Monthly statements are available on the web for review by cardholders and others. Administrators, meanwhile, "have more time to be good managers, because they don't have to push mountains of paper through the pipeline," Walueff says.

UD's push toward an electronic campus results in more efficient administration, as well as improved resources for the entire academic community. In the Hugh M. Morris Library, for example, an electronic system for processing book orders now increases operational efficiency and provides patrons with more complete information about collections. In the not-so-distant past, reports Josie Williamson, head of library acquisitions, acquisitions were based on paper files. "The library staff had these multipart forms filed all over the place," she says, "and it was very difficult to keep track of them. Now, it's all electronic and patrons who use the DELCAT [computerized card-catalog system] can quickly see when an order is due to be delivered."

In addition to DELCAT, which is accessible through U-Discover!, UD's award-winning campus information system, the library maintains multiple networked databases, covering topics ranging from folklore and nursing to political science. Since fall 1996, meanwhile, two journal databases, IAC Expanded Academic Index ASAP and Business Index ASAP, have provided access to thousands of complete and full-text journal articles online.

Another new UD library resource, the Current Contents/Table of Contents system, lets faculty and students log onto the Internet to scan content pages and article abstracts from 7,000 scholarly journals. Says Susan Brynteson, director of libraries, "UD is moving from a 'just-in-case' library procurement to 'just-in-time' document delivery." Updated weekly, the system includes 200 searchable subject categories—from art to zoology, explains Gregg A. Silvis, assistant director for library computing systems. From any faculty office computer and those in most faculty residences, a faculty member can access an abstract or summary of a desired journal article. If the UD library does not own a copy of the journal, the faculty member can order it online. With orders almost always completed within 48 hours and often within 24 hours, faculty members have been enthusiastic about this remarkable convenience.

UD's reengineering of administrative processes has helped curb overhead, has resulted in significant savings campus-wide, and has made available expanded resources for academic functions. Between fiscal year 1990 and fiscal year 1999, funds allocated for academic units have grown by 57% (5.1% compounded annually), while administrative budgets grew by 28% (2.8% compounded annually), according to a nine-year analysis completed recently by the university's budget office.

The growth of academic budgets, made possible in part by computer-driven advancements in administrative efficiency, coupled with a more than 130% jump in private gifts between 1990 and 1998, also helped support a dramatic increase in student financial aid, which more than tripled during the same period, budget director Carol Rylee reports. Moreover, she says, the growth in funds allocated to academic units would be even greater except for the fact that fringe benefits (a category that increased by 63% over the nine-year period) are not budgeted in the academic units.

Along with fringe benefits, academic salaries at UD have increased. When compared to 24 other top-rated public and private universities in Delaware, Pennsylvania, New Jersey, Maryland, Virginia, and the District of Columbia, the university's total compensation for full professors was highly competitive, ranking sixth in 1998—up from 16th in 1990. Similar improvements have been achieved in terms of compensation for junior faculty, and staff salaries are well above the national and local medians.

A clear result of UD's management strategy, the university's salary and scholarship progress was achieved despite the national financial downturn of the early 1990s, a period when the university's appropriation from the state of Delaware remained modest, increasing by about 1.3% annually.

A faster, leaner administration, happier faculty and students, and more advanced electronic resources all help make UD a better buy and a more rewarding experience for incoming students. UD was named a best buy by *US News & World Report* and by *Money* magazine, where reviewers also included the university among the top 25 publicly supported US universities in 1996.

'ONE-STOP SHOPPING' IMPROVES STUDENT LEARNING

Tory Windley, now purchasing director, was a UD freshman in 1969. In those days, she says, many students complained of the difficulties they encountered trying to complete administrative tasks such as course registration and fee payments. "Everybody went to drop and add courses on the same day," she recalls. "You had to wait in a long line. Courses with open seats were posted on big boards, but the seats were usually gone by the time you got to the front of the line. It took all day just to drop and add courses. My first semester was a disaster because I didn't understand the process."

Those days, fortunately, are long gone. In August 1992, the university opened a centralized student services building, providing students with "one-stop shopping." At the new facility, it was possible for students to quickly register for courses, change course selections, print copies of their course schedules, or complete any of the numerous other administrative tasks required of students. Since later in 1992, the services that are electronic have been made available as web-based services at all places and at all times of the day and night.

The electronic system and centralized services "save students several days of administrative work each semester," says university registrar Joseph V. DiMartile. Staff also benefit because students can independently update and maintain much of their electronic files. A new address or a new telephone number, for example, can be added quickly to the database by the student, freeing UD staff from the task of maintaining such data.

In this way, UD has once again "captured the keystrokes" of students. That's because the information system is open to the entire campus, while providing needed confidentiality. Developing this accessible yet secure system required overcoming many technological hurdles, notes Carl W. Jacobson, director of Management Information Services (MIS).

"The big issue for UD is customer service," Jacobson says. "MIS 'customers' are students, parents, faculty members, and researchers. Originally, our administrative software systems, just as had been the case for the earlier paper files on the students, were off limits for students. To get service, students had to go to a counter and ask a person to go into that computer system and help them. Today, the administrative software systems no longer serve as a locked filing cabinet. Our students themselves can gain access to any data maintained about them."

As a result, student files are more accurate. Students also report a higher degree of satisfaction with the services they receive from UD staff. Camilla "Kay" Morris is a case in point. When UD publicized a national search for a new academic provost in 1993, Morris, a cashier in the student services building, was promptly nominated for the job. Morris had won the heart of student Rob Wherry, who sang her praises in an editorial published by UD's student newspaper, *The Review.* "For two weeks every semester, this woman is flooded with thousands of students who need to pay bills, sign their financial aid checks, and take care of many other nagging things," Wherry wrote, yet "the smile is always there, always."

With her smile and soft North Carolina accent, Morris exemplifies the spirit of a student-friendly institution—one of UD's four key goals. "When someone comes to my window as a customer, I try to put myself in their place," says Morris. "I think about my own children. They were college students, too, and I wanted people to treat them well. Freshmen are sometimes frightened to be so far from home. It's up to us to help them feel at ease."

Working in the student services building requires patience and a sincere commitment to students, Morris and others say. The building houses a team of generalists who answer a broad range of questions. If they are stumped by a student's question, they pick up a telephone to track down an answer and then request approval to provide that answer to all students who later present that question. And, student questions definitely keep generalists on their toes. "One student came in because his mom had ordered sheets for his bed," former generalist Linda Diehl recalls, with a laugh. "He wanted to know where to go and pick them up because he wanted to go to bed that night and he didn't have any sheets. We tracked down the information for him. It was all part of the job."

A BETTER LIVING AND LEARNING ENVIRONMENT

Across campus, and at every step of their education, UD students encounter computer-based technologies. Indeed, many incoming students first browse the UD network while completing an electronic admissions application. Grade transcripts still must be sent to UD through the mail, but new optical scanning technologies at UD soon will also make that process electronic. By contrast, the university no longer mails grades to students; instead grades can be accessed by either telephone or computer.

At the graduate level, there is an online process that allows faculty members to review and communicate about applications via the intranet. Our improved student services provisions have generated significant interest among administrators from competing institutions—an average of two institutions per week since 1994 visiting the Delaware campus to view our unique system. Also, an online undergraduate admissions process was launched in 1996 when 394 prospective undergraduates used it to complete their applications; 1,423 did so in 1997 and, by early May 1998, UD had received 2,423 online applications for the fall semester.

Once enrolled at UD, all new students receive an email account and a voice-message mailbox and have a digital ID photo taken. The digital photos are network accessible to assist advising, student life, and other needs. Before they can make use of these resources, however, incoming students must successfully complete an Electronic Community Citizenship Examination (ECCE). "ECCE" in Latin means "behold," and it is part of a campus-wide Responsible Computing Awareness Program designed to promote the productive use of technology, while delineating abuses and their consequences. ECCE was selected for a 1995 Award for Best Practices in Higher Education Information Resources from CAUSE.

Supplementing the ethical computing exam, an entry-level course in computers and information systems offered each semester by the department of computer and information sciences, plus a variety of continuing education courses, provide new and returning UD students with basic computing skills. Fundamental use of computing is integrated into the freshman English course. On a day-to-day basis, students can always receive technical support from UD's Information Technologies Help Center or from the Technology Solutions Center which provides assistance in setting up and operating differently configured workstations.

The remarkably pervasive nature of technology at UD, coupled with the strength of two key units—the department of electrical and computer engineering and the department of computer and information sciences—means that students within every discipline are continuously introduced and reintroduced to some of the most sophisticated voice, video, and data technologies currently available at any global corporation or university.

Within the department of art, for example, UD students learn the HTML computer programming language. Basic programming skills give them a leg up on the competition for internships and jobs because students who understand HTML coding can display their work in electronic portfolios.

Students like Kevin Kruger, a 1997 graduate who created a web site for UD's Visual Communications (VC) Group while earning his degree, are well-prepared to enter the increasingly computer-intensive business environment. Kruger, now a multimedia designer at the Lyons Studio in Wilmington, Delaware, fine-tuned his skills by working with VC Director Ray Nichols, an artist and designer of Authorware, a multimedia software program for teaching graphic design. Kruger spent many hours in UD's Art Computing Site, where a variety of workstations include 19 web-connected G3 Macintosh computers capable of capturing sound and full-motion video images.

In the department of English, the approximately 100 students concentrating in business and technical writing can create literary essays or technical manuals using sound cards and compact discs, as well as words. Of course, with pervasive access to the Internet, would-be writers at UD also may view the original manuscript of *Beowulf*, the first major literary work in English and any of numerous other manuscripts.

"Any writer who manipulates technical information must be able to interface productively with current technologies," notes Deborah Andrews, professor of English and editor of the *Business Communication Quarterly*, the leading US publication in business communications pedagogy. UD's efforts to enhance business communications through technology are so well respected in the field that the National Council on Programs in Technical and Scientific Communication held its 1998 annual meeting at UD, Andrews says. The program's faculty roster includes such luminaries as John R. Brockmann, award-winning member of the Society for Technical Communication, and other prestigious professional organizations, Andrews adds.

The college of business and economics also has parlayed UD's strength in information technologies to expand academic opportunities for students and help graduates compete more effectively for jobs. At the graduate level, UD's business faculty recently began offering a concentration in information technologies, allowing students to investigate emerging issues such as electronic commerce. At the undergraduate level, a minor program in management information/decision support systems (MIS) helps prepare students to serve as effective liaisons between technical professionals or "computer people" and "business people"—the managers in charge of day-to-day operations and other end uses.

In 1998, at the urging of Delaware's Business Roundtable, the state agreed to initiate funding for a large expansion of the MIS option in the College of Business and Economics. This will involve curricular revision so that information technology becomes a major part of the academic program for all business and economics students with additional courses available to non-business majors. There is also financial support provided for new equipment and new faculty lines.

Students like Clement Bason, a recent UD graduate and former MIS program participant now working for Andersen Consulting, tackle problems such as how best to develop an inventory management system for a large firm. Solving such problems may require, for example, the development of a new algorithm, selection of appropriate accounting software, or memory upgrades to existing computer technologies. "The MIS projects address functional areas of business, and therefore, they support UD's major programs in accounting, business administration, economics, and finance," economics professor Erwin Saniga says. "The goal is to solve the problem and to be able to use all appropriate technologies."

In the department of electrical and computer engineering, meanwhile, the addition of a second major in 1996 resulted in a doubling of enrollment figures as well as externally funded research. Faculty member Daniel W. van der Weide—one of only 19 researchers in 1998 to receive a Young Investigator Program Award from the US Office of Naval Research and one of 20 scientists in 1997 to win a National Science Foundation Presidential Early Career Award for Scientists and Engineers—recently was named director of a new $2.88 million Center for Nanomachined Surfaces. Supported by Governor Thomas R.

Carper and the Delaware economic development office, the center has been tasked to develop the highest-precision polished, or "nanomachined," photomask surfaces for patterning computer chips.

Another faculty member in that department, Guang R. Gao, director of the sprawling Computer Architecture and Parallel Systems Laboratory (CAPSL), will create the entire blueprint for a superfast petaflops computer, capable of processing one million-billion commands or floating point operations per second. Guang, a leading expert on the multithreaded program model, a processing strategy gaining attention from high-performance chip and system designers, has already proposed a new computing concept to address a key technological hurdle. To bridge the "speed gap" between the machine's superconducting microprocessors and its memory units, he says, information from different sites within the lower-memory hierarchy must be converted into uniform "capsules" or parcels of information—before processing.

Professor David L. Mills, also of the department of electrical and computing engineering, was a key architect of the Internet, vice president Susan Foster reports. "David was considered the right hand of Vinton Cerf, who is described by most as the 'Father of the Internet.'" Foster now directs UD's participation in the national effort to develop a second Internet, which she describes as a kind of "high-occupancy vehicle" lane for research and educational institutions. The effort received a boost in mid-April, when Vice President Al Gore announced plans by three major communications companies to install a megafast national data pipeline for at least 100 US universities. As an early and active participant in the Internet II project, Foster says, UD will be a direct beneficiary of these faster computing speeds.

UD's ECE program allows students to "look at the big picture, such as the interaction of operating systems with hardware," says Gonzalo R. Arce, associate department chair. Students who want to focus on the intricacies of various computer languages, programming principles, and algorithms typically enroll in the computer and information sciences (CIS) program.

Currently serving approximately 300 undergraduate majors and 100 graduate students, enrollment in the CIS program "has increased by 30% over a five-year period," the department's associate chair, Richard Albright notes, "and the numbers seem to be growing more rapidly all the time." New contracts and grants, meanwhile, have jumped by at least $1 million annually for the past several years.

Among the department's 18 full-time faculty members and three research scientists, three received UD's Excellence in Teaching Award within the last five years. "Given the size of the department," Albright says, "that's an extraordinary accomplishment. It means that our faculty take the job of teaching very seriously, and they are doing a good job."

Computational facilities available to the departments of ECE and CIS are among the most advanced on UD's Newark campus. Two central facilities, shared by the ECE and CIS groups, connect an extensive network of approximately 200 workstations. All are connected to a high-speed Ethernet switch providing high performance coupled with security. A Cray J90 high-speed system and a series of Silicon Graphics workstations also are included on the long list of systems available to students enrolled in those programs

TRANSFORMATIONAL LEARNING EXPERIENCES

As technology has become pervasive across the UD campus, it has transformed the teaching and learning process, too. Life-changing learning experiences in the classroom, supported by computing technologies, can help undergraduates compete more effectively for jobs by allowing them to think more creatively. In the 21st century, says Harold B. White II, a professor of chemistry and biochemistry and a national leader in techniques related to problem-based learning (PBL), "Students will need to be problem solvers, who understand the value of 'metacognition'—that is, the art of reflecting upon the way we learn."

To help students master this skill, he notes, "We must change the way we teach." UD educators are meeting this challenge, in large part, by customizing PBL methods, which require students to solve real-world problems through meticulous research, just as a scientist would put a promising theory to the test. In associate professor Chandra Reedy's art conservation classes, for example, undergraduates investigate the authenticity of a sixth-century BC sculpture. "Instead of lecturing to my students, I turn them into art detectives," Reedy explains. "They learn about art history, archaeology, and chemistry. They also have to talk about business ethics and whether or not they should purchase a sculpture that might be a fake."

Working hand-in-hand with PBL techniques, computer technologies also have played a key role in UD's shift toward more active learning in classrooms. Mastering abstract concepts, such as an object's resistance to electrical flow, becomes easier when students can view a step-by-step illustration of the process, George Watson says. Web-based instructional materials help take students out of the "passive, listening-to-a-lecture" mode, he says, prompting them to actively visualize problems from many perspectives. By interacting with a computer, with each other, and with instructors, Watson says, "students develop skills with lasting value, such as effective communication, mastery of analytical thinking, teamwork, independent learning, and strategies for making the best use of all available resources."

The Institute for Transforming Undergraduate Education (ITUE), established in April 1997 with a $200,000 National Science Foundation grant, allows an interdisciplinary UD faculty team to explore a broad range of active-learning strategies, including online resources for instruction. A host of similar initiatives at UD include a recent teaching, learning, and technology roundtable, which resulted in detailed recommendations for the appropriate use of technology in classrooms. In the fall of 1998, the university was informed of an upcoming announcement of an additional, large grant from one of the leading private foundations in support of the involvement of many additional faculty and students in problem-based learning.

Through UD's department of continuing and distance education, meanwhile, a new course on Internet literacy "uses the Internet to deliver a course about the Internet," says Mary V. Pritchard, manager of the division's credit programs and student services. Open to returning students as well as traditional undergraduates, the course covers the conceptual background and online skills students need to become Internet literate, she says. Teaching this new program will be UD faculty member Fred T. Hofstetter, creator of Podium software. Still at the forefront of multimedia tools for incorporating audio and video clips into classroom lectures, Podium is commonplace now in classrooms nationwide.

Another new course allows students to become certified webmasters. Through the continuing education program, older and returning students also may complete a more comprehensive computer applications certificate program. In its 30-year history, this program has served 4,428 students, says T. Gregory Lynch, senior program manager for computer and information technology education.

UD's efforts to promote technological literacy have not been limited to the campus community. Faculty and staff routinely reach out to surrounding neighborhoods, businesses, and government agencies through continuing education services and other outreach initiatives.

English professor John R. Brockmann, for example, helps nonprofit groups and companies develop web pages and newsletters using current technologies. Organizations such as Homeward Bound Inc., a homeless shelter, benefit from these types of collaborative efforts. So do UD students, who inevitably gain an enhanced understanding of their role as productive citizens in their communities— and the ways that technology can make our world a better place to live, work, and learn.

WHAT'S NEXT

The University of Delaware will continue efforts to address the goals mentioned earlier (a student-friendly institution, competitive faculty compensation levels, an increase in financial aid and scholarships, an excellent living and learning environment), and technology will be important to our success. On the instructional front, further faculty uses of technology will be facilitated by continuation of the desktop/laptop refreshment program. That program, whereby approximately one-third of the faculty receive a new computer each year, has completed a three-year cycle. A similar program, whereby machines appropriate for the tasks in question are provided for administrators, has also completed a three-year cycle and will be continued. There have been, and will continue to be, upgrades to all other hardware and software support for UD's instructional, research, outreach, and administrative programs.

The university's efforts to have a more efficient administration will be facilitated by completely integrated software support. We have concluded that the commercial marketplace does not currently have any offerings that fully meet our requirements, but we will rely upon and assist the vendor of a recently selected human resources system in efforts to implement a completely integrated system. This implementation should enable the university to conduct essentially all of its internal, and much of its external, business electronically.

Efforts to more widely use technology for instructional support will continue. Software and courseware development will be recognized in considerations related to personnel actions, including promotion and tenure and sabbatical and other paid leaves. Also, short courses on a variety of topics will be offered by information systems staff, and the Center for Teaching Effectiveness will continue its sponsorship of sessions on problem-based learning supported by technology and other related topics. The university is well positioned for the upcoming availability of large amounts of additional bandwidth. It will then be necessary to support efforts of our faculty to capitalize upon the educational implications of this additional bandwidth, such as easier adaptations of full-motion videos.

Our ability to capture the first keystrokes and the consequent improvements and reduction in costs of the university's administrative processes has been a crucial element in the progress made versus the goals set forth in 1990. We are indebted to the resourcefulness of our support staff who adapted to make these changes a reality.

As a result, our living and learning environments have been transformed. Students and faculty often say that the university's investments in technology have enriched their classrooms, while extending learning and collaboration beyond the classroom walls. We want to stay abreast of upcoming opportunities and expect an even more promising future.

2

Rethinking "Rethinking Administration": A Cautionary Tale

Michael Finlayson

INTRODUCTION

This account is very much a report on work in progress. The University of Toronto, with 52,000 students, 2,700 faculty, and 4,000 staff, is the largest institution of higher learning in Canada and among the largest in North America. The university has experienced more than six years of massive budget reductions. These cuts have reduced our faculty by 8% and our administrative staff by 18%, while our student complement remains virtually unchanged. In 1998, we rolled out a new Human Resources Information System (HRIS), the fourth module of an ambitious and demanding Systems, Applications, and Products in Data Processing (SAP) and SAP-based Administrative Management System. In 1999, we plan on rolling out a new Software Atkien Geselleschart (AG, German for Share Holding Company) Student Information System. The completion of these Year 2000–compliant systems will permit many of the dreams described in this chapter to be realized.

THE "RETHINKING ADMINISTRATION" PROJECT

On April 30, 1992, Robert Prichard, the energetic new president of the University of Toronto (and former dean of its law school) announced his intention to "embark on a major rethinking of the administrative work" of the university. His goal, he said, was to make our administrative activities, structures, and practices more "directly responsive" to the academic mission of the university and to ensure "complementarity between activities undertaken centrally and in the divisions." A prime motivating force, he added, was his desire to "reduce the total cost of our administrative work without undermining the university's capacity to pursue its academic mission while still meeting our public obligations of accountability." Above all, the president indicated, he wanted the University of Toronto to be known, *inter alia*, for the exceptionally high quality of its streamlined and simplified administration. To assist him in carrying out this daunting task, he hired Ontario's senior civil servant and deputy treasurer, Bryan Davies, as his vice president of business affairs and chief administrative officer. Thus, the beginning of the "Rethinking Administration" project at the university.

Influenced by the innovative work that was then (and still is) going on in the University of California system and remembering his own sometimes frustrating experiences as dean of a small professional faculty, President Prichard was acutely aware of the apparent paradox of a highly centralized administrative structure attempting to manage a fiercely decentralized academic community. What particularly concerned him, he said, was the incongruity of a central bureaucracy exercising—for reasons both good and bad—a control function over faculties and divisions that were academically autonomous. To resolve the paradox, he felt, the bottleneck of administrative processes needed to be redesigned completely, decentralizing authority to the lowest feasible level. "It is my view," he added, "that at present many of our administrative processes are overladen with unnecessary work, duplication of effort, multiple levels of approval, and daunting complexity. Too often, we separate the point of decision within the administration from the location where the operational results of the decision will be implemented or felt."

The original goals of "Rethinking Administration," therefore, were to make administrative structures reflect and support academic ones and to locate administrative responsibility with academic authority. In considering how many PhD students to admit in a given year, for example, a faculty would henceforth consider not only academic questions such as fields of study, availability of appropriate supervisors, and the like, but also resource questions involving the connection between doctoral enrollment and departmental or faculty resources.

The long-standing disconnect between the administrative center and the academically autonomous divisions, however, was not the only pressing problem the president wished to address. Like many other universities, the University of Toronto was reeling from funding cuts which, unknown to Prichard and Davies at the time, were to become much more severe in the next six years. Students were being expected to bear a larger proportion of the total costs of an education delivered by a shrinking complement of full-time faculty and staff. At the same time, the university was expected to maintain or increase its teaching and research productivity and was therefore obliged to seek and manage unprecedented levels of private support. These difficulties made "Rethinking Administration" a hard sell in the university community. That it was in part a cost-cutting exercise immediately raised suspicions, especially among administrative staff, that paring costs was the only reason for undertaking the project. Academic administrators, both at the center and in the divisions, were also wary. To many of them, the goal of "Rethinking" seemed to be to devolve work, not to enhance autonomy or improve services. It was in this fog of skepticism that Bryan Davies and his steering group of central administrators began their uphill climb.

They were not unaware of the difficulties that lay ahead. "I have been charged with heading up our efforts to institute fundamental change in our administrative practices and procedures," Davies wrote in a fact-finding letter to Gail Salaway, UCLA's administrative vice chancellor, in April 1992, "and I am struck by the need to obtain a buy-in to this effort amongst our administrative staff and their clients, the academic cadre. The atmosphere for this is less than ideal at the present time, in that severe budget pressures have led to a high degree of job security anxiety on the part of administrative staff and increasing levels of criticism of administrative activity from academic staff, who see these functions as draining away funds otherwise available to support the academic mission directly."

As a first step up the mountain, Davies took advantage of a pro bono offer from McKinsey and Company (a consulting company) to assess the university's administrative processes with a view to identifying those that might urgently be rethought. The McKinsey analysts identified about 40 distinct processes that could and should be scrutinized. They then held a series of workshops involving both central and divisional administrative staff who were asked to rate existing processes on a number of criteria, including the amount of effort expended on each, the number of people involved, and the potential benefits of reengineering. The analysts recommended that initial efforts be concentrated on 10 or so distinct financial management processes identified in the workshops.

A university-wide survey of time currently being devoted to each of these processes further defined candidates for "Rethinking." It indicated that the buying and paying process consumed by far the greatest amount of staff members' time, followed by human resource payroll and budgeting processes, with the labor-intensive administration of grants and contracts cutting across all financial processes. The results of the survey persuaded Davies to concentrate on two projects first: buying and paying, and grants and contracts, to be followed by two more: human resource/payroll, and donations management. The budget process, responsibility for which resided elsewhere in the university, he decided, was too pervasive to be successfully reformed in the first iteration and should be left to a later date.

The McKinsey analysts did good work. However, their deliberations and recommendations, and some of those made by the university's own "Rethinking Administration" team in the early days, were couched in language that baffled everyone more accustomed to academic discourse. The high-level, essentially corporate, nature of their analysis soon gave "Rethinking" a sour reputation in the university for impractical and theoretical nonsense, an image it never really shed. It also exacerbated anxiety in the community at large about the true purposes and likely outcomes of the "Rethinking" exercise.

Nevertheless, the workshops and survey had identified a number of genuine problems, some unique to individual processes and others common across several of them. Among the most commonly noted were:

◆ Too many confusing options, rules, procedures, and policies

+ Too many hand-offs, too many approvals and people involved in each transaction
+ Duplication of effort and multiple data entry
+ Poor access to information
+ Unfriendly and often inconsistent systems

The four processes chosen for "Rethinking" in late 1992 shared many of these problems.

The "Rethinking" team, which would soon include more than 30 staff members seconded half-time from the central administration and the divisions, were mindful of the need for a consistent approach. The overriding goal of the exercise remained the same: to decentralize data and move the responsibility for information and accountability to where the action was taking place. This constituted a massive paradigm shift in an institution accustomed to having administrative decisions delivered from on high, irrespective of how autonomous the divisions might be in academic decision-making.

The team set about gathering a group of administrative staff members whose day-to-day work involved the targeted process, either at the central or the divisional level. With the help of a facilitator, these groups scrutinized the processes and redesigned them through much of 1993 and early 1994. Team members then took the reengineered processes to some of their colleagues and to their managers and divisional heads to make sure they made sense. This was a critical step in ensuring that the new processes—not the ones they replaced—would be reflected in the new human resource and research information systems planned for the near future.

This is the first reference in this account to the introduction of new systems. Yet while all this process redesign was going on, other groups of senior, mostly nonacademic administrators were purchasing new off-the-rack information systems at considerable expense. This resulted from a decision by the central administration that the university should no longer try to develop its own in-house systems, but rather should buy canned software. Inevitably, this approach to systems renewal reflected past practices and traditional structures. Because of the compartmentalized way the university was organized, we were not inclined to take an integrated institutional approach to the problem of data management. Instead, it seemed to make more sense to allow each functional area—finance, human resources, and research, among others—to make independent decisions about which systems would best meet its needs.

The decision to purchase a new financial system, for example, was made when "Rethinking" was working with frenetic energy on finance projects on a parallel, and largely separate, track. The decision was driven almost entirely by the need to replace a 20-year-old, outmoded system. The rethinkers were not involved, nor were the sponsors of the other systems that, four years later, would be inextricably linked with the new financial system. Unknown to any of us, we were hurtling toward fully integrated administrative management systems at a time when we were still relying on the old nonintegrated, silo-based administrative organization to make decisions.

At the time, the University of Toronto used at least 15 separate automated information systems to support its administrative processes. It is hardly an exaggeration to say that the 15 different systems used 15 different sets of assumptions and definitions and that these assumptions and definitions were often inconsistent. For example, the definition of a full-time equivalent employee used by the financial system was different from that used by the human resources system. This inconsistency made it difficult, perhaps even impossible, to answer the simple question, "How many employees do we have this day, or this year?" The patchwork of systems—many of them in the process of being replaced—also made it difficult, sometimes impossible, to draw data together from different sources to address issues that cut across their boundaries. For example, the graduate school could not readily obtain data about its students' financial situations because the teaching assistantship data on the human resources system was not integrated with the student registration system.

The existence of so many distinct and nonintegrated systems posed other problems as well. Because they were more than 20 years old, most had become anachronistic and were both expensive and complicated to maintain. In addition, many of them were no longer capable of adequately serving the purposes for which they had been developed. Worse, because the systems had been designed to serve a highly centralized administration, many divisions and departments had developed their own "shadow" systems over time to support their own needs. Often these systems bore scant resemblance to the databases they superseded on a work-a-day basis. It is interesting to recall that no one involved in finance or human resource system renewal in 1992 or 1993 referred to the problem of Year 2000 compliance.

In hindsight, it is clear that this attention to systems came very late in the piece. To understand why, it is necessary to consider the structure of the university's senior administration. In the late 1980s, a previous administration had created a separate and distinct computing and communications portfolio, with a vice president reporting to the president. By the early '90s, this organization had become dysfunctional. There were at least three different cultures within the central administration, each with its own assumptions and agendas at work, and the institution was finding it impossible to reconcile them. In computing and communications, the information technocrats were striving to find technical solutions to technical problems. "Rethinking Administration," for its part, was not seriously involved in discussions of the new information systems and was trying to develop a university-wide perspective that tore down departmental barriers while finance was simply trying to replace an outmoded system with a new one.

The decision-makers in finance were disinclined to accept advice from computing and communications because its technical specialists were not perceived as sufficiently sensitive to the needs of the central users. Nor did they think that the "Rethinking" team could contribute much to the selection process surrounding the choice of a new system. (Tension within computing and communications, and between it and the other administrative portfolios, would come to a head over the choice of the new financial system. In May 1994, the president decided to abolish the computing portfolio.) Meanwhile, on the academic side of the house, the recently appointed provost had initiated a white paper planning process which was not connected in any meaningful way with any of these initiatives.

Only gradually did we come to understand how sweeping were the changes implicit in both the "Rethinking" exercise and the introduction of the new systems as well as in the complex interrelationships between them. If information was to be generated and acted upon locally, we came to realize, such localized information must be democratized in fully integrated systems, a paradigm shift that, potentially, would alter every aspect of the way the university conducted its internal business. Furthermore, if successful, our plans would change in subtle ways (and in some ways not so subtle) the fundamental culture of a conservative, rule-bound institution in which the central bureaucracy dictated and policed every administrative operation and policy.

The "Rethinking" process, we began to see, was much more radical than many of us had realized. When the new processes came into effect, academic and administrative managers would be responsible for the management of their own units and would be fully accountable for their own actions. In the future, newly empowered divisional academic and administrative managers would be expected to consider both the interests of their own divisions and those of the university as a whole in the performance of their duties. They would come to discharge their new responsibilities in a competent fashion for which new accountability mechanisms would be developed. Many would need to be persuaded to accept their new responsibilities and would require sophisticated training and support systems. Administrative staff would also, of course, need to be convinced that this was not simply a downsizing exercise designed to eliminate their jobs. This proved to be a difficult task, given that the "Rethinking" team was on record predicting that the first phase of the exercise would save more than $4 million in base budget, with the majority of the savings to be found in "reduced work effort." That $4 million was equivalent to about 80 staff positions.

The central administration, for its part, would have to abandon its traditional obligation to monitor, oversee, and control the day-to-day activities of the divisions. It would continue to develop policies and procedures to ensure compliance with legislative requirements and with collective or other employee agreements; it would continue to develop and maintain administrative systems to provide efficient and effective operations; and it would still be charged with ensuring that divisional interests and actions were consistent with the university's overall interest. Central administrators would need to develop models of best practice for divisional administrators to encourage uniform standards and quality control. They would need to persuade the entire university community that the focus of all administrative processes and systems must be on the customers, who, depending on the process, might be students, employees, alumni, or grant and contract

providers, among many others. But in the future, the central administration would not behave as it had behaved in the past, as a top-down
issuer of edicts and decrees which were enforced by highly centralized
control processes.

Over time, this bureaucracy-busting—many would say Utopian—
approach came to be seen by some as entirely consistent with the
architecture of the new systems. By making all data theoretically
accessible to all users, it would be much easier for divisions to exercise
their authority responsibly, taking into consideration the financial consequences of their independent academic decisions. With the introduction of integrated systems and a seamless database, local administrators would be able to make informed choices and would be less
likely to hide behind the central administration. Moreover, the new
principles, if successfully embodied in systems and process redesign,
would be fully consistent with the public expectation that the university must be more accountable and open.

While these splendid principles appealed to a handful of visionaries at the center, they had not even been discussed by our academic
colleagues, either at the center or in the divisions. One outcome of this
lack of communication was that when the first lot of the new systems
were actually rolled out to the divisions in 1996 and 1997, deans were
uncomfortable with the open architecture and insisted that a highly
complex system of access restrictions accompany them so that the
business officer in Faculty A would under no circumstances have
access to data in Faculty B. In multidepartmental faculties, deans were
also unwilling to allow departments to gain more information and
authority over their administration. In short, one of the great virtues of
the new systems, their open architecture, was anathema to divisional
heads who knew virtually nothing about any of the systems until roll-
out, either because no one had consulted them or, more importantly,
because, when consulted, they had little to say, systems not being
especially important to them at the time.

There were other problems. How responsibility and accountability
would be reconciled with real devolution of authority was one. How
could it be ensured that the funds provided by the provincial government, a declining but still major portion of the university's operating
budget, would be spent responsibly? As the center abandoned its traditional function of overseeing divisional expenditures, how could the

university's audit committee be assured that the funds were responsibly spent? Moreover, in the faculties and departments newly empowered by devolved authority, how could it be ensured that academic and administrative employees would be treated consistently in negotiated agreements that crossed divisional lines? And, did the devolution of authority simply mean that work would be transferred from the center to the divisions, enabling the central administration to take budget cuts at everyone else's expense? (In 1999, this is a suspicion that has not receded.)

The answers to many of these questions, and to a multitude of others like them, clearly lay partly in education and training, partly in the development of performance indicators for academic administrators and their senior administrative managers, and partly in the development of the audit function. Whereas in the past, the center had tried to control the divisions, now it would have to rely on after-the-fact audits. To make all of this possible, academic administrators, many of whom are new to the task in any given year, would need to know precisely what their responsibilities were and how they were to be carried out. They would also need to be assured that the university would support them in the exercise of these new responsibilities. In addition, we came to realize that there must be a genuine reduction in the number and complexity of policies and procedures which govern administrative work. Only then would it be reasonable to apply performance indicators designed to determine success or failure objectively.

As "Rethinking" scrutinized the institution's business and administrative processes in order to simplify them, a countervailing current threatened to undermine the exercise. Understandably, current users of existing systems wanted the new systems geared to old ways of doing things, not to new streamlined processes with which they were totally unfamiliar. Not only were reluctant people going to have to learn to use complex new systems; for many of them, the very nature of their work was about to change. Under these circumstances, it was hardly surprising that many employees feared for their jobs. It must also be said that for some the challenge did prove to be too daunting, the fears too overwhelming. A few employees simply could not cope with the new systems, while many others coped, but continued to be uncomfortable.

Another area of unexpected turbulence was the tendency for everyone to want all their pet peeves addressed under "Rethinking." "We began, and continue, to receive many suggestions of administrative activities and processes needing attention," Bryan Davies noted in 1993, one year into the exercise. "The difficulty is in keeping our attention focused on the so-called 'core processes,' while, at the same time, not ignoring the perceived and real needs being brought to our attention." He began to keep a separate list of issues that could be resolved under existing procedures.

The guinea pig system was the financial information system (FIS), purchased in 1993 by the finance department from the German software company, SAP. Based on client-server technology that employs the desktop computers already on most of the university's financial and business officers' desks, the new system promised to revolutionize routine administrative chores. Moreover, because its software permits users to develop local adaptations without requiring that data be entered twice, it also promised to render existing shadow systems superfluous.

At the very early stages of vendor evaluation, SAP's presentations had focused on a client's need to reengineer prior to acquiring its systems. In our determination to solve our archaic systems problem, we were not as responsive to this important advice as we might have been. Moreover, as with every new system, the relationship between the system we thought we were buying and the one we received was not exact. In choosing to purchase software from SAP as opposed to other vendors more commonly used by North American universities, the University of Toronto was embarking upon a bold experiment. We were consciously choosing a more complex, but more flexible and adaptable system over alternatives that carried with them the rigidities that would have hobbled future "Rethinking" capacity. In making this choice, we were the first university to make such a commitment to this European company, and inevitably, we were a beta-site for many parts of the developing system. Purchase price savings achieved by beta-site status, we soon discovered, can easily be consumed by an unpredictable implementation schedule.

In retrospect, it is clear that we were facing fundamental structural problems in 1993–94. The old systems we were replacing were entirely central. Inevitably, it was the central departments, notably finance, and later, human resources, that were best equipped to make decisions about the new systems that would replace them. These new systems, however, were highly decentralized and would have dramatic impact on the work of the divisions, who had never had much to do with the old systems, and, when asked, had little to say about the new ones. (It is exceedingly difficult to interest academic administrators in the selection of a new system, even though it will be of great importance to them when implemented. At that time, of course, they will complain and wish to change it. Only when a system is rolled out do they comprehend how it works, and by then, it is usually too late to react to their complaints.)

Even in the center, the departmental structures that matched the separate legacy systems caused us to make questionable decisions and to take measures that would soon become anachronistic. When the decision to purchase FIS from SAP was made, for example, I, a complete systems neophyte, asked the senior technical advisor to that process whether the decision would have a steering effect on the soon-to-be made decision on a new human resource system. I was assured that as long as HR chose an Oracle-based system, I need have no concern. A year later, when the HRIS decision was being made, the same person informed me that the prior decision on FIS had virtually eliminated choice on HRIS. It had to be SAP.

Bryan Davies viewed FIS as an opportunity to put "Rethinking" into practice. "Putting in a new financial information system affords us a marvelous opportunity to reexamine, in a fundamental way, what we currently process and where we lodge the processing activity," he pointed out. While it was theoretically possible to address these matters in sequence—that is to introduce new systems and then to re-jig assigned responsibilities for generating and processing data—it made a great deal more sense to reengineer and redelegate concurrently. "This is a critical project, one that will influence our ability to adopt other, new, administrative relationships between the center and the divisions," he insisted. "It is important that we get it right."

Getting it right was not easy. The enthusiastic conviction of the "Rethinkers" that reengineering could smoothly accompany the introduction of a brand-new system was not fully embraced by central finance, which was preoccupied with its need to buy a system that would solve its immediate problems. Moreover, we continued to encounter widespread resistance at all levels, both central and divisional, in the university. In a highly decentralized academic institution, it is not easy for even the most talented and highly qualified individuals, who do not hold professorial title, to achieve significant change. Furthermore, the university's business board, many of whose members come from the corporate world, was also skeptical. In a particularly gloomy assessment of the situation, Bryan Davies lamented in a May 1993 memo to central administrators that "a number of recent comments" had caused him to recognize that he had not done an adequate job of explaining the objectives of "Rethinking" to the "key group of leaders in this institution . . . whose full understanding, commitment, and endorsement is needed to make 'Rethinking Administration' work."

In fact, Davies had devoted countless hours to explaining the goals of "Rethinking" to countless committees. That his words fell on deaf ears says much more about the culture of the university than about the quality of his efforts to bring about reform. Still, he persisted. "In its essence," he reminded the recalcitrants, "['Rethinking Administration'] is changing the administrative culture of the institution, and that cannot and will not happen unless all the leaders in the central administration embrace the objectives and understand the processes involved in achieving this cultural change. Change," he added, "can only be achieved via the commitment of significant resources to the effort, in an atmosphere that has all the senior leadership of the university embracing and contributing to the program."

Many senior academic leaders, however, openly resented the presence of the "Rethinkers." As one team member commented after fielding objections from a dean to the presence of outsiders poking around in his faculty, "His resistance is not, I think, resistance to change as much as it is resistance to any third parties engaging in change within his operations, given what else he has to contend with." Indeed, the widespread conviction among academics that outsiders simply could not understand the culture of a university was, and to some extent continues to be, an ongoing threat to success.

At various times, we made use of the services of several sets of consultants. As with the McKinsey analysts, the results were mixed. Most of my senior colleagues, academic and nonacademic alike, developed a profound aversion to them—to their vagueness, to their jargon, and especially to their fees. In turn, the consultants found the university baffling, with its endless consultative processes and its caste-ridden and territorial hierarchies. Nevertheless, the consultants did make a significant contribution to the process of change. Our successes probably would never have come about in their absence. We were amateurs; they were professionals, albeit from a different planet.

With FIS as the model, we began to develop plans to replace and integrate all our systems. We now understood that a disaggregated approach to systems renewal was simply not going to meet our needs and was likely to create terrible problems in the future if not corrected. As FIS was being configured, a separate group decided to purchase the human resources system from SAP. (We had by then realized that only this decision would ensure complete integration, making data entered for one system accessible to the other and eliminating the artificial distinction between financial and human resource data.)

To ensure that the new HRIS reflected the new world, not the old, "Rethinking" would scrutinize all of the administrative processes involved in hiring/paying/benefit enrollment activities, with a view to streamlining and decentralizing them. The decision made in 1994 to rethink all of our HR processes demonstrated an impressive ability to learn from the mistakes made with FIS. However, once again, it was a decision made by central administrators, this time in my own department, human resources, and when the time came to implement, divisional staff felt ill-equipped and unwilling to perform the new reengineered tasks. In 1994, we also decided wisely that there should also be a new, fully integrated research information system (RIS)—replacing the homegrown Tauris system which was still being implemented—to provide information about research grants, contracts, and related international and research activities as well as a new development information system (DIS) to facilitate fundraising. We would have to develop these two systems ourselves, but they would be fully compatible with SAP software.

In May 1994, Bryan Davies accepted a senior vice presidency with the Royal Bank of Canada, and my own involvement with the "Rethinking" project escalated. As vice president of human resources, I had been working fairly closely with the project and pushing hard to decentralize the personnel services—recruitment, staffing of administrative positions, job evaluation, labor contract administration, and staff development—for which I was directly responsible. At about the same time, the president eliminated the position of vice president of computing and communication and redistributed the responsibilities of the portfolio to me, to the provost, and to the chief librarian. New faces appeared on the "Rethinking" team, too, as we sought ways to bridge the understanding gap between the theoretical center, the technicians, and the eventual users of the new, "rethought" systems and processes.

In the fall of 1994, after members of the university's audit committee had expressed concern about the loss of adequate controls in the face of decentralization, we asked a major international consulting firm to review FIS, which was then scheduled to be rolled out on May 1, 1995, as well as associated "Rethinking" projects. The report was not reassuring. It noted an uncertainty in many constituencies as to the interrelationships between the new systems and "Rethinking" and suggested that the absence of an "overall architecture expressing an agreed future vision of the university" had caused confusion, lessening a "true buy-in and a commitment to substantive change." The analysts pointed out that too little time had been devoted to training, that no roll-out plan had been developed, and that major users were unsure of precisely what would be delivered to them. They added that the "degree of true, meaningful communication between the 'Rethinking' team and the FIS team had been minimal at best" and that integration of the projects had not been attained.

The analysts also pointed to the continuing belief in the university that authority, responsibility, and accountability were to be pushed downwards with no clear organizational or policy framework in place to provide an appropriate degree of control. In addition, they found no clear reward/punishment systems or mechanisms to address misbehavior or control violations. "This is potentially a classical case of a technical success (provided that the technical risks noted are dealt with) and complete failure to gain real and positive benefits from new systems and business processes," they warned ominously. Certainly, "Rethinking's" successes to that point were exceedingly modest. The project team had identified eight processes to be rethought, with only buying and paying and grants and contracts completed.

In response to this report, in December 1994, we seconded a project manager, Nigel Kelly, from KPMG Peat Marwick, a consulting company. His first task was to analyze the four modules of what we now described as the administrative management system and their relationship to "Rethinking." Kelly focused our attention more sharply on several issues that we had already begun to understand, among them that we should not have been surprised by the discomfort of the users and should have taken their concerns much more seriously at the outset. Although we knew that in recent years, many attempts to build large multicomponent systems at other large institutions have ended in failure because they did not win the loyalty of those who must use them, we had seriously underestimated the time and effort needed to win that acceptance. If few in the user group care about the success of a system, we now understood, it is doomed.

Similarly, we had discovered through experience that if a new system cannot win the loyalty of its sponsors, especially, in our case, academic administrators, some of whom viewed the goals of the "Rethinking" exercise as a challenge to the primacy of academics as the proper and legitimate leadership of the university, it is most unlikely to be successful. Also, we had learned that it is even less likely to be successful if reluctant administrators feel that they have no guidance, yet will still be held accountable for their actions.

Knowing such things in the abstract, however, is one thing. Acting upon them effectively is quite another. By the spring of 1995, donations management and human resources/payroll had progressed through the "Rethinking" analysis and design phase; changes were in the implementation stage. By then, we had tightened our organization significantly. Each project now had an implementation manager accountable for making sure that the plans created by the original teams were carried out. Each of those managers had been added to the appropriate software development team to ensure that new software reflected the reengineered ways of doing business rather than replicating past practices.

Three more processes, solicitation management, hiring and termination, and management of employee absenteeism, were in the early stages of being rethought. A list of candidates for the next round of reengineering (remodeling the dental clinic, reorganizing the school of graduate studies and the faculty of law, developing a campus card to streamline identification and purchasing, redesigning the faculty of medicine's salary and benefits recovery program, and completing the restructuring attendant upon the merger of the Ontario Institute for Studies in Education with the University of Toronto) was being compiled. Team members were acting as internal consultants to faculties and departments wishing to rethink significant portions of their activities.

"Rethinking Administration" achieved some real successes in 1995 and 1996, but only when a particular dean (e.g., law, education, graduate studies, or dentistry) saw a real benefit in the special techniques employed by members of the "Rethinking" team. Gradually, however, it ran out of steam as an activity separate from systems renewal. This was signaled clearly in July 1996, when Chris Handley, who had been the director of "Rethinking Administration" since 1993, became director of both the administrative management systems and of organizational and systems effectiveness.

Nigel Kelly also focused our attention on the needs of other constituencies, especially students. "A potential customer should not be forced to go through arbitrary and inconvenient steps to use services provided by the university," he stated in a June 1995 memo. "A potential customer should surely not have to go through a registration and payment session in a separate location for each course, nor should a potential customer have to register and pay separately in different locations for food, parking, library, computer access, and accommodation. . . . The wishes and attributes of the customer should be paramount."

None of the systems mentioned heretofore has much to do with students and the integration of student data. Yet it was widely known as long ago as 1994 that the old student information system was not Year 2000–compliant and would need to be replaced. As a result, consultants were hired to oversee process reengineering in anticipation of a new system. But because student affairs were in the provost's office, organizationally separate from finance, human resources, payroll, and development, "Rethinking Administration" had no involvement in the process reengineering that accompanied the development of the student information system, scheduled for implementation in November 1998. (Because SAP did not offer a student system, because student affairs lay within the purview of the provost's office, and because "Rethinking Administration" was primarily of interest to nonacademic administrators, there was little linkage between the two sets of activities.)

The university, Kelly pointed out, was in effect proposing that information systems spanning the whole field of customer service be developed and maintained by two separate organizations, administrative computing, and academic computing. Each would have to keep track of names, addresses, accounts receivable, and the like. The prospect of any significant integration across the boundary was remote. "Almost certainly," he warned, "the systems will use different software, different hardware, and different architectural approaches. . . . The result will be a long-term systemic lack of integration [and] the university's customers will suffer because they will have to do apparently senseless things to complete simple business transactions."

It remains to be seen whether his gloomy predictions will come to pass. In spring 1998, the University of Toronto implemented HRIS, the fourth module of its administrative management system. In 1999, we will be implementing the new student information system. We are optimistic that some integration between the systems will be achieved, but we have no idea how complete that integration will be.

All of us, I believe, have become much more sensitive to the needs of users, as Bryan Davies had told us from the beginning we must. For example, the project with which I was most closely involved, the development of HRIS, established a resource transition team, in an admittedly only partially successful attempt to make certain that the move to the new processes would be as smooth as possible. The team has worked closely with implementation managers and supervisors to define new organizational structures and job functions, trying to ensure that current employees will be adequately trained to do the new work. It has also worked closely with career counselors to help employees make some difficult transitions.

The delayed launch of FIS in November 1995 taught us some useful lessons about the importance of fuller communication. When the system was rolled out, many people in the university were still not convinced of the necessity or wisdom of the "Rethinking" project, and many users were still deeply concerned about increased workloads and how the new processes would affect the nature of their work. We resolved, therefore, to concentrate more energy on providing better information to them. *The Changing Times,* an internal newsletter distributed periodically on the university's three campuses, appears online monthly, discussing various "Rethinking" projects, answering specific questions, profiling staff members involved in a wide range of new activities, and providing retraining and career planning information. A hotline puts users in touch with liaison teams who can answer their questions. A help desk and FIS Bulletin Board provide further information and assistance. Workshops of various kinds, organized by the individual project teams, reach more and more employees. At the same time, we have begun to develop performance indicators that will give us some idea of how we are doing, beginning with a questionnaire to a randomly selected group of faculty and staff members to measure current satisfaction levels as a baseline for the future.

It is difficult to overemphasize the importance of genuine communication in an exercise such as this. As we learned, there is no reason to believe that people working feverishly to solve complex technical systems problems will understand, or have much sympathy for, the needs of the eventual users of the systems they are perfecting. When a system threatens to drive processes and policies, beware! Unless the gap between theory and practice is aired and discussed, and rethought if necessary, there will always be suspicion in the field that the central administration is up to no good.

We have found that one solution to this problem is to seek out those rare people who can bridge these chasms, and then to give them the time to listen and talk, and then to listen again, for as long as it takes. Even then, misapprehensions will remain. The fact is that many academics mistrust the motives of central administrators, just as many administrative employees are suspicious of the motives of both the central administration and academics. Are they wrong to be suspicious? Probably not. Because the new functions are more general than specialist in nature, they do require employees with broader knowledge and skill sets. It follows that these jobs will likely be more interesting and, in some cases, more challenging. It also follows that there will likely be fewer of them and that not all employees will be able to meet their demands.

So the "Rethinking" exercise continues sporadically at the University of Toronto, although it ceased to exist as a separate entity three years ago when it was subsumed in the Administrative Management System (AMS) which arose, phoenix-like, from the ashes of the critical consultants' report. AMS now oversees both systems renewal and administrative reengineering. It is still very much a work in progress.

With the four basic administrative modules in place as of May 1998, it is a challenge to see if the new systems facilitate greater efficiency and if the university can take advantage of the integration they provide. Despite our best efforts, our structures, it must be said, still tend to reflect old processes.

In the six years since President Prichard began the drive to "Rethink Administration," the University of Toronto has experienced great change. The massive reduction of public funding for universities inevitably resulted in a change in the preoccupation of the central administration. As the money vanished, the cost-saving aspects of "Rethinking" became more prominent in our discussions than they had been before. As the systems become operational in each division, for example, I often found it necessary to reassure academic administrators that not only will we be able to provide better service by eliminating many steps in processes that have become anachronistic, but also that we will help them save money.

This kind of talk may be reassuring to academics, but it is also confirmation of much that the administrative staff has feared all along. Some administrative staff reductions have been facilitated by the work of "Rethinking," but many more have resulted from old-fashioned budget reductions. Yet the fact remains that when the "Rethinking" exercise began, our analyses indicated that about 30% of all administrative work in the university was redundant, much of it innocently created in an effort to get jobs done. This work has been accumulated vertically, but can only be removed horizontally, in a workplace where people naturally confuse removing work with firing people.

Our successes so far? I have already referred to a significant number of major reengineering exercises in divisions whose leaders were not discouraged by the language and culture of "Rethinking." Any authorized staff member may now order goods to a value of up to $5,000 on a purchasing card, eliminating 80% of purchase transactions (and causing a tiny, temporary flurry of criminal activities as staff adjusted to the new audited, but not controlled, culture of decentralization). Personal expense reports are handled without central monitoring and the turnaround time has been reduced from a week to a day. The elimination of double and triple handling of routine financial and HR transactions is permitting the central administration to eliminate staff positions in purchasing, payroll, and human resource data processing, while departments now enjoy unprecedented access to real time information. This access enables them to do their work more cost-effectively and efficiently, although the departments still argue that the elimination of work at the center is possible only because we have added to the workload in the divisions. There has been a significant reduction in the size of the employee complement since 1992, mostly among administrative staff. This is due at least in part to "Rethinking" and systems renewal.

There is little doubt that there has also been a profound change in the relationship between the central administration and the divisions in the past six years. As Marty England, the university's senior planner, put it in an April 1998 memo, "there has been a fundamental cultural shift over the past few years . . . [in that] we expect the divisions to develop credible multiyear plans, but we then grant them considerable day-to-day flexibility." Whereas in the past, the central administration monitored and controlled the divisions' activities, now they provide enormous freedom and rely on an expanded audit function to ensure compliance with policy and accountability. In many important ways, the goals President Prichard articulated in 1992 have been realized.

The ultimate success of the new systems, however, will best be measured by the elimination of departmental shadow systems. There we have a long way to go. Many faculty and staff members still tend to be reactive rather than strategic, and because there is no shared vision for the institution among them, they see no reason to change. As a result, every change still meets some resistance, both from those involved in the change process and from those in other parts of the organization.

So far, the University of Toronto has spent about $18 million on the purchase, development, and implementation of the four modules of AMS and the related "Rethinking" process, not including the salaries of regular staff members who are involved in these activities. Compared with other organizations with which I am familiar, this has been a massive exercise in systems renewal on a shoestring. For complex reasons, one-time-only money was not as difficult to find as it might have been. This circumstance did not have a completely salutary effect on the project. Fewer hard questions were asked of the advocates of each of the modules in the early days than should have been asked. Moreover, the relative ease with which we found the funds meant that the institution did not suffer through the inclusive process of making hard decisions and, therefore, did not commit itself to systems renewal.

Finally, we should not have argued for the new systems and processes on the ground that we would "save money" (i.e., reduce the staff complement). Linking "Rethinking" and systems renewal with downsizing was not wise. Today, we are digging out, successfully I hope, from the consequences of having done so. We are almost at the point of having replaced our old technology, although the real advantages of the new integrated systems still lie in the future. We may even be at the dawning of a new institutional awareness of the exciting possibilities the new systems offer.

And what of our administrative staff? Many find the new levels of responsibility inherent in the new systems stimulating and career-enhancing. Some have taken early retirement or enriched severance packages. Still others, I suspect, are deriving some satisfaction from the success of the campaign mounted by the United Steelworkers of America to represent them.

ACKNOWLEDGMENTS

I am grateful for assistance in writing this chapter to Ann Finlayson and for the comments of Bryan Davies, Jack Dimond, Marty England, and Gayle Murray.

PART II

Emerging Administrative Strategies

3

Understanding e-Business

Martin C. Clague

N o longer for just the digital elite, the phenomenon known as
e-business has achieved mainstream status. Businesses, universities, and government agencies around the globe are tapping its potential to help them work smarter and faster.

Using the Internet as a new channel to communicate and to conduct business, e-business promises to profoundly change the way
companies promote brands, sell products, communicate with customers, and manage suppliers. It will also fundamentally alter how
colleges and universities conduct the business of higher education,
how professors teach, and how students learn.

So broad and far-reaching are the implications of e-business that
those not intimately involved with the Internet may find it difficult to
grasp. In the few short years since the Internet gained prominence,
thousands of businesses, educational institutions, and government
agencies have begun to exploit the opportunities offered by e-business. Although education is not a business it can benefit from innovative practices whether they derive from business, education, or government.

This chapter examines how business is done on the Internet and
what it means through real-world examples across a wide array of
enterprises. Highlighted are some of the best practices of successful

web sites. The rise of the Internet-based business has created a more competitive marketplace than ever before. Also identified are the factors that will continue to fuel the growth of Internet-based business as well as obstacles that could hinder its success. We will close with a glimpse of the future.

e-BUSINESS ENABLED BY TECHNOLOGY

The focus of e-business is on the benefits, opportunities, and best practices of doing business on the Internet, not on the enabling technologies. Even so, it was technological developments that transformed the Internet from a network for programmers into a viable new channel for business and education.

An important technological component of the Internet is TCP/IP, a base communications protocol that allows computers to talk to each other regardless of manufacturer or operating system.

The Internet and TCP/IP have been around for more than a generation. Both are central to the new world of net-based business. However, it wasn't until the early 1990s that the World Wide Web (WWW) opened the Internet to the masses. e-business owes its existence to the creation of the World Wide Web, to web browsers, and to servers. The development of the WWW created a new channel through which to conduct business.

- ◆ Unlike the original text-based Internet, the World Wide Web is made up of graphically oriented pages that are visually pleasing and simple enough for virtually anyone to use.

- ◆ What makes the web accessible to all is a piece of software called the web browser—a universal client that provides a standard interface that runs on any PC and allows it to communicate with any server—including mainframes, mid-range machines, and personal computers—which runs web server software.

Web browsers also serve as the interface—the front end—to the traditional information systems that businesses and universities have used for years. It is important because it does away with the high cost of developing custom interfaces for each computer application. In addition, it allows web sites to access traditional information systems where critical business data is stored. That allows individuals to tap into pertinent information or to search through literature stored on huge servers. The web enables colleges, universities, schools, and companies to leverage their information technology investments.

IT'S NOT e-COMMERCE, IT'S e-BUSINESS

Internet commerce is about much more than taking payment for goods and services sold on web sites. "e-business" is a more apt term than "e-commerce." Gaining in popularity, the term "e-business" encompasses a wide array of business functions including those carried out by universities and public service organizations.

e-business includes the following activities:

- ◆ Selling goods and services
- ◆ Providing service
- ◆ Promoting brand awareness
- ◆ Extending market reach
- ◆ Distributing information
- ◆ Delivering distance learning
- ◆ Managing business partners
- ◆ Launching a web-based business

Although each of these segments has a distinct primary purpose, many of the segments also overlap. For example, virtually all e-business sites, regardless of the segment they are designed to serve, provide some means of communicating with customers or colleagues. And a site that sells merchandise typically also extends market reach. A site whose primary purpose is to promote brand awareness probably doesn't sell products, but it might provide customer care. A site that delivers distance learning is, by definition, also distributing information. And those designed to manage business partners typically sell products, albeit to a closed, select audience, made up of resellers, distributors, and other partners. This overlap is expected to continue as companies strive to develop increasingly sophisticated sites that deliver all of the services customers demand.

Selling Goods and Services

At the heart of e-business is commerce: the selling of goods and services over the Internet. Drawn by the prospect of low overhead, 24-hour customer access, and global reach, selling over the Internet seems like a dream.

To be sure, the opportunity to exploit the Internet as a sales channel is enormous. But in reality, companies trying to make money online face many of the same issues they face offline—as well as a host of tough, new challenges unique to the Internet.

Chief among the challenges of doing business online are addressing security concerns, linking web sites to order fulfillment and other back-end systems, creating a satisfying online shopping experience, and reconciling web sales and processes with those of other channels.

On the web, security is as much a state of mind as it is a technical issue. Today's technology enables safe web transactions, but even a state-of-the-art security scheme won't encourage online orders if customers don't believe a site is safe. So, in addition to providing secure payments schemes, successful sites post messages that convince customers their credit card numbers and other sensitive data are protected.

Established companies—those with brick and mortar counterparts—that succeed on the web do so largely because they have done a good job of integrating this new sales channel with existing ones, regardless of what business they are in. That is, they see the Internet as a new way to serve some of their present and future customers, not as a replacement for their offline operations.

No matter what type of product a company sells online, every successful site has one thing in common: They all treat the customer well. Creating a pleasant, efficient environment for customers entails designing an easy-to-use interface, offering personalized services, and implementing convenient, efficient payment schemes, among other things.

Direct merchants were among the first to set up shop on the web. And it's no wonder: Because their business model lends itself naturally to the Internet, the opportunity was easy to envision. Publishers of paper-based catalogs could create electronic equivalents. Customers could point and click their way through online forms instead calling toll-free numbers and placing orders with a phone representative.

When sales of home computers equipped with modems began to skyrocket, direct merchant Lands' End foresaw that opportunity to sell its clothing and other wares online. The company views its Internet effort as a logical extension of its core business. Its web site (www.landsend.com) does not replace its phone-based, mail-order operation. It simply offers a new way for some of its present and future customers to shop.

The site allows customers to view the merchandise and place orders online. It is intuitively designed and easy to use. And, because its "look and feel" conveys the down-home, solid Midwestern image the Dodgeville, Wisconsin company wants to project, web shoppers feel right at home. It even includes the magazine-like feature stories its printed catalog is famous for.

This site succeeds for two reasons: It provides online customers the best of the traditional Lands' End buying experience, making it easy for them to shop. And it does a good job of allaying the two big fears the web has given rise to: security and privacy. Realizing that failure to address these concerns is among the biggest inhibitors of e-business growth, the site takes a no-nonsense approach. It takes the time to tell customers clearly and informatively why it's safe to use credit cards online, how the personal buying data it gathers about them might be used in the course of business, and where that data is stored.

Another key to Lands' End's success is that it was able to leverage its existing information systems, using them as the back-end engine to drive the web site. Since it connects to an order-entry and inventory system, the site is able to instantly confirm orders for web shoppers in much the same way representatives do for customers who prefer to buy over the phone.

Let's look at another retail operation that is also achieving success on the web. Since Brookstone opened its first store in 1973, the company has always strived to create a fun, interactive shopping experience for customers. Its upscale retail stores, which sell hard-to-find tools and innovative products, are designed to let customers try before they buy. Sales people encourage shoppers to treat their feet to the Shiatsu Foot Massager or to peer through the Ultra-Compact Binoculars.

Designed to sell the same line of products featured in its stores and catalog, the company's web site (www.brookstone.com) delivers its own version of the personalized shopping experience. The site combines the look and feel of the popular catalog as well as the colors and merchandising approach of the retail stores. It allows site visitors to page through the various categories of items, walk down the aisles, or even request buying assistance by searching for items in particular price ranges or by plugging in keywords.

By creating a preferred member club, Brookstone offers special services to registered customers. Membership allows shoppers to bookmark items for future consideration, to order products on subsequent visits without reentering shipping information, to create a friends and family address book, to locate items they are most interested in quickly, and to receive updates on new and featured products. More important still, it allows Brookstone to collect pertinent data about the shoppers who browse its site. By offering this service, BrookstoneOnline is taking advantage of the unique attributes of the web. Not only does the site offer customers a personalized, efficient, and fun shopping experience, but also by gathering information about their preferences, it creates opportunities for proactive selling. Using the compiled personal profiles, Brookstone can alert customers to the availability of items they are mostly likely to be interested in. Brookstone, like other successful sites, is using customer information to market and sell creatively.

Like Lands' End, Brookstone does a good job of allaying fears about privacy and security. It assures customers it's safe to enter their credit card numbers online, and explains how, in the course of business, it uses the personal data it gathers about them.

Almost all colleges and universities do the equivalent of selling goods and services over the web when they advertise programs and recruit students via web sites. An increasing number of institutions allow students to enroll online as well. Indications are that virtual campus tours and other features of campus web sites help attract students. The interactive nature of the web also makes it easier to find the right information at the right time.

Providing Customer Care

The web is poised to fundamentally redefine what it means to provide service. Because it cuts costs and offers unprecedented ways to keep customers coming back, the Internet has the potential to transform customer care from a labor-intensive, expensive post-sales operation to a strategic initiative on which future profits depend.

While countless companies are selling products on the Internet, very few fully exploit the web's capacity to deliver customer care. Today, many sites offer features aimed at servicing customers, such as the ability to read through lists of frequently-asked questions or to send a query via email. These capabilities represent a good first effort, but they fall far short of solving all customer problems all the time. So, by and large, most companies still rely entirely on the telephone to deliver customer service.

That will begin to change as more and more businesses tap the Internet's potential as a customer care channel. Driving the change is the high cost of delivering telephone-based customer support. Analysts estimate that while a telephone call costs a company between $25 and $30, serving that same customer on the web runs just $2 to $3. Compounding costs is the fact that customers tend to ask the same questions over and over again. Analysts estimate that the repeat rate runs anywhere from 50% to 70%.

Sophisticated Internet applications empower customers to serve themselves. This enables companies that deliver service online to achieve some economies of scale. In other words, instead of paying to solve the same problem over and over again, they simply solve it once for many. Taking charge of their own cases, customers with web access can search the knowledge bases on the company web site, access key information about their accounts, and request diagrams, photos, and multimedia documents that help them resolve problems.

What's more, the real rewards of Internet-based customer care extend far beyond keeping customers satisfied. The opportunity for companies who deliver customer care on the web is enormous. Not only do these applications reduce costs and provide personalized service, they can help generate sales, identify future products with high-profit potential, and provide valuable insight on how to refine existing ones.

Customers willingly provide more, and often better, information in exchange for services they find valuable. In fact, it's almost impossible to use a customer service application without revealing personal information. Every question asked, menu item selected, or form filled out provides data that can be used to build a customer profile. Those customer profiles can help companies hone their online efforts, adjust the products and services they offer, perhaps even lead to new ventures.

Companies that take advantage of this data source before their competitors do can gain an edge. In short, companies who are ready to exploit the web to its full potential can transform their customer care operation from a cost center to a profit center.

It's no surprise that today only a handful of companies are on their way to making that happen. Let's look at an example of a company that has achieved success selling its wares over the Internet and recently began to deliver customer care from the same site.

1-800-Batteries, the largest supplier of batteries and accessories for laptops, cell phones, and camcorders in the US, recently redesigned its web site to deliver customer care features to better serve the mobile professionals who buy its batteries.

The site (www.1800batteries.com) offers customer care features such as email notification, which alerts shoppers that their orders have been received and shipped. It allows them to check the status of their accounts without having to speak to a telephone rep.

It also provides a new service called battery life expectancy notification, which sends customers an email message when it is time to purchase a new battery. The service works by automatically logging the type of battery purchased by the shopper in a database noting the average life expectancy of the brand. That feature is not only useful to customers, it's also an example of how the company uses the customer information gathered on the site to proactively generate new sales.

In higher education, many IT support centers are using the web to provide customer service. Frequently asked questions lists can help many users answer their own questions. Online human resource systems allow individuals to check the status of benefits, enroll for programs, or review job listings.

Promoting Brand Awareness

Contrary to popular opinion, not every business looks to the web as a sales channel. Many name-brand companies, especially those that sell cars, soft drinks, and other consumer mass market products, have no intention of using the Internet to move merchandise. For some of these companies, Internet sales don't make sense. Car buyers, for instance, will happily comb the web looking for comparative price and feature information on cars they're considering in much the same way that they would read the printed version of *Consumer Reports*. However, they aren't about to forsake the test drive and place orders for such a high-ticket item online. By the same token, no one sees the Internet as a viable channel through which to sell consumers soft drinks.

Instead, these companies see the web as a significant new channel for promoting brand awareness. Designed to convey the image they want customers to associate with that brand, the sites deliver sophisticated, well-packaged content. Typically, they share the look and feel of the print and TV ad campaigns the company runs. Among the most sophisticated examples of e-business on the web, brand awareness sites sport features such as store locators. They entertain visitors by offering interactive quizzes and hosting contests. And they provide information on the events and causes they sponsor.

Levi Strauss & Co. is an excellent example. Using sophisticated animated images, its site (www.levi.com) says more about the young buyers it's trying to attract than about blue jeans. It flashes messages such as "A Cultural Revolution Is Inevitable." It sponsors a contest for up-and-coming musicians, provides information on musical events it hopes will help convey its image, and lists links to interesting music web sites. It even matches up site visitors with the perfect mate, thanks to an online, interactive personality test.

For Levi's and companies like it, the web offers a unique, low-cost way to promote brand awareness and convey image.

Colleges and universities promote their image through web sites as well. In fact, many potential postsecondary students turn to web sites for information on colleges and universities well before they contact the institution directly or take a campus tour. Hundreds of institutions choose to have their campus represented in online services that aggregate information about colleges and universities. The purpose is to promote brand awareness.

Extending Market Reach

Because the Internet is global, it offers companies a powerful, inexpensive way to extend their reach without having to open new stores and set up distribution networks in each location they hope to serve. That was true for Wolferman's, a purveyor of specialty foods and signature baked goods.

Ever since it opened its doors as a corner grocery store in Kansas City, Missouri, 100 years ago, Wolferman's has been moving into new markets. Its famous English muffins are available in supermarkets and specialty stores around the country. Over the years, the company has built a thriving mail-order business as well.

Wolferman's was looking for an additional sales avenue—a new way to deliver customers the same quality products they bought in stores or ordered from the catalog. The Internet offered that opportunity.

First among Wolferman's priorities was to build a web site (www.wolfermans.com) that graphically resembled the print catalog and offered a way for buyers to securely purchase baked goods. The second concern was to create a pleasant shopping experience. That meant building a site which could download pages quickly and keep the number of registration screens to a minimum. Otherwise, why would customers bother placing orders online?

Since the site went live in October 1997, the company has achieved its global marketing goals. It is attracting customers as far flung as the US embassy in Athens. For Wolferman's, the Internet solution offers unprecedented opportunity to extend market reach and provide customers with goods as fresh as those it sold in the corner grocery store 100 years ago.

Hundreds of colleges and universities are extending their market reach by offering courses and degrees over the Internet. In a networked environment, learners can come from well outside the institution's traditional geographic service area. The bulk of these institutions have not reduced their traditional on-campus programs, they have expanded their market by attracting learners worldwide.

Distributing Information

When the web first gained prominence, one of its primary uses was to distribute information. Since then, sites have become capable of carrying out far more sophisticated business functions. But for some web sites, distributing information is their business.

How do 435 congressmen, 100 senators, and 18,000 congressional staffers keep track of where 17,500 Washington lobbyists stand on the thousands of bills introduced each year?

With the increasing complexity of legislative issues and the escalating number of lobbyists who represent thousands of corporations, trade associations, unions, and other special interest groups, it was imperative to find a new way to communicate.

The Internet-based INCONGRESS (www.incongress.com) was the answer. Prior to its establishment, no such resource existed. Now customers, who buy the service on a subscription basis, can search on an issue by issue basis through public policy statements, press releases, studies, and other documents used by interest groups to lobby the Congress.

For an annual fee, this web site lets lobbying groups submit their issue papers and press releases in real time to the entire Congress while simultaneously making this information available to the media and general public. In addition, these same organizations can also make available to Congress more cumbersome reference documents, such as studies or legal briefs.

Launched in January 1998, several hundred Congressional staff members have subscribed, as well as members of the White House staff and employees of the media and foreign embassies.

The nonprofit organization Immunet is another good example of how the web is distributing information that once was available only from limited sources. Aimed at physicians and AIDS organizations throughout the world, Immunet's web site provides worldwide access to the latest AIDS information and treatment therapies. Its offerings include a comprehensive archive of *AIDS Treatment News*, a highly respected international reference.

By offering Immunet's accredited continuing medical education training programs, where medical professionals can earn credit for courses they take online, the site also plays an educational role. The courses make learning easy and practical, offering features such as online participant registration, the ability to post questions to faculty, and instant evaluation of tests. The course materials are developed by medical experts and reviewed by a panel of internationally recognized experts in the research and treatment of AIDS.

Many of the world's web sites that distribute information are owned and developed by educational institutions. Information ranging from nutrition to entomology to Shakespeare is distributed by colleges and universities. This is a natural activity for institutions that create, manage, and disseminate knowledge. In fact, it is increasingly common for students to develop web sites to share information they have acquired and organized as part of their educational experience.

Delivering Distance Education

Distance education, delivered over the Internet, allows colleges and universities to extend their reach by offering quality education to students who don't have access to a nearby campus. This eliminates the capital investment cost of building new facilities and offers the benefits of a college education to students who might not otherwise receive one.

The Monterrey Tech System, Sistema Instituto Tecnológico y de Estudios Superiores de Monterrey (ITESM), in Monterrey, Mexico hoped to reach more students without creating new campuses when it embarked on its distance learning program. Founded in 1943, the highly respected technological institute has 70,000 students at more than two dozen campuses (http://www.sistema.itesm.mx.).

Distance learning is part of its long-range plan to modernize its academic environment and prepare professionals to contribute to society. Among its goals: to create more and better jobs, to improve Mexico's competitive stance among industrial nations, and to graduate students ready to compete in advanced technological fields.

By establishing a virtual university, ITESM could prepare more students for Mexico's future. The university would realize immediate savings by being able to provide additional classes and curricula without incurring the cost of building new educational facilities. The virtual university is based on a family of collaborative computing and educational software programs, which are delivered over the Internet. These interactive teaching and learning tools allow students to communicate with their instructors and to participate in discussions with their fellow students.

This new educational model puts the student at the center, with open access to professors, other students, and a variety of multimedia learning tools and resources. Learning in this type of environment will result in better prepared students who can more readily obtain jobs because of their familiarity with leading-edge technologies.

Managing Business Partners

Another way companies are reaping the benefits of e-business is through the use of extranets. Unlike the public web sites, open to anyone with Internet access, extranets are private. They are designed to communicate with business partners, resellers, distributors, suppliers, and other parties with whom the company has ongoing relationships. That might include distributors who resell the company's products or suppliers who provide the parts to manufacture those products. Increasingly, extranets are also being used to sell products to select customers, who are steady repeat buyers.

These extranets, which automate the buying process, are designed to carry out business-to-business transactions. They cut costs by dramatically reducing cycle time. Automatic online ordering is replacing time-intensive, high-cost business processes traditionally transacted with paper-based purchase orders.

Looking to manage its retail outlets more efficiently, Office Depot de Mexico developed an extranet application that would allow the stores which sell its products to access the company's inventory information on their own. That way, stores could monitor stock and automatically replenish products when numbers fell below pre-set levels. They could also check on the status of shipments, billing, and other aspects of the order process without having to contact Office Depot customer service personnel over the phone. In other words, they could serve themselves on an as-needed basis, instead of requiring one-on-one service.

By making this happen, Office Depot has realized significant benefits. The company has increased revenue through an expanded sales base, enhanced customer satisfaction by providing additional services, improved inventory management, reduced overhead costs by expanding sales without additional labor, improved relationships with providers, and streamlined the purchasing process.

Another company that is using the web to connect buyers and suppliers is Ace Hardware. In business for more than 75 years, with 5,300 stores that sell its brand of hardware across the US, last year the company launched a private web site that links 1,000 hardware stores to Ace Hardware, allowing them to place orders and check inventory. By 1999, it will connect all 5,300 Ace stores.

Ace is finding that the extranet application is paying for itself in saved paper costs and avoidance of purchase orders. The stores love it, since it allows them to serve customers better, by placing an order and giving a delivery date thereby keeping customers from shopping elsewhere.

Some colleges and universities are beginning to use extranets to make purchasing more efficient. Office supplies, chemical reagents, groundskeeping items, and cleaning supplies are just a few of the types of items that can easily be procured through extranets.

LAUNCHING A WEB-BASED BUSINESS

Because it all but eliminates the physical overhead associated with traditional startups, the Internet has given rise to thousands of new companies that use the web as their sole channel of doing business. But low overhead alone is no ticket to success. It's still difficult to make it on the web. Those that are succeeding do so largely because they are offering something their offline competitors can't. In other words, they give customers compelling reasons to shop on the web.

Let's look at a company called Kozmo.com, Inc. When the online video store opened its doors on the Internet last year, the company set out to fill a void that the traditional video rental market had not yet met: to provide home or office delivery within 30 to 60 minutes of placing an order online. As a web-based business, Kozmo.com can carry 10 times the inventory of offline competitors in a quarter of the retail space, and it can rent videos at a competitive price point. Capitalizing on the opportunity of electronic commerce and catering to the consumer's appetite for convenience, www.kozmo.com offers other services its brick and mortar competitors can't. The site allows movie buffs to browse and search through thousands of titles, read what the critics have to say about their favorite films, publish their own reviews online, and watch trailers on new releases.

By offering value-added content and premium services while keeping overhead low, Kozmo is an excellent example of a startup that is truly taking advantage of the Internet.

Since 1996, nearly 100 online universities have been established. They offer their services without the need for a brick and mortar infrastructure. In fact, several operate as brokers or consolidators of courses offered by others. The Southern Regional Electronic Campus offers courses from 42 institutions. Its online catalog serves as the access point to a large inventory of learning resources from the Southeastern US. The California Virtual University operates in a similar fashion. Its "inventory" of over 700 courses comes from 100 accredited public and private higher education institutions in California.

FUTURE OF e-BUSINESS

Now that we've seen how e-business has begun to change the way institutions everywhere conduct business, let's get a feel for some facts and figures. How many people use the Internet? How big is the market for e-business? We'll explore some of the factors that will fuel its growth—as well as those that could potentially hinder success.

Surveys abound and, not surprisingly, numbers vary widely. Nua, Ltd. (www.nua.com), highly regarded for its "How Many Online?" feature, estimates the worldwide figure in April 1998 at 115.75 million people or 2.4% of the total population.

In February 1998, Intelliquest (www.intelliquest.com) estimated that 62 million or 30% of US adults (age 16 and over) had access to the Internet. That represents a 32% growth from the 46.8 million users reported a year earlier.

Despite the fact that most of the population is not on the Internet yet, the e-commerce market is expected to grow dramatically in coming years. Activmedia (www.activmedia.com), a research firm, predicted in April 1998 that the e-commerce market would double to $75 billion in total revenue from 1997 to 1998. The firm predicts that number will skyrocket to $1.2 trillion by 2001.

Fueled by Java, sophisticated web browsers, scalable servers and technologies that enable secure transactions, and rapid-fire growth of the Internet is expected to continue. In the last six months of 1997, the number of hosts has increased by 21%, bringing the total to 19.5 million. Domain names are up by 43%—.com sites are responsible for 23% of that growth; .edu for 15%; .net for 11%; .jp for 5%.

As we've seen, that growth is driven not only by technology, but by the increasing number of businesses and educational institutions tapping the potential economic efficiencies of e-business. These trends are expected to continue—provided web site operators and users take measures to address problems that could otherwise stall growth.

What, if anything, could cause that to happen? We see two critical challenges that need to be overcome: ensuring privacy and educating future citizens. Unfortunately, these problems have no easy answers, no technological solutions. They are issues that society needs to embrace and solve. The growth of the Internet depends on assuming responsibility for providing the next generation with the skills and resources to harness the power of the Internet—at school, work, and home.

It also depends on solving the privacy issue. On the Internet, privacy refers to how personal data—such as email addresses, consumer shopping habits, and financial data—are used. We have seen how the ability to gather such data and target consumers makes the Internet powerful and how it can increase sales and engender customer loyalty. The solution is not to put a stop to this practice, but to police it effectively.

Web site operators and users need to band together to develop and adhere to appropriate privacy policies that protect personal information made too readily available by the Internet. Web sites need clear, consistent postings about data collection. Most sites do not do that today, but displaying such policies is an essential ingredient to successfully conducting e-business.

As e-business continues to combine the broad reach of the Internet with the vast resources of traditional information technology systems, changes more profound than most of us can imagine are coming. The Internet as we know it today has already begun to change the way business, education, and government connects with customers, students, and the constituencies they serve.

Put another way, the true impact of e-business is yet to be realized. Today, for example, thousands of companies are selling products over the web. But in the not-too-distant future, web sales will begin to account for a substantial percentage of overall sales for many companies. And applications, such as distance learning, will become the rule, not the exception.

When that happens, the web will no longer be seen as a novelty, but as a preferred way for companies to sell products and deliver customer care, as a profitable medium for advertisers and marketers to promote brands, as an efficient, cost-effective means to educate students and distribute information.

We have seen how these things are beginning to happen today. But in order to move beyond their initial efforts, e-business adopters need to effectively synchronize their web efforts with offline channels. That means, for instance, giving customers a choice of how they want to do business with the company—on the web, over the phone, or a combination of both. To make that happen, both those who provide phone support as well as customers will use the web browser as a means to access essential business information stored in databases companies have used for years. That means integrating our existing information systems with the Internet.

The web has leveled the playing field to the point where a mere presence is no longer a strategic advantage. It's a requirement for doing business. That's the paradox of doing business on the Internet today. While the web has enabled companies that exploit it well to gain an edge, it has also has created a business climate where competition is more fierce than ever.

On the one hand, the web makes it easy for companies to find new customers and to gather marketing information on them. On the other hand, because the web enables buyers to compare products and prices more easily than ever before, its very existence increases the likelihood of losing those customers to competitors.

Despite the challenges ahead, no company, college or university, or government agency can afford to ignore the opportunities e-business offers. The facts are clear: For those who are savvy enough to exploit its potential, the Internet provides a more efficient and effective way to get the job done.

4

Distributed Computing Support

Polley Ann McClure, John W. Smith,
and Teresa W. Lockard

INTRODUCTION

Over the past 25 years, the pervasiveness and the nature of information technology (IT) resources in our institutions have changed dramatically. Many of us have participated as our institutions deployed mainframe batch-style computing, transitioned to time-shared services, adjusted to the dizzying proliferation of personal computers, and stretched to manage the networked computing environment.

It's fun to reminisce about the "old days" before we all had computers of our very own and before we even had remote access to the computer center's machine. In the late 1960s, local computers and access devices were introduced to our academic departments. Before this, if you wanted to compute, you carried your cards to the computer center and returned to pick up the printout from the output bins. The experts were also housed at the computer center and you went there to seek their counsel when your program wouldn't work. Some of us were allowed to run our own jobs, even allowed to set the switches on the remote job entry machine, but the vast bulk of responsibility for operating and managing the computers was "theirs."

Today, we are all system managers, and the computing systems we are individually managing are more powerful and complex than the one encased in glass with its own brotherhood of dedicated technicians in the old days. Our institutions operate at least 10,000 times that amount of computational capacity today, but our support resources have not increased by anything like that proportion.

Of course we shouldn't increase support resources by 10,000-fold, but we probably do need to think harder than we have about how best to deploy the existing resources. Many of our institutions are still behaving as if we are managing that single computer. Others have realized that things have changed, but are behaving as though the distributed desktops are independent, self-contained environments like they were when the "personal" in personal computer meant just that. Today's networked machines can no longer be treated as simply personal.

The past few years have witnessed a resurgence of interest in distributed support mechanisms (http://www.cause.org/information%2Dresources/ir%2Dlibrary/subjects/support%2Dissues.html) brought on at least in part by the increasingly evident failures of the current model (McClure, Smith, & Sitko, 1997). The purpose of this chapter is to:

- Review reasons why distributing support is important
- Identify high-level goals of most distributed support programs
- Consider several dimensions along which support can be distributed
- Describe some design considerations
- Provide a few real examples of distributed support programs in action

All of this is aimed at assisting higher education institutions in designing programs that are likely to produce the desired outcomes, given the particular idiosyncrasies of individual environments.

We use several terms that describe different models of support:

- "Central" or "centralized": a model or the part of a model of support in which most of the resources are managed and provided by a single entity for all or most users.

- "Decentralized": a model in which a formerly centralized organization is divided into parts, with the parts then assigned to subunits of the institution and managed independently, with no unit taking an institution-wide perspective.

- "Distributed": a model in which both centralized and noncentral resources exist, with the noncentral resources assigned to parts of the institution. Sometimes distributed models are well-coordinated among the parts, and sometimes they are not.

- "Haphazard": a model that often results if no one in the institution exercises leadership, and support mechanisms develop through various independent processes driven by self-interest alone.

Keep in mind that these models are not discrete categories, but points along a continuous dimension.

THE REASONS FOR DISTRIBUTED SUPPORT

Computing Has Become Distributed

Even when the computing hardware was highly centralized, some level of distributed support existed, if only in the form of peer support among users. But as the bulk of computing has moved to desktops that are linked to the rest of the world through powerful networks, the need for support has developed outside of the computer center as well as within. It is both ineffective and inefficient to provide only centralized support in a distributed technology environment. It is ineffective because central staff cannot understand the diverse needs and abilities of users as fully as support staff who focus on specific subsets of users. It is inefficient because many problems are relatively easy to resolve if the helper is at the user's desktop, but much more difficult when the helper is physically unable to experience the desktop directly.

Scalability for Support Systems Has Limits

As organizations grow, the processes of communication and coordination consume more and more resources, subtracting from those directly available for productive work. This curve often is steeper for organizations that engage in work which is more highly dynamic in time and in which many specialties must be integrated to produce a single product. Loaded down with "self maintenance," such organizations become less effective. Very large universities, in particular, might profit from smaller units of support.

Technology Systems Are Very Complex and the Environment Is Heterogeneous

No single person or group can fully understand either the technology or the range of applications desired by diverse users. Complete self-support by each user now is out of the question. Where groups of relatively similar applications and needs are clustered, as in academic departments, targeted support staff are more likely to provide very high-quality support. This is especially true if they concentrate on their departments' unique areas and if they have good access to central staff who concentrate on common needs and basic infrastructure.

Distributed Computing Systems Are Linked through Networks and the Flow of Common Information

The need for coordination in a distributed support system derives not only from considerations of efficiency, but also from the integrated nature of the system being supported. Today's desktop computers as well as their sources and sinks of information are linked in increasingly interdependent relationships. If the people who provide support do not also function in a linked relationship, it will be increasingly difficult to provide effective services and support. This point is clear when you consider the interconnectedness of a simple use, such as looking up an entry in the library catalog. In this case, the desktop is probably managed by the user or, at best, the user's department; the local area network is usually managed by the department; the wide area network is managed by the telecommunications department; and the Internet connection may be provided by an external state or regional network. The local servers might be managed by what used to be the computer center, or perhaps the library, and the application might be managed by the local library or, sometimes, by a remote state consortium of libraries. Each of these technical links is managed by different people with different work priorities and different cultures. In our experience, as complex as the technology is to make work, getting the human support network to function as well is much more difficult.

Distributed Computing Costs Exceed Our Ability to Pay

While experts argue about calculations of the total cost of owning a desktop personal computer, they generally agree that hardware and software account for less than half of that total cost. As the number of PCs in our institutions has increased, the costs of technical support, training, and management of the desktop environment have created the crisis we now face. We need to lower the total cost of support, while improving its quality. One way to accomplish this is to manage the standard parts of a standard desktop environment in a standard way, centrally, through the network, while focusing distributed support staff on unique applications and needs.

A Haphazard Model of Support Will Evolve Naturally, But It Will Not Produce Good Results

Ignoring the question of IT support models (which we believe many institutions are doing today) will almost always result in the natural evolution of what we call the haphazard model, not no model. People will find ways to get the support they need. Positions will be created, decisions will be made, and support will be provided. Costs will be high, support will be inconsistent and inefficient, and staff will naturally take independent and inconsistent positions on important technical and support issues. These institutional discontinuities will result in a wide variety of problems ranging well beyond first-level waste. Email attachments may not be easily shared across the institution, faculty and students whose work crosses the borders between service domains may receive inconsistent and conflicting technical advice, and mistakes on such fundamental levels as cabling types may occur. Once a haphazard model has become well established, it can be difficult to replace because of intense vested interests in the status quo, even if the status quo is acknowledged as being inadequate. Some administrators lack courage to challenge these fiefdoms to the overall detriment of their institutions.

PROGRAM GOALS

The ultimate goal, of course, is to help institutions provide the best possible opportunities for learning, research, and outreach. We believe that IT support programs contribute directly to achieving these goals by enabling faculty, staff, and students to funnel their time and energy directly and effectively into learning activities and institutional support processes rather than wasting resources struggling with computers, applications, and networks.

The goal of a distributed support system, per se, is increasing the total level of effective support delivered to end users for a given level of institutional investment. This goal incorporates both the concept of effectiveness (end users can really accomplish more of their primary missions) and efficiency (we can provide the support with as few people and little money as possible, so as to leave more of those resources for direct academic activities).

The following strategies can help achieve this goal:

◆ Tighter coupling of institutional infrastructure and standards to real needs and priorities of end users

◆ A reliable and robust infrastructure that provides users with a guaranteed level of functionality

◆ A managed distributed environment that assures all of the users' needs are met

Steps to support these strategies include:

◆ Better communication among users, local support staff, and central staff

◆ Increased and more consistent skill levels among local and central staff and users

◆ Greater focus of local staff on unique and discipline-specific user needs

◆ Greater focus of central staff on infrastructure and institutional standards

ENVIRONMENTAL CONSIDERATIONS

Given the complexity of both the institution's information needs and the contemporary technology environment, there are an infinite number of ways in which support for technology can be distributed.

How does the institution find the most appropriate model? Factors influencing that decision fall into three general categories: culture, demographics, and technology.

Culture

The culture of the institution is difficult to translate into the management and engineering parameters needed to design and implement a distributed support scheme. Any model that ignores the culture, however, will fail, no matter how well managed or engineered. Academic mores, governance, and the institution's sense of the role of technology are important cultural considerations (Smith, 1990).

Academic mores. The customs and values of higher education differ significantly from those of corporations or civil service entities. Academic independence, for example, is a primary value in higher education. Faculty members (and academic staff) are very protective of it and are generally mistrustful of and quick to react to anything that appears to threaten it. The diffusion of authority and responsibility inherent in distributed support can be perceived by many members of our community as loss of control and diminished service.

Another important characteristic of faculty is sociological identification. All faculty interact with others in their discipline, department, school, and institution, but identify most strongly with one group to the exclusion of the others. The intensity of expression of these mores varies across types of institutions, perhaps reaching a peak in research institutions.

Governance and management. Governance in higher education can vary from *laissez faire* to strong central micromanagement. The distribution of power among departments, schools, and the institution varies considerably among different institutions. The distributed support model will need to be different in an institution where schools have primary control over personnel, budget, and technology, compared to one with strong central control. Another important governance consideration is egalitarianism. In some institutions, it is important to distribute technology resources equally, even though needs may vary considerably.

Technology. The perception of technology is itself an important cultural value. In some institutions, technology has high value for its own sake. In others, technology is perceived as subverting other highly held values. In the latter, the distributed support scheme must address *why* as well as *how*. Any distributed support model must take into consideration the distribution of people on the technology assimilation curve (Moore, 1991). A campus with large numbers of innovators/ early adopters and few laggards (persons who embrace emerging technologies and incorporate them into their work versus those who do not) is significantly different from a campus where technology has not become mainstream.

Demographics

Size, wealth, and geography are important considerations in the development of distributed support.

Size. Large institutions are likely to have a pool of deep expertise available, and some resources can be redirected for greater efficiency. Their size makes it both necessary and highly beneficial to exploit economies of scale. Distributed support programs in large institutions need to focus on improving communication, coordination, and control. Although small institutions often have an easier time maintaining effective communication and coordination, they typically have very little margin in support resources beyond those required to deliver basic services. The distributed support program in small institutions needs to focus on developing technological depth and breadth.

Wealth. Wealthier institutions can afford to duplicate facilities and services and worry less about efficiency. They are in a much better position to optimize at the individual or departmental level. They can undertake risky exploratory efforts without the fear that failure will jeopardize basic services. Poorer institutions must focus upon efficiency. They must eliminate duplication and avoid dissipating resources on too many activities. They must avoid risky endeavors and manage their technology environment to most directly achieve their academic goals.

The distribution of wealth, as well as its absolute value, is an important consideration. The institution that centrally controls dollars and other resources can create a distributed program that balances support at all levels, from individual to institution. It can use its resources to create a more easily supported environment and connect it with users via a path of least resistance. Where resources are controlled by schools or departments, distributed support systems tend to optimize for the controlling unit and more indirect methods will be needed to achieve the most effective balance.

Geography.   The geography of the campus plays an important role in a distributed support environment. A small, compact campus allows local support staff and central personnel to be colocated, thus facilitating communication and coordination and achieving a critical mass. A large campus or multiple campuses may require central support staff to be dispersed in order to provide timely support. Where like disciplines, such as the physical sciences, language, or business, are physically close, discipline-specific support staff can be housed in the same building or part of campus.

Technology

In many cases, the current campus technology environment, which is of strategic importance, evolved in response to numerous tactical problems and through the uncoordinated efforts of numerous people. The base of facilities and expertise constrains what can be done and how quickly.

Facilities.   The support scheme will be very different on a campus where all the servers are housed, maintained, and operated centrally, compared with one where every department has its own. The campus where most of the desktops are similar is significantly different from one with large numbers of Wintel, Macintosh, and UNIX platforms. Similarly, support requirements differ where machines span many generations, as opposed to a few, or where old computers with limited power must be accommodated.

Expertise.   Effective support involves the broad, general knowledge needed to answer the questions of new/naïve users and the deep expertise needed to help power users and to design and implement a reliable infrastructure. On some campuses, the central IT organization views itself as the sole repository of technical expertise. Although it may be obvious that the central organization can no longer fulfill that role, central staff can be reluctant to share the responsibility and authority with others. Where a school or department has developed high levels of technical expertise, it is likely to see distributed support as a threat, even though it may be having difficulty meeting all of its support needs.

SUPPORT TOPOLOGY

In this section, we consider several dimensions along which institutions can organize the distributed elements of support and discuss the definition of responsibilities. The specific organization chosen should reflect the way other activities within the institution are organized. The way we define responsibilities for the central and distributed elements of the support system does matter to the program's overall effectiveness.

The following possibilities are not meant to be exhaustive or mutually exclusive. Indeed most campuses will be a mixture of some or all. We list them separately as a way of bringing issues of structure into focus.

Organization

Administrative unit. This is the most common model. Each organizational unit, usually defined by budget responsibility at some level, has one or more support staff managed on behalf of members of the unit. Sometimes the unit is large, for example, a school and the sizable staff make up an organized group that specializes in certain functions, applications, or technologies. In other instances, the unit is a small department and a single generalist comprises the support group.

Discipline. Another effective model groups departments into clusters based on disciplinary similarity. Examples are clusters in foreign languages, humanities, physical sciences, biomedical sciences, social sciences, and fine arts. Discipline-based organizations are probably less common because many institutions' budgets do not correspond to these groupings, which makes it difficult for units to cooperate and share resources across departments. The model has much to recommend it, however, if departmental politics and budget structures can accommodate it. The most obvious benefit is that better support can be provided for very small units which, on their own, may not be in a position to dedicate even a single person to IT support.

Less obvious, but perhaps more important, is that such an organization makes it more likely that common problems and issues can be addressed efficiently. Foreign language word processing is an example. The effort required for each language department to identify, implement, and develop expertise in such functionality would be much greater than if they worked on the general problem together. Another advantage is that IT support resources often serve as a vehicle for collaboration among faculty across disciplines.

Precincts.   In this model, the physical campus is divided into contiguous units. IT support staff are assigned to support buildings in close proximity. This model works well when the support staff is primarily focused on the infrastructure rather than the application level, or on common standard applications and/or when the units in a discipline are widely dispersed across the campus. It serves to minimize the transit time of support staff and keep them available at or near a base of operations. It can also help bond staff to their customers and create a greater service orientation. Because many of our campuses are laid out such that disciplines are clustered physically into precincts, the discipline and precinct models are often the same.

Function.   In this model, specialized support groups are organized to serve different institutional functions. For example, individual support groups might include research computing, instructional technology, and administrative processes. These may or may not report to and be colocated with the central IT support staff. The research group may report to the vice president for research, the instructional technology group may report to the provost, and the administrative processes group may report to the chief financial officer. The advantage of this scheme is its focus on core activities that are identifiable by faculty and staff. It can lead to greater depth of expertise, but it also can run into trouble if responsibilities for all common hardware and software support are not clearly delegated elsewhere. A single faculty member is at the same time a researcher, a teacher, and, sometimes, an administrator. All aspects of that person's work should occur in a coherent environment.

Technology. Especially at key stages in the emergence and evolution of technologies, separate support units may be set up to focus on support for a new innovation. When personal computers first made their way onto our campuses, some computer centers were slow in realizing their responsibility to support these new devices. One response was to establish a small computer support group under the dean for research or some other sympathetic office, especially to provide this needed support. Later, after the computer center developed a broader perspective, it was possible to fold such a unit back into the larger organization.

DEFINITION OF RESPONSIBILITY AND AUTHORITY

Definitions of responsibility and authority for the central and distributed components are not usually independent of the organizational model, but we separate them here to make clear that both should be considered.

The list of possibilities that follows clearly is not complete. But the models indicate some ways of thinking about how to define the missions for distributed and central staff so that we can take the greatest advantage of the distributed arrangement. If we invent a distributed support system but fail to define responsibilities, then the most likely result will be overlap, support gaps, waste, wars, and finger-pointing.

The first model divides responsibilities along some physical demarcation such as the wall-plate, with everything on the users' side of the wall-plate being the responsibility of distributed units and everything behind the wall the responsibility of central staff. While having an advantage of apparent clarity of responsibility, this design is usually the least efficient since all distributed support staff will need to manage common desktop hardware and software independently. These independent environments will likely diverge from any institutional standard over time, and there will be greater possibility of finger-pointing across the wall-plate when it comes to resolving users' problems.

Another model is to assign all user-support responsibility to the distributed elements and focus central elements on technology management. This probably has some efficiencies in assigning staff to roles that are well-suited to their personal skills and preferences, but it has great difficulties in bringing about the delivery of "whole products" (Moore, 1991) where user support and enterprise technology must be seamlessly coordinated for users' benefit. It also can result in undergraduate student support becoming no one's job.

A third model is to charge distributed staff with all first-level support for faculty and staff (usually this is used in conjunction with an administrative unit-type organization), but to assign direct student support and enterprise technology responsibilities to the central organization. The rationale here is that undergraduate students usually do not belong to a single administrative unit, and they can often be supported effectively and efficiently with pools of student assistants managed centrally. This model suffers the same problems in delivering whole products as the second model.

A fourth approach assigns first-level support and training for all users to distributed staff, with central staff serving as secondary or back-up support to the distributed staff and also providing training for the trainers and technology management. This offers better use of scarce deep expertise among central staff as well as a vehicle for coordination. Depending on where undergraduate student general support is focused, this model may have the problem identified in the second model.

A fifth possibility is to focus distributed staff exclusively on discipline- or business function–specific applications and to centrally provide all general desktop support, training, and enterprise technology activities. This is likely to be the most efficient and effective model, especially in more mature technology environments with desktop standards and at least some level of remote desktop management. This is not a good model for an institution with a primitive or overloaded network or where automated management is not established because remote support is too difficult or expensive to do manually.

DESIGN CONSIDERATIONS

We have explored the necessity for distributed support, looked at the goals it should strive for, investigated the considerations that impact it, and suggested ways in which distributed support can be structured. This section will discuss specific design considerations.

Information technology must address the information needs of the institution, of each faculty member and student, and of all organizational units in between. Providing efficient support to the integrated distributed environment is challenging. The design of a distributed support system must pay special attention to integrative efforts that span the entire institution, while not inhibiting individual creativity. Five areas crucial to the design and implementation of a distributed support program include institutional commitment and leadership, planning and design, communications, training, and infrastructure.

Institutional Commitment and Leadership

The "distributed" part of distributed computing can be difficult for many leaders and many institutions to embrace. Authority and responsibility, as well as the technology, are distributed and management links and hierarchy are diffused or nonexistent. In spite of this, institutional leadership and commitment are essential for the creation of an efficient and effective distributed support program.

Leadership. Although the central IT group might seem the best locus for leadership, the group may have a style and history that make it unlikely to succeed in an expanded role. People will be reluctant to follow a central IT group that has attempted in the past to impose its will on others. The organization that still thinks "center," even though it is no longer called "computing center," may not be able to broaden its perspective enough to lead the whole campus. Academic leaders (provost, deans, etc.) have a better perspective on the whole institution but often do not fully appreciate the technical complexity of the contemporary information environment.

The key to providing the needed leadership is to make sure that someone has responsibility for IT management at the institutional level and that the person exists in a structure that facilitates—indeed, mandates—interaction with the entire campus. How this is accomplished and the division of power between formal and informal are largely determined by the campus culture. A high-level information council, advisory committees, and working groups can provide interaction on technical and policy matters. It is important to avoid the common mistake of selecting only the technically expert for advisory committees: They no longer represent the user community at large.

Institutional commitment. Central to the concept of distributed support is the notion that information technology is institutional in scope. Without institutional commitment, a distributed support program is unlikely to succeed. The institution must commit both start-up and ongoing resources. Once developed and running well, a distributed support program should be able to deliver significantly greater service with few additional resources. As with most new programs, however, it is much more likely to be successful if initiated with extra resources.

It is also important that the institution fund the costs of IT needs where the benefit is primarily institutional in scope. A common failure in this area is using institutional funds to buy computers for a department but not providing a maintenance and upgrade budget. The local economic decision is that faculty members will spend two days finding the money to fix their broken machines. Institutionally, these are two faculty days that have not produced research or instruction. Another example is a department buying less expensive but nonstandard machines so that it can afford one for each faculty member. If the institution subsidized the difference, it could meet the department's needs and still maintain a more standard environment, with all the benefits that it entails.

In addition to resources, the institution must also be willing to commit to the decentralized responsibility and authority inherent in the distributed support model. Distributed support requires a level of cooperation and coordination that, while not counter to higher education culture, is not natural to it. If central IT resources are diverted to meet responsibilities that should be schools', departments', or individuals', the institution is unlikely to develop an adequate infrastructure. Inefficiency and ineffectiveness will result if schools, departments, and individuals have responsibility for their local environment, but not the resources and authority to create and maintain it.

Planning and Design

Planning. In the distributed information environment, many different technologies, under the control of many different units, must work together to deliver seamless and reliable services to users. This environment is far too ubiquitous, complex, interconnected, and rapidly changing for this to happen without some process of planning and design (Smith, 1994).

The ubiquity of today's technology creates two problems. The first is that the dollars and personnel invested in technology are very large. The central portion of this investment is obvious in the central IT group budget, but the distributed part, which is as large or larger in most institutions, is dispersed and hard to determine. It is difficult or impossible to make good cost-benefit decisions when the true costs are unknown. Introducing a new technology or updating an old one for the whole campus is costly enough to require several budget cycles. Planning helps the institution focus its resources on the technology and activities that have the greatest institutional impact. It allows resource allocation to be considered in light of the whole campus and over a period of several years. The second problem is that the scope of information needs over the entire campus is huge. Planning helps the institution determine which needs are general and are therefore best delivered centrally and which are unique to a discipline and are best delivered locally.

The complexity of today's technology makes it impossible for a single person, or even a single unit, to understand the whole environment. Yet the interconnectedness means that all the parts must work together. Planning allows developers to break the whole system into components small enough to be thoroughly understood and to integrate them into a reliable and functional whole. Planning provides the overview that allows users to develop technology solutions to their unique problems with the assurance that they will be compatible with the institution's infrastructure. When developed under the guidance of a plan, these individual efforts can be integrated into the infrastructure, thus contributing to the campus' common good.

Everyone acknowledges the rapid evolution of technology, but few institutions do anything but react to the change. Numerous examples exist of expensive technology that was obsolete before it was fully exploited because ad hoc implementation neglected a critical component of the whole solution. Planning mechanisms render visible the whole of a system so that timely solutions are developed for all problems. Planning that looks two to four years into the future can predict changes in technology and in user needs. With this foresight, the institution can anticipate capability and capacity problems and solve them before they escalate to crisis stage. It can redirect resources from old technologies to new ones based upon rational, cost-benefit criteria, rather than emotional or political reactions.

Many people claim that higher education is too diverse and disorganized, and technology too rapidly changing, to allow for effective planning. This is certainly true if you hold to the classical business model of planning or if you consider planning to be purely a rigid, deterministic process. Planning can be adapted to the academy, however, and any institution that needs to make its distributed information environment more effective and efficient must make the effort.

Design.   Planning is a process that sets priorities and results in goals and objectives. Design is the process of converting goals and objectives to engineered realities. Design is also the manifestation of an architecture, specifications, and technical design. Architecture determines the basic elements of the information environment and their interactions, and it provides the linkages between information and technology. A good design will layer information upon technology, rather than embed it. This makes it possible to provide new technology with minimal disruption to users. Seeing where a particular technology might be applied in a new way or in a new area is easier with a holistic perspective of architecture.

Architecture leads to specifications and specific technical designs. This provides a well-defined environment that allows individuals to act very independently with new and unique technologies and solutions and with the assurance that they can fully use the whole of the information environment. The Internet and World Wide Web are examples of architectural designs that provide both extreme flexibility and guaranteed utility. It is important to note that architecture and design should be distributed processes. As with distributed support, leadership and coordination are essential, but units and individuals can contribute to, as well as take from, a well-designed environment.

Planning and design should be conceived not as special, stand-alone processes, but as part of the management continuum. Managers who do not use the plans, or plans that are not relevant to day-to-day decisions, indicate fault in the planning process or management, or both. The same thoughts apply to architecture that does not provide a sense of direction and to specifications that are deemed irrelevant by the majority of the campus. These management tools are important in all cases, but are critical to the success of the distributed environment.

Communications

If any single element is crucial to a distributed support program, it is communication—between support providers and users, among providers, and communication that works in both directions.

Providers and users. The distributed environment, where authorities and responsibilities are always hard to pin down, is guaranteed to fail if good communication does not exist. User-provider communication has two important goals. The first is to help the technology group understand users' needs; the second is to help users understand the limitations and constraints imposed by technology. It is inevitable that the form of the solution shapes the problem to some extent; hence the communication of needs and solutions must always be interactive and iterative.

Among providers. A typical contemporary problem and its solution will bridge the technology areas of desktops, servers, networks, and applications. These four areas may be the responsibility of four different administrative units. Because finger-pointing is an all too common phenomenon in troubleshooting problems in this extended environment, strong provider-provider communication is key.

It is important that service providers communicate with each other when designing and implementing the information technology system. A change in network routing can disable the users' working environment until changes are made in their desktops. From the other perspective, the faculty member who gives a web-intensive assignment to 100 students can seriously disrupt the network. We cannot expect all faculty members to understand the implications of their use, but a local support provider who is aware of what faculty are doing can get the word out in time for the networking people to fix the problem before it even occurs.

Communication mechanisms. In the distributed support model, the amount of information is huge, some of it is very esoteric, and most of it is irrelevant to a particular user or support provider. The eternal communications paradox is that if you provide all the information, most of it will be ignored, including the relevant parts. The only realistic solution is to provide all of the information in as many formats as possible and to provide selection and filtering mechanisms to route the correct information to the people who need it, when they need it. A local support provider who is knowledgeable about the usage and needs of his or her department and who is aware of technology materials can be the bidirectional filter. The providers pass on to their people only the technical information that is relevant to the users' needs.

Because no single communications mechanism will serve all the users, it is important to use every possible mode, from personal contact to articles in the campus newspaper. With clever planning and design, information can be organized to fit into multiple formats with minimal extra effort (e.g., the announcement of a change in service can be placed in the IT newsletter, the campus newspaper, on bulletin boards, a list-serve message, the IT announcements web page, and the distributed support providers' news group). It is still necessary, however, to place some priorities on messages. Although everything is important to someone, not everything is important to everyone.

Matching the communications mechanism used with the mechanism favored by the individual is essential. Some people prefer impersonal electronic messages. Others need human contact in order to best receive the message. Some people look forward to weekly or monthly meetings, while others go to great lengths to avoid them. It is easy, particularly when dealing with limited resources, to say, "We made it available; it's your fault if you didn't take advantage of it." Communication is so important in distributed support that every reasonable effort must be made to make the information easily available in the style best received by those who need it.

The need for information in IT can develop in a very short period of time. It is important to establish communication mechanisms that let users control when, as well as how, they get the information they need. For example, users don't need to understand mail-merge in detail until they need to send out 100 letters. Even if they were given that information in an introductory course, they are likely to have forgotten it by the time they need it. Short and simple messages can announce new information, with greater detail available via electronic or human linking. Indexing and cataloging of information are important tools in helping both users and providers find the information they need at the most appropriate level of detail.

Training

Many institutions made an initial attempt at distributed support a decade or more ago by appointing IT staff to be departmental representatives or departmental staff to be IT representatives. These efforts were not very successful for a number of reasons. Among the most significant problems was that representatives were not given the knowledge and skills demanded by their new responsibilities.

The home-grown support person in the department or school may be a true expert in the local environment, but often lacks a comprehensive knowledge of basic information technology. The result is often idiosyncratic systems that only the particular support person can maintain and that lack compatibility with campus and industry standards. Their first introduction to a technology is often trying make it work, resulting in inefficient learning and poor system configuration.

A comprehensive training program for distributed service providers greatly increases their efficiency. By making them aware of best practices, training increases the reliability and serviceability of the environments they create. An institution can guide people toward standard information environments by emphasizing training in standard hardware and software systems. A pool of uniformly trained support staff helps reduce single-person dependencies and provides lateral mobility for support staff.

Training is also important for central support staff. Most of the arguments given for distributed support personnel apply to central staff. Additionally, high reliability requires that problems be found and fixed before they disrupt the system. It takes more expertise to do this than it does to fix a part that is obviously broken. Proactive training, rather than ad hoc learning, is needed to create this expertise. Training must be forward-looking, including more than just those skills that are currently needed. Too often, we train staff in the new operating system as we are installing it. It is not surprising that the introduction of a new technology is often traumatic and disruptive. Well-trained users require minimal support. Once a critical mass of knowledgeable users is created, many questions are answered by other users, reducing the load on service providers. It is easy for IT professionals to forget, however, that technology is not the focus of most users' days. They are not particularly interested in it, nor do they want to waste time learning it. User-oriented training needs to focus on functions to be performed (writing reports) rather than technology (word processing). It needs to give users enough information to allow them to meet their needs, but no more. It should be available to users when they need it, not just at the beginning of the semester, or even once a month. It should be available in different modes to accommodate different learning styles.

These needs clearly cannot be met with an ad hoc or marginal training program. Significant effort is required to develop training that is comprehensive, effective, and timely. User training, in particular, has tough requirements. No central unit can provide the variety of training needed by individuals, when they need it, how they need it. A distributed training program is the logical answer to distributed training requirements. Local support providers can provide local training if they themselves are well trained and have access to good course synopses and training materials. Central support can most efficiently deliver training in IT fundamentals and can justify the effort of developing good courses to be used by everyone in the institution.

Infrastructure

In higher education, each faculty member has dissimilar information needs, since each is an expert in a unique area of knowledge. Although the immediate information environment must be unique, a large number of information services are common throughout the campus. Printing, using electronic mail, sharing formatted documents, and backing up electronic data are examples of common information services. On most of our campuses, the delivery of these basic services is highly inefficient. How many times have you been unable to read a document emailed by a colleague? How many times have you had to resubmit a print job because the printer did not work properly? Aggregated over the whole institution, this is a huge waste of resources. One reason for this inefficiency is that we have not paid enough attention to infrastructure reliability and robustness.

A second cause of this inefficiency is lack of campus standards. The fact that a standard technology environment will not meet all of the needs of every user does not mean that a large portion of the environment cannot or should not be standardized. Few people disagree with the 80–80 rule—that we can create a standard information environment that will meet 80% of the needs of 80% of the users (McClure,

Smith, & Sitko, 1997; Smith, 1997). Standardizing 80% of the environment produces huge gains in institutional efficiency and effectiveness.

Infrastructure considerations are important to the concept of distributed support in two ways. A technology infrastructure that is unreliable and unresponsive to users' basic needs so severely hamstrings an institution that any support program—centralized, decentralized, haphazard, or distributed—will have limited effectiveness. If a distributed support scheme does not work well, it can be difficult to say whether the design is at fault, or if it was given an impossible challenge.

The 80–80 rule suggests a way that authority and responsibility might be apportioned in a distributed model. Significant resources and effort are required to create an environment that is reliable and robust. The costs are reasonable if they can be amortized over the entire institution. Deep technical expertise in several areas is needed to design and implement a reliable environment. A single school or department would find it difficult to hire and maintain such a collection of experts. In all respects, it makes sense for the central IT organization to take on primary responsibility for the design, implementation, and maintenance of the basic information infrastructure.

School and departmental support staff freed from supporting basic technology can devote their time to the special technology needs of their discipline. Users who can depend upon these combined baseline and discipline-specific services can target their efforts on the unique needs of their research and instructional programs. The combined efforts lead to a 100% solution that is both effective and efficient.

Infrastructure plays a special role in distributed support in that it is both a goal and a critical success factor. Few campuses have the ability to create a reliable infrastructure without the full use of their distributed resources, yet any distribution scheme is likely to fail if it is applied to an unreliable and unresponsive infrastructure.

EXAMPLES OF DISTRIBUTED SUPPORT PROGRAMS

Many institutions of higher education have implemented distributed computing support programs. No two models are exactly alike—each having been adapted to fit unique institutional parameters. In this section, we discuss how four institutions implemented distributed computing support models.

Indiana University (IU)

Institutional profile and IT history. Indiana University is a major public research university composed of a residential campus in Bloomington, an urban campus in Indianapolis, and six other campuses located throughout Indiana. In 1997–98, IU had 92,000 students and employed nearly 17,000 faculty and staff, making it one of the nation's largest institutions of higher education. The Bloomington campus had 35,000 students, 1,600 faculty, and 4,000 staff. Indiana University–Purdue University at Indianapolis (IUPUI) had 32,000 students, 1,400 faculty, and 3,500 staff. Other campuses are not a part of the distributed support model discussed here (Alspaugh & Voss, 1998).

The campus culture at IU is characterized by responsibility-centered budgeting and management, wherein a great deal of decision-making is made at the campus, school, and department levels. Faculty governance is well established, and the departments maintain a certain level of independence.

University Information Technology Services (UITS) provides leadership in technology appraisal for teaching and learning technologies and in research applications. Its primary role is the facilitation of a rich, diverse IT environment that offers abundant support.

The academic and administrative areas at IU have long had their own technical staff. In the academic areas, it may have been faculty supporting their own research; in administrative units, it was primarily personnel supporting their own unique systems. These technical contacts had always interacted with central IT staff. When the academic and administrative computing units merged, an opportunity for increased resource leveraging appeared. The administrative computing support staff had been developing technical staff liaisons with users by providing mainframe report-writing training and support at the office systems level. This liaison between the computing coordinators in departments and UITS was part of the foundation for the distributed support model.

Distributed program structure. An early adopter of a distributed computing support model, IU began its program in the late 1980s. Rather than fight the inherent decentralized nature of the university, the Partners in Computing Support (PICS) program sought to work within that context. The program was voluntary but provided a strong tangible benefit to encourage participation.

The program's evolution was grounded in the increasing need for more effective and efficient front-line computing support. As technology changed, an outreach program was initiated to link users and UITS and to provide training and support for the increased power at users' desktops. Although rich in talented technical staff, UITS did not possess the resources necessary to keep up with the burgeoning demand for support. In response, some departments began hiring their own support staff.

The Distributed Support Assistant Program was established on the Bloomington campus because some departments were not progressing in the use of technology, and some were unable to fund computing support internally. Five-hundred thousand dollars of seed money was used to hire, train, and manage Distributed Support Associates (DSAs). UITS trained the DSAs, who were placed in departments. In the first year, UITS covered the entire cost of the position for the department. The department assumed half the cost of the position in the second year and the full cost in year three. As central money was freed up, it was used to expand the program to other departments. Participation in the program was voluntary, but the seed money served as a strong incentive. In addition, departments not directly involved in the program recognized the benefits of local support and hired their own staff without the central funding.

In conjunction with the Distributed Support Assistant Program, UITS reallocated $1 million and distributed it to the deans on the Bloomington campus. The funds were provided on a matching basis to create an account in each school for a fully funded replacement cycle for faculty computers. The result was a dedicated pool of funds to provide faculty workstations.

Support and training for the DSAs were enlarged to include existing, de facto support staff in departments, resulting in the Partners in Computing Support (PICS) program. Participants in PICS are called LSPs, local support providers. Designation as an LSP carries no minimum requirements, and LSPs include administrative staff, faculty, and professional staff. PICS provides a vehicle for fostering continuing technical education, human networking, and tool-sharing as well as communication of strategies on an ongoing and consistent basis. LSPs at Indiana do not have regularly scheduled meetings. The Partners in Computing Support Program has a staff of 20 and a budget of $1.3 million to provide support, training, and services to LSPs at the two campuses.

Benefits provided to LSPs include a directory of services, a mail list, workshops, and forums. The program includes a server that is reserved for LSP use and that enables centralized software distribution, which further enhances the benefits of standardization. The server also provides free and convenient access to electronic libraries and utilities, such as Computer Select, a database that delivers comprehensive and complete information on computer products and industry information, Microsoft TechNet, and Novell Support Connection.

Despite the program's breadth, the round-the-clock need for answers for students, faculty, and staff could not be satisfied with a central help desk or LSPs. To help address that need, $500,000 was used to establish the Knowledge Base, a frequently updated, online support program that contains answers to approximately 5,000 IT-related questions. LSPs may request on-site Knowledge Base classes for users.

Through time, the constant change in technology required more highly technical education for LSPs. The PICS EdCert program, implemented in 1994, is targeted to LSPs, faculty, and staff in technical leadership positions. The program has helped hundreds of IU employees develop the expertise they need to provide computing support to their departments. Although comparable to commercial classes, most EdCert classes are offered at no charge to registered local computing support providers on any of Indiana's campuses.

Results and lessons learned.   The fact that IU's distributed computing support model has been in place for a decade testifies to the program's success. In 1998, IU had more than 380 LSPs, with only the smallest departments lacking representation (Alspaugh & Voss, 1998).

The program has succeeded for a variety of reasons. The relationships developed over time are good ones, and the long-standing working partnership between administrative computing staff and users is one example of how this facilitates expanded collaborations. For one thing, it meant a more relaxed program environment and relatively little distrust at the onset of the PICS program. No formal governance structure was needed. Indiana's historic commitment to information technology and a strong central technology organization allowed for the allocation of resources for the development of the PICS program. Institutional leadership provided the vision and the advocacy necessary to make the PICS program successful.

What lessons has Indiana University learned? In designing a program, it is important to build on the institution's strengths. For IU, that meant exploiting the existing relationship with technical staff in departments. Some universities may not have that advantage but will have other strengths on which to build.

Good two-way communication and trust are essential. Create a formal program, identify LSPs, and keep them informed about the central IT organization efforts. Work to build trust in the technology support community, which includes central IT staff as well as LSPs. The idea of distributed computing support must be sold to both the central and departmental staffs, as it takes a while before everyone can be convinced that the partnership is worth the effort.

Use a positive approach in the program's design and implementation. Explain the program's mission in terms of how it will result in better computing support. Do not say you are reducing support or transferring support to departments. Explain that support needs are increasing far beyond what a central IT organization can meet and that leveraging technical resources will result in more effective and efficient user support.

Although planning is crucial, do not over plan. It is more important to try something with the intent of evaluating it and changing it, if needed. As the LSPs mature, their needs change, so the program must be flexible and proactive.

University of California, Davis (UCD)

Institutional profile and IT history. The University of California, Davis is a land grant, research institution. It has just over 24,000 students, 2,000 faculty, and about 12,000 staff, including medical center personnel. The campus governance is very decentralized, and departments are highly autonomous.

The computing environment at UCD evolved as a result of the general decentralization of campus services, changing technologies— particularly the rising use of the Internet, and the proliferation of personal computers. No technology standards are stipulated, and many departments had already hired their own computer support staff when the distributed support program was implemented. UCD had migrated from a mainframe environment for most administrative applications to a client-server architecture. Despite major changes in campus computing, very little had changed in the formal structure of user support through the early 1990s.

Distributed program structure. The Division of Information Technology, which provides centralized communication and large-scale computing services, implemented its Technical Support Program (TSP) in July of 1995. The program's mission was to address needs presented by the major changes in the institution's computing environment. UCD's decentralized governance and its distributed computing environment resulted in the development of a program that is completely voluntary. Aside from requiring the department head's signature on the enroll-ment form and requiring the support staff member's attendance at a one-hour orientation, no requirements for participation exist.

Front-line information technology support persons are known as Technical Support Coordinators (TSCs). Many TSCs landed in their roles by being "super-users" and had received no credit or recognition for their additional responsibilities. In designing the program, the IT Division sought to provide TSCs with a sense of recognition. TSP mail lists and gatherings are open only to TSCs. This exclusivity is an important perk to the departmental staff participating in the program and one that they guard ferociously.

The Technical Support Program coordinates local department ser-vice personnel in an integrated training and support organization, and it provides technical needs assessment and planning services to departments. A key element of the TSP is the single-point-of-initial-contact strategy. TSCs are the first point of contact for computing sup-port for all faculty and staff in their department. A TSC is, in turn, assigned a designated IT Representative (ITR) as her or his one point of contact within the Division of IT. ITRs provide referrals and track any problems they cannot resolve. UCD's help desk, IT Express, is the single point of contact for students and is exclusively for their use. Faculty and staff who call there are directed back to their TSC. With this program, the ITR's role became one of second- and third-level support, and any confusion regarding where to go for support has been eliminated.

UC, Davis' strong campus commitment to staff development resulted in a programmatic emphasis on free training for Technical Support Coordinators, which is the heart of the TCP. It provides compelling incentives for participation while improving services to faculty and staff. The program's ongoing training for TSCs includes customized courses as well as high-level technical training. TSCs are also given access to outside technical support services and IT-sponsored events. They participate in regularly scheduled informal gatherings and beta test programs. Special interest groups created and maintained by the TSCs have proven quite successful in promoting peer collaboration and problem solving. UCD's long-term use of mail lists made email a natural vehicle for collegial interaction and problem-solving with and among TSCs.

UC, Davis was financially able to dedicate resources to the implementation of a distributed computing model. The TSP was initiated with four ITR positions, with two full-time professional positions and 12–15 half-time student positions for the help desk. The budget for both the TSP and the help desk was approximately $700,000. Since the program's inception, the number of ITR positions has increased to six (Kava, 1998).

Results and lessons learned. By all accounts, formal surveys, and informal feedback, the UCD program has been very successful. During the 1995 pilot phase, 21 TSCs were enrolled; in 1998, the program included 304 TSCs and 202 departments (Kava, 1998). It is often used as a model for other institutions.

The program has succeeded in forming closer alliances between the central technology organization and individual user departments. The relationships developed between the ITRs and the TSCs have improved computing support provided to departments. The enormous amount of activity and quick resolution of problems over the TSC mail lists illustrate the success of improved communications and the creation of a viable support community.

What lessons has UCD learned? UCD's strong Technical Support Program results from good planning. UCD spent two years planning before implementing the TSP. During that time, the IT Division was able to forge bonds through a cooperative and collaborative design process. Buy-in from the TSCs, administration, faculty, staff—including IT Division staff—was crucial to the program's success.

The program continues to flourish, at least in part because it is responsive to the changing needs of TSCs. Programs are under frequent review and revision. As technology shifts and the skills of the TSCs improve, new training programs are developed to advance the support offered.

University of Virginia (UVa)

Institutional profile and IT history. The University of Virginia is a state-supported research university with a 1997–98 enrollment of 12,000 undergraduates, 4,220 graduate students, and 1,700 professional school students (http://www.virginia.edu/Facts/Glance_ Enrollment.htm). The nine schools that comprise UVa are as different in their technology needs and resources as they are in their curriculum, ranging from a nationally ranked law school with the perception of minimal technology needs to a research-intensive engineering school with sophisticated and pervasive technology use. UVa has 1,800 faculty and approximately 8,500 staff (University of Virginia, 1997).

Governance at UVa is extremely decentralized, with great authority for resource-allocation pushed to deans and department heads. UVa is an old institution steeped in tradition. Faculty are afforded a great deal of autonomy. This decentralization resulted in little standardization and a disparity in the resources dedicated to information technology from school to school; some schools were perceived as "haves," while others were perceived as "have-nots."

Central computing services at UVa are provided by the Department of Information Technology and Communication (ITC). At the time the Departmental Computing Support program (DCS) was initiated, relations between ITC and user departments were strained. Communications were poor, and years of central control of IT resources had created a culture of distrust. Departments accustomed to a decentralized culture in most areas relished the autonomy gained by the change to a distributed computing environment. They did not want to give that up and were suspicious of ITC's efforts to partner.

However, the crisis in IT support, which was faced by most colleges and universities in the 1990s, brought UVa to the point of change. In just a decade, the number of desktop computers increased from about 10% of faculty, staff, and students to almost 80%. The old central support model did not work in this large and diverse distributed environment. Individual departments began hiring their own computing support staff to address their unique needs. The haphazard model was neither planned nor coordinated, but emerged to meet a growing need. Although the hiring of local support staff was generally positive for departments, communication between ITC and departments was poor, local support was inconsistent, and technology implementation was piecemeal. To address department-level computing support needs more effectively and to leverage shared resources most efficiently, ITC implemented the DSC in January 1997.

Distributed program structure. The University of Virginia's Departmental Computing Support program is an alliance between ITC and user departments. Its goal is to help departmental support staff provide effective front-line information technology support. By developing local resources, this program empowers user departments to sustain their own desktop computing endeavors. The program seeks to create a more efficient support community. Better general base support will allow local staff to focus on more discipline-specific needs. Departments wishing to participate are asked to select one or more staff members to act as front-line information technology support persons, or Local Support Partners (LSPs). LSPs must have computing support, which is loosely interpreted, in their job description to qualify for inclusion in the program. Some smaller departments in related disciplines share one LSP.

Given the decentralized nature of governance at UVa and the extent of autonomy of the schools, all aspects of the DCS program were made voluntary. Participation was encouraged through tangible incentives, but no department was required by ITC to identify an LSP. A mandatory program would have failed from the start. The DCS program was developed and billed as a formalization of the existing situation rather than wholesale change. In developing the DCS program, ITC made a great deal of effort to reestablish trust with user departments. Focus groups of LSPs were brought together to shape the program, and governance of the group became a joint ITC-LSP effort.

Departmental computing support is divided into three phases: assessment, implementation, and the LSP program of ongoing support. In the assessment phase, the client department conducts a comprehensive survey of its current technological state. This assessment may include an inventory of the department's hardware, software, and technical support resources; an evaluation of its user training and technology funding, and the ways in which it is using computing resources to support its mission; and a list of technology-related goals, with a plan for achieving them. ITC provides whatever tools and specialized expertise the department requires for its self-assessment, and it can direct the entire assessment process if the department so prefers. ITC helps formulate financing strategies for implementing technology upgrades. To avoid alienating user departments, all aspects of the assessments are conducted jointly with the department. ITC limits its involvement to the level of comfort of the department chair and faculty, an approach which has gone a long way toward proving good will and opening doors. The final product of the assessment phase is a report of findings, which incorporates a plan for deployment of hardware, software, training, and technical staff within the department as well as financing options.

From the outset of the implementation phase, ITC personnel assist the LSP with the procurement and configuration of hardware and software. If the department's plan specifies a major technology overhaul, ITC provides help in finding funding sources. Once the pieces are assembled, ITC's implementation team assists department personnel in all aspects of the new computing infrastructure: delivery, installation, integration with the existing environment, and orientation of users. The implementation coordinator works closely with the department's LSPs to ensure their technical mastery of the new environment.

The cornerstone of the DCS initiative is the LSP program of ongoing support. Through the program, Local Support Partners are equipped to provide basic computing support and technical training to the department. The program offers regular liaison activities, including monthly meetings, special interest group sessions, and semiannual conferences. At these events, LSPs are given advance notice of central IT plans and directions. Peer-to-peer collaboration is encouraged through mail lists and has proven very effective. LSPs are provided high-level access to ITC resources and staff and have been integrated into ITC's planning and budgeting process. The LSPs shape the program through an elected steering committee of their peers. ITC staff members dedicated to the LSP program are available to assist with computing needs and problems as they arise within the department.

The academic and administrative leadership recognized the need for a distributed computing support model and provided resources to help establish the new program. DCS was implemented with four ITC positions dedicated to the program and a budget of approximately $300,000. At the same time, ITC transformed its help desk from one staffed on a rotating basis to one with a full-time, dedicated staff.

Because the central resources provided to establish the program were insufficient to stimulate participation among departments, ITC leveraged existing resources and services to offer tangible benefits to users. The promise of assistance in securing funding for technology initiatives is a powerful incentive for participation in a DCS assessment, since funding for technology equipment and support at UVa is the responsibility of each school or department. Other incentives, such as free training, access to ITC knowledge bases and tools, and the semiannual conferences were developed to encourage LSP participation.

Results and lessons learned.   In its first year, the DCS program at UVa has proved very successful. More than 140 LSPs participate in the program. Communication between ITC and user departments and among user departments has improved dramatically. Suspicions of ITC have waned, and relations have improved. LSPs have bought in to the concept of a partnership with ITC and have gained tangible and intangible benefits from the partnership. LSPs are better informed, better trained, and in touch with resources to assist them. For its part, ITC has gained valuable perspective about emerging user needs and concerns from direct interaction with front-line support staff.

What began as an initiative advocated by a small group within ITC has become a part of the university's fabric. The terms "departmental computing" and "LSP" are well-known and frequently used around the campus. Faculty, administrators, and LSPs themselves now advocate for the DCS program.

What lessons has the University of Virginia learned? Success for UVa meant overcoming barriers and establishing trust. To be successful, the program had to be a true partnership with recognizable benefits to both LSPs and ITC. Providing tangible benefits, such as free training and tools, encouraged LSP participation. However, the less tangible benefits of improved communication, input into the project planning and budget process, and peer-to-peer collaboration have kept participation high. Recognizing and admitting a benefit to ITC helped alleviate suspicion and build trust. Buy-in from departments and particularly LSPs was crucial. ITC staff sought LSP input about user needs and responded to what they heard. Being involved in developing the program and seeing their ideas incorporated into the plan drew LSPs into the partnership.

Although planning is an important part of implementing a distributed computing support model, UVa spent only six months planning its program. This was possible because ITC staff were able to build on the lessons learned by the University of California, Davis and Indiana University, both of which had previously implemented distributed support programs. The design of UVa's program is based in large part on what had proven effective at these institutions. An important lesson to learn from the UVa program is the value of taking advantage of the expertise and experiences of other universities.

The DCS program must develop and evolve as technology changes, and constant evaluation is necessary to keep the program fresh and on-point. In the year-and-a-half since its inception, the program has already been evaluated and adapted. The successful elements have been expanded, while less successful elements have been adapted or eliminated.

The Wharton School

Institutional profile and IT history. In the previous three examples, we have examined distributed computing support models from a university-wide perspective. The Wharton School, however, is a subunit of the University of Pennsylvania and exemplifies how distributed support is applied at a school level.

Wharton is one of the country's preeminent schools of management, offering undergraduate, master's, and doctoral degrees as well as executive education programs. In 1997–98, more than 4,650 students were enrolled in its degree programs, and approximately 9,000 managers participated in its executive education programs. The faculty total 188 and are organized in 11 academic departments (http://www.wharton.upenn.edu/wharton/wharfacts.htm).

Wharton itself has a decentralized structure. Responsibility and authority for budgeting and administration are delegated to the departmental level, and the heads of these units have discretion in allocating resources as long as the expenditures are consistent with school-wide directions. Although the Wharton School has several academic departments, it is relatively homogeneous.

The University of Pennsylvania and the Wharton School had a history of decentralized computing support that dated back to the late-1980s. Wharton perceived that the school-level IT organization was out of touch with the differing needs of departments. The school was haphazardly moving to a distributed computing model as several departments began to rely more heavily on department-based support. Improved mechanisms for ongoing communication between the school-level computing support group and departments were critically needed.

Distributed program structure. In response to its computing problems, Wharton decided not to abandon the principle of decentralized management, but rather to adapt the existing model to fit the distributed computing environment. It was clear that departmental computing, already well established in several units, was key to meeting the varying computing needs of faculty. The result was a structure that combines elements of centralized computing and departmental computing.

The goal of the hybrid model is to create an effective working partnership between the school-level computing organization and departments. The program retains a school-level computing support operation for the infrastructure and core technologies and services, and it places staff directly in departments to provide locally oriented faculty support. Although distributed computing personnel are physically located in the department, with space and equipment provided by the department, they operate under both central and local management.

In this partnership, the department and the school computing group jointly hire and evaluate distributed staff. They also share training and staff development responsibilities. Funding for the position is provided by the department, with some cost-sharing by the central IT organization. The department sets the work priorities, and distributed staff manage the day-to-day work under the central group's general direction and technical supervision. A total of 14 distributed staff positions have been created through this program (Eleey, 1993).

Essential coordination functions and information-sharing are accomplished through mandatory participation in regularly scheduled meetings held by the school computing group. Departments renew participation in the program annually (Eleey, 1993). To date, all departments have renewed.

Results and lessons learned.   Wharton's distributed program's success has generated much demand across the campus. Since the program's inception, participation by academic departments has grown steadily, with one or more departments joining the program each year (Eleey, 1993).

Much of the program's success comes from the fact that it addresses the school's needs on several levels. The distributed staff approach is consistent with the school's budgeting and management philosophy and with the campus culture. The model complements rather than duplicates IT services provided across the school, and it leverages scarce resources. In addition, the program encourages change and adaptation. As priorities shift and technology changes, Wharton's distributed staff program is flexible enough to meet changing service needs. And lastly, the program provides effective channels of communication, cooperation, and coordination.

The program's configuration works well because of the school's relatively small size and homogeneity. These factors allow, for example, the requirement of mandatory meetings that might not be possible at a multicampus university.

CONCLUSION

The specific examples of distributed support programs differ in:

+ Maturity (IU started its program over a decade ago, while UVa's program is less than two years old)

+ Level within the larger institution (UVa, IU, and UCD are institution-wide, while Wharton is a single school within the University of Pennsylvania)

◆ Requirements for participation (UVa has a minimum requirement of 50% computing support in the job description, Wharton hires the computing professionals, and IU and UCD have no requirements)

◆ Use of regular meetings (UVa and Wharton have regularly scheduled meetings; IU and UCD do not)

Despite the programs' differences, however, they share many common elements. Each institution was experiencing a crisis in computing support and because the central organization could not meet all of the institution's needs, departments were hiring dedicated support staff. A distributed computing support model was developing in a haphazard manner. Also in each of these examples, institutional leadership advocated for the development of a more effective distributed support program. All of these schools allocated financial and human resources to make the program a reality, and they all provided some kind of incentives for participation.

In each example, the implementation of the distributed computing support model took into consideration the campus culture, and specific programs were designed thoughtfully to maximize success within that culture. All used the "departmental" topology. For each institution, a crucial step in the implementation was careful planning, although, in part because of the existence of the others as models, that planning required less time for the more recently implemented programs than it did for the earlier ones. In all, planning included negotiating with all stakeholders in order to secure their buy-in at the very beginning. The extensive use of mail lists and the provision of training to local support personnel were key elements of each of the programs described. Possibly the best way to summarize common elements of success is that the programs were all implemented with genuine good will, looking for win-win outcomes.

At this stage in their evolution, the programs cited have primarily focused on improving communication and coordination between central and local staff and increasing skill levels for local staff. We do not currently see a clear emphasis on differentiating the focus of local staff on unique, discipline-specific needs from an increased focus of central staff on infrastructure and institutional standards. At least at our own institution, we intend for this to happen. Early in our program, we faced so much pent-up demand for basic desktop support that all hands have been required to attempt to fulfill the need. As we quench that demand, our intent is to more intensely refocus central staff toward proactive infrastructure management and implementation of institution-wide basic standard desktop management in order to free local staff for more high-level, discipline-related support activities. We view this as a critical element in harvesting the greatest value for the institution.

REFERENCES

Alspaugh, G., & Voss, B. (1998, April 14). Correspondence.

Eleey, M. (1993, Fall). Managing to change: The Wharton School's distributed staff model for computing support. *Cause/Effect, 16* (3), 53–55.

Kava, P. (1998, March 11–13). Presentation handouts at the ACM SIGUCCS Computer Services Management Symposium 25.

McClure, P. A., Smith, J. W., & Sitko, T. D. (1997). The crisis in information technology support: Has our current model reached its limit? *CAUSE Professional Paper Series, 16.*

Moore, G. A. (1991). *Crossing the chasm: Marketing and selling high-tech products to mainstream customers.* New York, NY: Harper Business Press.

Smith, J. W. (1990, September). The interaction of technology, economics, and culture as a basis for understanding academic computing support needs. ACM SIGUCCS User Services Conference 18.

Smith, J. W. (1994, October). User's guide for shadowy crystal ball: Practical tips and techniques for planning the future. ACM SIGUCCS User Services Conference 22.

Smith, J. W. (1997, December 5). A whole-product approach to standards. CAUSE annual conference.

University of Virginia. (1997). *Data digest.* Charlottesville, VA: University of Virginia.

Note: The authors wish to thank Melinda Church, assistant to the vice president and CIO, University of Virginia, for her outstanding skill, tactfulness, and hard work in turning three very rough drafts into a single chapter that people might read and understand.

5

The Shifting Ground Between Markets and Hierarchy: Managing a Portfolio of Relationships

John C. Henderson and Mani R. Subramani

INTRODUCTION

E ducation institutions face the challenge of improving their performance with limited resources. Critics of higher education point out that the cost of education has consistently increased at a rate disproportionately larger than the public's ability to pay (Kaganoff, 1998). In fact, many experts are predicting a massive restructuring of higher education not unlike that experienced by health care (Benjamin & Carroll, 1996). While such radical projections of transformation may be overstated, it is evident that college and university administrators are rethinking their investments and patterns of resource allocation. They must ask how each investment dollar contributes to the institution's strategic direction and whether it represents a core competency for the institution.

For those academics who have watched the private sector restructuring during the past decade, these are familiar questions. It was the critical examination of strategic directions and core competencies that led many enterprises to outsource information technology (IT) during the 1990s. While a direct comparison between organizations in the private sector and educational institutions may seem tenuous, some lessons are applicable. Among the most important lesson is that those IT executives who fail to proactively address these questions will soon find themselves swept up (or out) in a tide of events with little or no ability to influence the outcome. IT directors and institutional leaders are being challenged to wrestle with the questions of strategic direction and core competency in constructive, innovative dialogues.

This chapter seeks to provide a framework for such a dialog. It does not claim to have arrived at a single, correct answer. Instead, our goal is to explore the concept of partnerships as one of an institution's choices for organizational structure. We believe that executives should view the organization on a continuum from direct ownership to virtual control of assets. Virtual assets are resources—often strategic resources—that are owned by another enterprise but which are deployed in the interest of the institution itself.

The relationship between the provider and the consumer can vary significantly. Relationships may range from those that are similar to a market exchange or those that are so seamlessly integrated that it would be difficult to differentiate between the buyer and seller. The point is not just to describe these alternative arrangements, but to recognize that different management processes are required to achieve effective performance. These management processes include selecting the right governance structure for the two organizations as well as the appropriate design of work processes and management controls that fit the structure chosen (Bakos & Brynjolfsson, 1993; Henderson, 1990).

This chapter begins with a brief theoretical discussion of alliances or partnerships as well as a description of the different kinds or typologies. Each type is illustrated in a retail context, a higher education context, and in the context of information technology. We conclude with a discussion of three key challenges that managers must address to achieve a high performing alliance.

THEORETICAL PERSPECTIVES ON RELATIONSHIPS

Transaction cost economics (TCE) can help explain the choice of governance structure in exchanges between organizations. There are three generic types of structures: markets, hierarchies, and hybrids (Williamson, 1994).

1) Markets. In the case of markets, the goods and services supplied are not differentiated, so price becomes the differentiator.

2) Hierarchies. There are times when goods and services require the investment of specialized assets (e.g., specialized tools or equipment, training for personnel, etc.). When the assets cannot be reused with another buyer, the investor is vulnerable if the buyer becomes opportunistic and goes elsewhere. To guard against that risk, assets are safeguarded by writing elaborate contracts to anticipate future contingencies. Another safeguard is to have these specialized assets under the control of the enterprise. Therefore, for exchanges that require specialized investments, hierarchical governance (or firm ownership) has lower transaction costs and is preferred. This is the traditional justification for "owning" an internal IT capability. Owning the IT assets minimizes overall costs and reduces uncertainty in the exchange between the IT service provider and the end customer.

3) Hybrids. Hybrid governance (alliances and partnerships) is intermediate between markets and hierarchies (Powell, 1990). Alliances or partnerships are preferred in situations where the need for specialized assets lies between the extremes of market and hierarchy. In these forms of organizations, the concept of asset specificity is central to understanding transaction costs, hence a deeper understanding of the factors that influence the performance of an alliance.

Oftentimes, an asset is *relationship-specific* (i.e., its greatest value is associated with a specific relationship). In a different relationship the value of the asset would be reduced or eliminated. In essence, the asset cannot be redeployed. The asset that is relationship specific can be physical, temporal, or a dedicated asset. An example of *physical asset specificity* is the investment an automobile parts supplier makes in specialized tools and dies. They cannot be redeployed elsewhere (Monteverde & Teece, 1982). *Site specificity* arises when the location of an asset (e.g., a supplier's warehouse located close to a customer's plant) makes the asset less valuable in serving other customers. In other situations, alternative uses of an asset might be impossible without a loss of productive time. This is *temporal asset specificity*. An example would be that of a cargo ship that may need to travel a considerable distance to another port to obtain cargo if it is not available from shippers at one port (Pirrong, 1993). Dedicated asset specificity derives from the scale of supplies that are not readily deployed (e.g., a large investment in plant capacity for a customer that may not be used in supplying other customers) (Williamson, 1994).

Each of these types of asset specificity can create risk in relationships. As the specificity increases, the dependency or cost of switching the relationship goes up. In the face of these costs, one partner may be taken advantage of by the other, either by increasing price or extracting price concessions.

The assets involved in *asset-specific* relationships need not be tangible. Asset specificity can derive from intangible investments (Williamson, 1979). The knowledge and experiences of the enterprise represent an intangible asset. In these cases of human capital asset specificity, the specificity is usually considered to be embedded in people (Williamson, 1994). More recently researchers such as Henderson and Clark (1990), Nonaka and Takeuchi (1995), and Davenport, Jarvenpaa, and Beers (1996) have pointed to explicit knowledge (i.e., databases, documents, or lessons learned, as critical types of intangible assets). These intangible asset specificities range from learning-by-doing of the personnel involved (Williamson, 1979), to jargon and specialized vocabulary (Monteverde, 1995), to specialized operating procedures (Venkatraman & Zaheer, 1994).

As we enter the post-industrial economy, intangible informational assets and resources are replacing physical assets as core components of the identity and positioning of enterprises (Nonaka & Takeuchi, 1995). The ability to leverage intangible, external resources and the ability to create value in coordination with other firms is a key source of competitive advantage (Dyer, 1996). With the increasing importance of intangible assets, they are likely to have significant influence on the nature of interfirm relationships (Glazer, 1990). Therefore, we must understand the risks and rewards of establishing relationships that uniquely use not only tangible assets but also intangible assets.

The typology of relationships we propose (illustrated in Figure 5.1) reflects the fundamental premise that two types of asset specificity, *process specificity* and *expertise specificity*, play a significant role in determining the nature of the interfirm relationship. We define process specificity as the nonredeployable investments made by a firm in changing and reconfiguring organizational processes to perform in the relationship. We define expertise specificity as the organizational investments in reconfiguring the knowledge base and expertise of the organization to execute effectively in the relationship. These investments are of less value in other exchanges.

Consistent with the logic underlying organizational economics (Williamson, 1994), this typology highlights the linkage between the nonredeployable investments in relationship specific processes and expertise and the nature of the relationship. Further, these concepts are consistent with the logic that interorganizational relationships are created and maintained by organizations to leverage specialized capabilities and resources that complement their own core competencies (Quinn, 1992; Venkatraman, 1997). In effect, the typology suggests that the confluence of process specificity and expertise specificity creates organizational contexts where management processes of different types are encountered. These relationships are suggested as intermediate between the extremes of managing the activity entirely within the firm (hierarchical governance) and executing it in a completely nonspecific, fleeting interaction with near anonymous parties (spot market). The typology frames the pattern of relationships in a manner that allows managers to explore both value creation in specific types of relationships and to articulate the key management processes required to sustain performance within them.

We label the four basic types of relationships, consistent with their distinctive characteristics, as *market exchange* (Mkt), *process dominant* (ProcD), *expertise dominant* (ExpD), and *strategic relationship* (Strat). Market exchange is the term used for exchanges in the lower left quadrant of the typology where both the levels of process specificity and expertise specificity are low. We term relationships in the opposite corner strategic relationships, reflecting the high level of both specialized processes and specialized expertise deployed in the exchange. Relationships in the off-diagonal quadrant marked by high levels of expertise specificity but lower than median levels of process

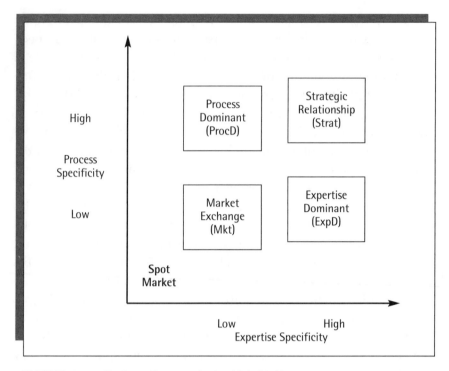

FIGURE 5.1   Typology of Interorganizational Relationships

specificity, we term expertise dominant. Those in the other off-diagonal quadrant characterized by a high level of process specificity but relatively low levels of expertise specificity are termed process dominant. Each of these relationship types embodies a unique value proposition for the organizations involved. In the following section, we explore each type and offer examples drawn from the retail context, the higher education context, and an IT management context.

Market Exchange

In the market exchange relationship, the level of process specificity and the level of expertise specificity are both low. The assets dedicated to the relationship are nonspecific and redeployable to other relationships if required. Also, the knowledge required to perform in the relationship is well understood.

Retail.   A typical example of a *transactional exchange* encountered in the retail setting involves the procurement of miscellaneous items like dishcloths, low-end necessities that retailers must carry. One retail manager, referring to these types of production service said, "the retailers can just pick up the phone and call parties in India and Bangladesh for the prevailing prices. They just buy them in bulk from whoever sells at the lowest price." The key issue in the relationship is the exchange of goods or services at the lowest cost.

From a market perspective, there are usually a large number of buyers and sellers, and since the level of process specificity is minimal, buyers' and sellers' processes are equivalent. The level of expertise specificity is also minimal: The knowledge required for an exchange is no more than the standard description. Current price and quality processes are undifferentiated.

This does not imply that such exchanges are always simple. There can be transactional exchanges around products or services that would be considered complex. The distinguishing feature of such market exchanges is that the knowledge base required by the parties are well specified and understood: The syntactical rules to encode and interpret the knowledge are commonly accessible (Kogut & Zander, 1992).

To illustrate this point, consider an exchange between the manufacturer of lawn mowers and John Deere, a large supplier of power-driven equipment. Deere needs to periodically outsource the manufacture of low-end lawn mowers to external manufacturers when their in-house capacity is committed to higher-value models. At these times, Deere procures the equipment from manufacturers who adhere to Deere's specs. Their equipment is offered for sale under the John Deere brand. There are a number of competing firms manufacturing to ISO 9000 standards with the capability to meet Deere's requirements. These firms often use orders, such as those coming from Deere, to absorb capacity that might be idle otherwise. These firms respond to RFPs. Contracts are awarded to suppliers—largely based on quoted prices—after an inspection of the facilities by Deere. Interactions between the manufacturer and Deere tend to be the minimal required for contract signing and contract execution. When the goods are ready, a manager said "they pick up the equipment at the loading dock, and we never hear from them again."

Note that the assets committed to executing processes in the exchange are entirely nonspecific: The manufacturers employ manufacturing facilities created for their own products. The processes used to deal with Deere are standard and nonspecific. The process specificity is consequently low. The knowledge and skills required to execute the exchange are completely communicated by the ISO certification and evaluated in an inspection of the facilities. "We don't have to talk very much," the manufacturing manager remarked. "Our quality procedures and our assembly processes speak for us." The knowledge and skills needed for the exchange are understood, while knowledge dependency is low.

Higher education. In a higher education setting, market exchange transactions are also quite prevalent. For example, professional schools often use adjunct professors to supplement their teaching capacity. These relationships, while ongoing, involve little or no customization on the part of the schools (e.g., the course context is not changed to suit the adjunct, and the adjunct professor can use the standard context in other teaching settings). An adjunct professor may teach a fairly standard course (e.g., Introduction to Accounting) for several different universities. In such cases, the profession may standardize the context, thus the professors' added value comes from their practical experience. Note that a relationship between the adjunct and the university does exist. Professional reputation and previous experience help to reduce the contracting as well as monitoring costs, so it is not a pure market transaction. However, the ongoing relationship in which the services are exchanged reflects a market-like relationship.

Information technology. In the technology domain, market exchange relationships are also quite common. Higher education institutions supplement their work force by subcontracting, as do many other enterprises. For example, the use of temporary programmers or service contractors for equipment movement and installation is commonplace.

Although some of these exchanges may reflect a pure market transaction, many of them involve ongoing relationships that allow the institution to specify various requirements—including quality of service—that are difficult to signal in a pure market setting. Of course, the market exchange relationship may become more efficient with time because both sides are familiar with the other's reputation or they communicate frequently. However, the level of specificity is low (both process and expertise) for both parties. Ultimately, competition remains a central tool to ensure best price and continuous innovation.

Expertise Dominant

Expertise-dominant (ExpD) relationships occur when the level of process specificity is low and the level of expertise specificity is high. We find these relationships when tasks require specialized expertise that is tailored to the relationship but where the assets and facilities are generic.

Retail. An example of an expertise-dominated relationship in a retail setting might involve the sale of clothes by a merchandiser who has a chain of stores catering to young men—a segment where the nature of preferences and styles are volatile and unpredictable. In the ExpD relationship between the retailer and the merchandiser, the merchandiser selects the assortment of goods and uses his or her specialized expertise to manage the "store within a store" to achieve the profitability and operational goals. As a senior manager of the retail store remarked, "In previous times, we have tried to hire buyers from successful specialty merchandisers to attempt to replicate the success the chain stores are having in the segments. We found that things don't work this way. There is something special about these firms' operations that is lost when you bring in just one key individual."

The level of knowledge dependency in such a relationship is high. However, from the perspective of the retailer, although the knowledge dependency is high, the processes are not specialized to a particular merchandiser: They could be applied to comparable suppliers in similar or different domains. In other words, the manufacturer could also operate a "store within a store" for a competitor. The level of process dependency is low. The relationship is characterized as expertise dominated to reflect the central motivation behind contracting for specialized expertise—to achieve specific outcomes.

Higher education. In higher education settings, examples of ExpD are growing in areas such as food service. Most student centers house a variety of food service companies (e.g., McDonalds or Pizza Hut). Institutions are getting out of the business of owning and running student-oriented food establishments. This trend is also reflected by the increasing number of organizations that contract with firms such as ARAMARK to run campus-wide food services.

Interestingly enough, these specialized services are having a direct impact on the context and delivery of courses. For example, a growing number of companies offer services that include the development and deployment of standard courses ranging from course context to administrative services (e.g., registration or testing). With the advent of the Internet and distance learning, examples of the ExpD relationship in higher education will continue to grow.

Information technology. In the information technology domain, higher education has been relatively slow to leverage ExpD relationships. The outsourcing of a data center, for example, is a classic example of an ExpD relationship. To be effective, the supplier must customize services to the unique environment of the client (requiring high expertise) while leveraging the assets of a common process (low process specificity). That is, an application must be delivered with customized features (e.g., capacity, reliability, responsiveness), but the application may be run in the same data center as a peer (or competitive) institution.

The value of an ExpD relationship is created when the buyer can leverage the competencies of a supplier to achieve consistent performance over time. These economies of expertise arise when the buyer does not have to invest in research and development, training, and process improvements in order to maintain market performance. Thus, a *performance contract* differs fundamentally from a market exchange in that these strategic investments are avoided, significantly reducing the buyer's investments. Of course, such rewards are not without risk. As the buyer transfers out or eliminates sources of expertise (e.g., those people who have the data center operations knowledge), the buyer creates a knowledge asset specificity similar to that of a specific physical asset. It is therefore essential for the buyer to adjust the management processes in ways that allow effective management of the relationships to manage these potential rewards and risks.

The number of ExpD relationships in other industries is exploding. The outsourcing of data centers and network and user support services have become commonplace. These trends will probably emerge in higher education as colleges and universities strive to optimize increasingly scarce resources and stretch tight operating budgets.

Process Dominant Relationships

Process dominant (ProcD) relationships occur when the level of process specificity is high and the level of expertise specificity is low. These relationships are typically found when the intent is differentiation in the delivery of a relatively standardized product or service.

Retail. One vendor of snow blowers and power tools described how they work closely with the retailer to introduce specially styled handlebars for blowers that allow the equipment to be operated with one hand. This feature was incorporated in the retailer's models exclusively under this retailer's brand. As part of the retailer's brand strategy, the retailer invests significant resources in creating quality standards that are revised every year to keep their products state-of-the-art. In addition, the retailer provides a team of trained specialists to work with equipment manufacturers to resolve manufacturing problems and improve quality standards. Furthermore, products sold by the retailer are serviced for ten years through the retailer's service division. This service requirement has resulted in sophisticated processes that enhance the interaction with vendors. For example, the service division tracks customer complaints by model, then works with the design and engineering team to resolve them and then disseminates the information to all field service locations. In addition, they periodically compile the list of proposed product design changes for inclusion in future products.

While these actions on the part of the retailer and manufacturer have resulted in a specialized process (i.e., dedicated assets, temporal specificity, and physical asset specificity), the expertise exchanged by both parties is not relationship specific. The quality processes and standards adhered to by the retailer are widely understood by manufacturers (i.e., they are standardized and encoded), hence they are redeployable. The information system for compliance tracking and shipping data is well documented and reflects the industry's best practice.

In essence, the uniqueness of the relationship is not in the context of the knowledge or information exchanged but the manner in which it has been implemented—in this case represented by dedicated capacity, commitment to timing requirements, and even specialized equipment designs. As a result, the relationship adds greater value than a market exchange because the processes are designed for optimization from end-to-end. This integrated process design creates a unique working arrangement between the two firms that allows an enhanced level of performance. Because of the commitment of specific assets, the relationship also incurs additional risk (e.g., opportunistic behavior by one of the parties). The executives for both firms must recognize this altered risk and reward profile and adjust their management processes accordingly.

Higher education.   The existence of ProcD relationships in higher education varies widely. Traditional purchasing organizations have, in some cases, pursued ProcD relationships for their material management in areas such as physical plant operations, supply of laboratories, or in services such as food operations. In many cases, however, higher education has not chosen to leverage their purchasing power across an entire system; rather they allow each institution to control purchasing decisions locally. Therefore, the incentives for the seller to enter into a ProcD relationship may be limited.

Information technology.   In the technology domain, ProcD relationships for most higher education settings have been limited. Until recently, most institutions have written home-grown applications or customized standard applications and related technologies. Suppliers have been kept at arm's length reflecting a market exchange relationship. Of course, a gift of vendor technology may evolve into asset specificity as the university deploys specialized skills (e.g., programming skills) that are unique to the gifted technology. We are seeing a rise in ProcD relationships as more and more institutions replace and redesign their administrative systems with enterprise-level software solutions (e.g., SAP, PeopleSoft, or BAAN). As this trend continues, we expect to see the number of ProcD relationships with technology providers increase.

Strategic Alliances

Where the levels of process specificity and expertise specificity are both high, the exchange relationship is a *strategic alliance*. In such relationships, unique expertise coupled with unique work processes offers the opportunity to deliver extraordinary value. However, the risks of these relationships are also significant. Partners often have access to each other's core intellectual assets. Because of the tight linkage of expertise and processes, mutual dependencies are created which are critical to the long-term survival of each party. This elevates the cost of opportunistic behavior to a strategic level.

Retail. For example, consider the previously discussed relationship between a retailer and a manufacturer of snow blowers and power tools. From the manufacturer's perspective, the level of process specificity is very high: They have invested significant resources in customizing manufacturing processes to conform to the quality standards of the retailer, particularly with respect to the service network. The manufacturer has also made investments in hardware and software to enable online access to quality inspection reports and to facilitate the electronic exchange of documents with the retailer (e.g., submission of invoices and delivery of shipping notices). These investments have limited redeployability to other customers.

The expertise specificity in the relationship with the retailer could also be high if the manufacturer depends on the retailer's service network as the primary source of feedback on customers' use of their products. Recall that the retailer's service network maintains products sold through the retailer for ten years. As a result, this service network also serves as the repository of systematically recorded data on component failures. These statistics become the basis for the manufacturer's recommendations about what stock should be on hand for repairs. These statistics also constitute an important input in new product designs, guiding the retention or improvement of assemblies and subcomponents in subsequent products. Clearly, the level of expertise specificity can become quite high. Thus, executives argue that the relationship with the retailer is strategic.

Higher education. Examples of strategic alliances in higher education are also increasing. Universities and colleges have long sought such relationships with major funding sources, supplying intellectual capital in exchange for research funds or educational programs. Increasingly, these arrangements involve equity positions by the university as a means to share in the expected long-term returns from patents, new products, or intellectual capital.

Information technology. In the technology domain, strategic alliances are also beginning to emerge. University systems are recognizing that they bring significant brand recognition as well as a strong affinity group. However, resource constraints significantly limit the ability of the university system to sustain the infrastructure investments required to make emerging technology readily available to their students. One possible approach is exemplified by the strategic initiative launched by the California State University System (CSU). CSU attempted to forge a multicompany technology alliance with Microsoft, GTE Corporation, Fujitsu Limited, and Hughes Space and Communications. The partners would use the university base of technology (i.e., 22 university networks stretching the length of California) and an affinity group of over one million people to create a technology and services organization. The alliance not only would have the means to provide new technology solutions to each campus but also, ultimately, could leverage the expertise on the campuses and among the business partners to offer courseware and technology-based products and services to the market at large (i.e., distance learning to educational institutions). Long-term research and development investments and the ability to upgrade and sustain a dynamic and innovative technology environment across all campuses would be funded through shared profits of these new offerings.

Needless to say, this initiative has proved quite difficult to execute, and two of the firms, Microsoft and Hughes, have recently announced their decision to withdraw from the alliance. Nevertheless, the structure and strategy of this plan clearly portrays a viable strategic alternative open to many educational institutions.

Another instance of a strategic relationship is between the University of Minnesota and IBM. In an agreement signed in March 1998, the university and IBM agreed to share the future development costs of a multimillion dollar integrated student information system. The system is to be based on the initial version developed by the University of Minnesota at a cost of $500,000 and currently in operation in the Twin Cities, Crookston, and Morris campuses. The system enables students to examine course information, to register online, and to view their fees using a web browser. The system integrates a range of university and class information for course planning, applying for financial aid, and purchasing textbooks online. The web interface serves as a unifying window to serve students. (See Chapter 7 for additional details.)

Through the strategic relationship with IBM, the partners will share the risks inherent in the venture. They will also pool their expertise and work jointly to develop the system that will be sold to other colleges and universities. The university expects to receive royalties on each sale.

ATTRIBUTES OF RELATIONSHIPS

The conventional notion underlying exchanges is that there is a spectrum with the polar end points ranging from low to high on a set of attributes (e.g., exchanges with low levels of trust lie on the end opposite to those with high levels of trust). This assumes that the attribute is linear and unidimensional. Our research indicates that exchange attributes differ qualitatively rather than quantitatively. The assumption of linearity from one end of the spectrum to another is a simplification that obscures the key differences. For instance, while trust is important in all four types of exchanges, the trust between the parties differs significantly, not in quantity but in the nature of the trust.

◆ In transactional exchanges, the trust is centered around the expectation that the other party will competently execute the contract as written.

◆ In ProcD relationships, the other party is trusted to execute their part of the contract with the expectation that they would perform irrespective of the contingencies that might arise. The trust, in this case, extends to the belief in their competence to overcome or anticipate adverse circumstances that are beyond the ability of the contracting firm to visualize or articulate in detail. Nevertheless, the firm executing the contract is expected to cope with all contingencies. In ProcD relationships, both parties implicitly recognize higher levels of unforeseeable circumstances and implicitly trust the competence of the other to behave nonopportunistically even though the potential to "hold-up" is high.

◆ In strategic alliances, the nature of the trust tends to focus on the belief that the vision for the alliance is realistic and that the direction is appropriate.

ISSUE	TRANSACTIONAL EXCHANGE	PERFORMANCE CONTRACT	SPECIAL RELATIONSHIP	STRATEGIC ALLIANCE
Focus	Exchange efficiency (e.g., lowest price, favorable terms)	Operational efficiency exploiting economies of scale, and scope	Achieve end to end efficiencies through process integration	Develop unique product/service capabili-ties
Opportunity leverage	Product/service requirements	Ability to deploy specific competencies	Ability to access specialized expertise and skills to complement competencies	Ability to probe, learn about market dynamics, trends, and the environment
Capability development	Market search, negotiation, contracting. Acquire info to improve future negotiations	Process specification	Process redesign, enable process innovations	Creation of new or unique competencies through synergy, innovation, alliance management
Planning horizon	Current deal	Ongoing, multiple exchanges	Medium term, loosely specified endpoint	Long-term, unspecified endpoint
Accountability assumption	Contractual accountability, contract performance relative to legal benchmark	Functional accountability, conformance to ethical, professional standards	Process accountability, institutionalized trust based on understanding of core values, non-opportunistic behavior	Value accountability to achieve strategic outcome, visionary trust, belief that direction is appropriate, trusted to share strategic direction
Information behavior	Market information prices/trends/terms	Synchronizing schedules and plans	Process metrics	Unstructured, sensitive information
Information mechanisms	Efficiency oriented (e.g., EDI based ordering, billing)	Structured MIS for decision support, management control	Integrated infrastructure, customized applications, analysis and decision support, development of joint capability, use of liaison	Unique and innovative technology deployment, co-location, joint planning, direct senior management contact
Risk management	Negotiation, compliance audit, noncompliance penalties	Establish service quality standards, service level benchmarking, performance bonuses	Process benchmarking, comparing against best practice, continuous improvement programs	Senior management review, market-based indicators

FIGURE 5.2   Management Processes in Different Types of Relationships

These fundamental differences point to a need to craft management practices that fit the nature of the relationships, as shown in Figure 5.2. In the next section, we will explore this theme in more detail.

MANAGING A PORTFOLIO OF RELATIONSHIPS

The relationship portfolio model allows one to explore how to achieve high performance across the full range of relationship types. Although there is a range of challenges facing relationship managers, three are particularly relevant:

◆ Value creation and appropriation

◆ Creating and sustaining trust

◆ The role of information technology in enabling effective relationships

The effective performance of an alliance requires a fit between the relationship type and the management process used to direct and control performance. The following section will explore the concept of fit in more depth.

Value Creation and Appropriation

Perhaps the most essential task of management in forming and sustaining an alliance centers on how this relationship will create value and the mechanisms that will ensure this value is appropriately distributed. Value is created both by the outcomes of the relationship and by the competencies or capabilities created during this process.

Market exchange.   From an output perspective, a market exchange relationship strives to produce an efficient transaction. By definition, exchange processes are standard and relevant knowledge codified. In such a setting, the product or service exchanged or acquired by one firm can be readily acquired by that firm's competitor (often from the same supplier). Thus, value is tied to price, product feature, and related issues such as timing and quality. Value is created by the relationship, over and above a pure market transaction, through investments that lower transaction costs such as the creation of standard contracts or timely information flows. These investments are quite modest and can be redeployed to other relationships. Value, beyond that of a pure market transaction, can arise from sources such as economies of scale or scope. Appropriation of value is managed through explicit pricing strategies (e.g., volume discounts or negotiated services). Examples in the technology domain are clearly visible in areas that allow for standard products. For example, a common practice is the negotiation of volume discounts for PCs for a university affinity group (e.g., faculty, students, and staff).

It is critically important to recognize how such relationships are structured to ensure sustaining value and innovation in both product and services. In a market exchange relationship, competition is the major mechanism. As a result, market exchange contracts normally involve a bidding process and the contract length remains fairly short (normally one year). Partners in a market exchange relationship are assured the right to bid or use processes that reduce the contracting costs. The direct market bidding process ensures that the products and services exchanged will reflect the market. Of course, the working relationship may allow both enterprises to better or more efficiently communicate requirements, thereby rewarding those partners with repeat business. Still, it is the use (or the threat) of competitive bidding that assures the market exchange relationship will achieve optimal performance.

Process dominant and expertise dominant. In the case of the ProcD and ExpD relationships, the direct market mechanism is not viable. Recall that each of these relationship types involves significant relationship-specific investments. Value is created in the relationships, in part, through these specific investments. Thus, two organizations that develop a unique end-to-end work flow process can outperform a standard market exchange process. Value is created by optimizing the combined process rather than optimizing subprocesses and coordinating the exchange. When significant efficiencies occur as a result of this end-to-end process optimization, the relationship creates value.

But how does each organization ensure that this value is appropriately distributed? What if one firm exploited the dependencies created through the relationship-specific investment in order to appropriate a greater share of the value? The relationship managers must deploy processes that help to guard against such behavior. Our work suggests two approaches: 1) the use of total quality management (TQM) practice across both firms, and 2) incentives that reward partners based on overall achieved business performance rather than on component performance.

In the case of ProcD relationships, the partners have no direct market comparison with which to gauge price or performance. By definition, the value is created through a unique workflow design. Therefore, the manager must look to continuous process improvement and best practice exchanges to help guide and motivate performance. Similarly, value is created by the deployment of an end-to-end process. Our work suggests that effective ProcD relationships tie rewards to the effective execution of the entire process. For example, in the deployment of an enterprise software solution, the buying firm may establish a ProcD relationship with the vendor (or consulting firm) that involves dedicated assets, use of a unique project management process, and so on. However, to ensure performance, the contract should tie significant rewards to the effective implementation of the entire solution in a manner that meets or exceeds initial expectations. Thus, if the enterprise solution is expected to achieve an integrated supply change that reduces the cost of inventory by 50%, rewards should be tied directly to this outcome. Such work relationships have emerged in the technology domain, particularly after the acceptance of redesign and process transformation concepts.

In the case of ExpD relationships, the process is standardized, while the expertise is customized, allowing expertise to be a source of value creation. By leveraging the core competencies of a partner, the relationship not only achieves immediate performance impact but can also sustain performance in the face of market uncertainties. For example, many firms that outsourced elements of their IT systems were able to quickly leverage the skills and investments of their partner in their efforts to develop a Year 2000 (Y2K) response. The technology vendor was clearly in a better position than the firm to acquire knowledge about Y2K solutions given their expertise base and experience across many firms. Our research has identified many examples of value creation that result from the ability of the enterprise to successfully leverage the core competencies of their partner.

However, achieving economies of expertise requires relationship-specific investments. How does management ensure that value is shared appropriately? Unlike a ProcD relationship, the ExpD relationship can use the market to compare price and product. By definition, the process is standardized; hence competitors may offer similar services. The value created in one relationship cannot significantly exceed market performance or that firm's competitor would simply acquire the same service (perhaps from the same supplier). The emergence of the technology service market (e.g., data center outsourcing) is an interesting example of this concept in the technology domain. The challenge for the relationship manager is to structure the contract to achieve the value of this extended relationship (e.g., reduced research and development investments, redeployment of assets, increased ability to focus on core competencies) without falling prey to opportunistic behaviors that could lead to submarket performance. Our research suggests that employing concepts such as dynamic pricing that is linked to industry benchmarks or gain-sharing incentive systems can be effective mechanisms to ensure the performance.

Strategic alliance. Finally, in the case of strategic relationships, the potential for value creation is high. Unique work processes combined with highly leveraged expertise create the potential for significant innovation. It is in this area that the rewards and risks of the relationship are greatest. Our work suggests that the direct involvement of senior executives is an essential element of success in these settings. Operating with a governance structure similar to a board of directors, these executives can help guide the relationship, continuously monitoring and negotiating issues of value sharing. In many cases, equity arrangements may also be used to ensure that long-term value is shared appropriately.

The risks of these relationships are also high. Beyond the concern that a partner will manipulate dependencies to inflate prices or reduce service levels, these relationships often expose core intellectual assets. Henderson and Clark (1990) describe these knowledge assets as architectural knowledge (i.e., the understanding of how to integrate activities or components into a whole system). The leakage of the core knowledge poses a strategic risk to the firm, yet is quite difficult to guard against. The complexity of such issues suggests that strategic alliances must incorporate deep institutional relationships where levels of trust are high and reputation is a dominant concern. Such relationships do not develop overnight and cannot be negotiated or captured in a control structure. They reflect a way of doing business that begins with the leadership of the organization. Without strong personal leadership—at both a vision and operational level—strategic relationships will be very difficult to manage.

Creating and Sustaining Trust

Trust is critical to the success of most relationships. Prior research confirms that the ability of firms to create trust serves as a foundation on which to build higher-value relationships (Gambetta, 1994). And yet, in today's turbulent, hyper-competitive world, any number of external events (e.g., a competitor moves or a market slows down) can impact the original vision of an alliance and undermine the trust between two organizations. In essence, one firm must alter its commitment, perhaps negating the relationship. In the face of such uncertainty, what is the meaning of trust? How is it achieved? And should a realistic management team even strive to achieve trust? One key concept is to create a fit between the level of trust and the type of relationship.

Market exchange. In the market exchange relationship, managers should work to establish *transactional trust* that implies that both parties adhere to legal and ethical conduct reflected by both the contract and society. Essentially, it means neither party will lie or cheat. Transactional trust also implies a level of information exchange that is transactional in nature. Firms clearly document outcomes and the fulfillment of contractual obligations. The firm can demonstrate the product or service was delivered on a particular date at a specified price and of the required quality. Lack of trust results in elaborate processes of verification. This lack of trust may be reflected in high monitoring cost. In contrast, for example, Wal-Mart instituted processes with Procter and Gamble that allows the elimination of event-oriented verification. Purchase orders and other verification mechanisms were eliminated in favor of an information-based system which automatically signaled a need, allowing Procter and Gamble to fulfill the need and bill Wal-Mart for products delivered. Of course, auditing mechanisms were instituted to guard against individual dysfunction (e.g., stealing), but these safeguards were efficient and did not undermine the level of institutional trust.

Process dominant and expertise dominant. In the case of ProcD or ExpD relationships, the levels of dependencies are significantly higher, and therefore a new kind of trust must be established. This type of relationship (*performance contract* or *special relationship*) requires process or informational trust. Process trust reflects the willingness of both parties to reveal internal processes and share sensitive, real-time information about work practices or work-in-process status. In order to improve overall operating effectiveness, the supplier shares sensitive cost data or opens up their processes for observation. The buyer is willing to include the partner in sensitive processes, such as strategic planning, in order to better communicate current and future needs. In essence, the firms establish integrated processes. Sharing information at this level, coupled with the personal relationships that are created through teamwork, raise trust to a new level. As a result, negotiating costs and monitoring costs can be significantly reduced. More importantly, innovation increases create an opportunity for the organizations involved to achieve a performance level neither could achieve alone.

Strategic alliance. Finally, strategic trust reflects the concept of identity. In essence, individuals must identify themselves as being part of a unique institutional relationship. In this type of trust, each organization is willing to make long-term investments in the individuals around them. Innovation and experiences are readily exchanged in an attempt to succeed. It is easy to see how knowledge at this level may be created and shared. The sharing of such core knowledge is both the source of potential performance improvements and the source of significant risks. The key issue for managers is to ensure that the knowledge exchange stays focused on those areas addressed by the relationship. This may not be an easy task when the objective is to create a relationship that projects a truly unique identity.

Role of Information Technology

The use of information technology to support information sharing and coordination varies in the different types of relationships.

Transactional exchanges. In transactional exchanges, enabling efficient, *partner-independent* sharing of coordination information is the goal of technology deployment. For example, a retailer may announce a policy requiring all vendors to adopt EDI technology and industry standards. This will allow the electronic dispatch of orders to vendors and the receipt of advance notices of product shipment with minimal delays and little need for attention by managers. The retailer has indicated that if the receiving report at the retailer's warehouse, the advance shipment notice (ASN), and the purchase order (PO) match, the accounting department should mail the payment, eliminating the need for paper documents such as invoices. The applications are also designed to generate statistics on the number of on-time/delayed deliveries and signal deviations from PO quantity, etc. These inputs enable more effective negotiation with the retailer in the next contract. This pattern of IT use for efficiency occurs in the automobile industry between suppliers and auto manufacturers. Bensaou and Venkatraman (1995) term this the "remote control" model.

Performance contract. In performance contract–based relationships, the application of IT is largely focused on enabling management control and monitoring. For a "store-within-a-store," the retailer and the specialized merchandiser would share information about sales trends, movement of products, and current margins. IT use would enable managers at the retailer's site to monitor the performance of the merchandiser and identify anomalous events using reports based on point-of-sale (POS) data, stock position in stores, and cash flows. Providing managers the ability to periodically check key indicators which verify the normal functioning of processes on the retailer's end (managed by the merchandiser) is the goal of IT deployment.

Special relationship. In the case of special relationships, the use of IT was focused on creating an integrated infrastructure to enable the review of detailed information on the status of both the retail end and of processes in vendors' production and logistics facilities. For instance, the vendor and the retailer shared a common database of inventory at different retail stores, the sales at each store, the number of days of inventory in the retailers' warehouses, and the production schedule to maximize product availability and sales. The information for coordination was very detailed, involving the discussion of inventories to be maintained at different stocking points before sales promotions. Such relationships were also characterized by extensive personal interaction between managers on both sides of the relationship, probably because the IT support was rudimentary, consisting of spreadsheets that the retailers and vendors shared and used as the basis for discussion over the phone. The focus of the deployment of email in these relationships was to share the interpretations of data online and keep each other abreast of market developments as they occurred so that coordinated plans for action (e.g., reacting to a vendor's promotion, reacting to unusual weather conditions that boosted the demand for snow blowers, etc.) could be formulated rapidly. The key elements of IT deployment are the sharing of an information infrastructure and common data analysis and management control applications.

Strategic alliance.   In strategic alliances, the IT deployment would tend to be unique and focused on providing both partners with the capability to maximize the synergistic advantages of the combination. The IT infrastructure and the technologies deployed tend to be leading edge and customized to the special requirements of the relationship. The deployment of IT to enable just-in-time deliveries to the retailer is a typical instance where both the vendor and the retailer have invested in customized hardware and application software. Further, IT systems also promote the creation and exchange of knowledge. Knowledge management technologies (Davenport, DeLong, & Beers, 1998) augment the infrastructure systems to help enable superior levels of innovation and operating performance.

CONCLUSION

Our data provide preliminary evidence for the existence of four types of interorganizational relationships: transactional exchange, performance contract, special relationship, and strategic alliance that are characterized by different levels of process specificity and expertise specificity in the exchange. Furthermore, our data indicate the existence of a set of key challenges in these relationships that are resolved differently depending on the type of relationship. A preliminary list of these challenges includes:

+ The focus of the exchange
+ The nature of competency exploited
+ The nature of competency upgradation

- ◆ The time horizon influencing decisions
- ◆ The nature of trust
- ◆ The information behavior
- ◆ Risk management

The four types of relationships, in the ideal form, are reflected in coherent configurations of responses to these challenges by managers in the relationship.

ACKNOWLEDGMENTS

The authors wish to thank Professor N. Venkatraman and managers participating in the workshops of the Systems Research Center for their input that allowed us to refine our ideas.

REFERENCES

Bakos, Y. J., & Brynjolfsson, E. (1993, Fall). Information technology, incentives, and the optimal number of suppliers. *Journal of Management Information Systems, 10* (2), 37–53.

Benjamin, R., & Carroll, S. J. (1996). The implication of the changed environment for governance in higher education. In W. Tierney (Ed.), *The responsive university: Restructuring for performance,* 92–119. Baltimore, MD, and London, England: Johns Hopkins University Press.

Bensaou, M., & Venkatraman, N. (1995). Configurations of interorganizational relationships: A comparison between US and Japanese automakers. *Management Science, 41* (9), 1471–1492.

Davenport, T. H., Jarvenpaa, S. L., & Beers, M. C. (1996, Summer). Managing and improving knowledge work processes. *Sloan Management Review, 38,* 53–65.

Davenport, T. H., De Long, D. W., & Beers, M. C. (1998, Winter). Successful knowledge management projects. *Sloan Management Review,* 43–57.

Dyer, J. H. (1996). Does governance matter? Keiretsu alliances and asset specificity as sources of Japanese competitive advantage. *Organization Science, 7* (6), 649–666.

Gambetta, D. (1994). *Trust: Making and breaking cooperative relations.* London, England: Basil Blackwell.

Glazer, R. (1990). Marketing in an information intensive environment: Strategic implications of knowledge as an asset. *Marketing Sciences Institute,* working paper.

Henderson, J. C. (1990, Winter). Plugging into strategic partnerships: The IS-Line connection. *Sloan Management Review, 31* (3), 7–18.

Henderson, R. M., & Clark, K. B. (1990). Architectural innovation: The reconfiguration of existing product technologies and the failure of established firms. *Administrative Science Quarterly, 35,* 9–30.

Kaganoff, T. (1998). *Collaboration technology and outsourcing initiatives in higher education: A literature review.* Rand Education report prepared for Foundation for Independent Higher Education.

Kogut, B., & Zander, U. (1992, August). Knowledge of the firm, combinative capabilities, and the replication of technology. *Organization Science, 3* (3), 383–397.

Monteverde, K., & Teece, D. J. (1982). Appropriable rents and quasi-vertical integration. *Journal of Law and Economics, 25,* 321–328.

Monteverde, K. (1995). Technical dialog as an incentive for vertical integration in the semiconductor industry. *Management Science, 41* (10), 1624–1638.

Nonaka, I., & Takeuchi, H. (1995). *The knowledge creating company: How Japanese companies create the dynamics of innovation.* New York, NY: Oxford.

Pirrong, S. (1993). Contracting practices in bulk shipping markets: A transactions cost explanation. *Journal of Law and Economics, 36,* 937–976.

Powell, W. W. (1990). Neither market nor hierarchy: Network forms of organization. In L. L. Cummings & B. Staw (Eds.), *Research in organization behavior,* 295–336b. Greenwich, CT: JAI Press.

Quinn, J. B. (1992). *Intelligent enterprise.* New York, NY: Free Press.

Williamson, O. (1979). Transaction cost economics: The governance of contractual relations. *Journal of Law and Economics, 22,* 233.

Williamson, O. (1994). Transaction cost economics and organization theory. In N. J. Smelser & R. Swedberg (Eds.), *The handbook of economic sociology* (1st. ed.), 77–107. Princeton, NJ: Princeton University Press.

Venkatraman, N., & Zaheer, A. (1994). Electronic integration and strategic advantage: A quasi-experimental study in the insurance industry. *Information Systems Research, 1* (4).

Venkatraman, N. (1997, Spring). Beyond outsourcing: Managing IT resources as a value center. *Sloan Management Review, 38,* 51–64.

6

The Colleges of the Fenway

Sister Janet Eisner, SND

I n 1995, I invited four colleagues, presidents of neighboring colleges, to consider the following questions:

◆ Would we enhance the educational opportunities of our students by working together?

◆ Would we find cost savings through economies of scale if we worked together?

We five presidents gave a resounding yes to these queries and resolved to form a new collaborative known as The Colleges of the Fenway.

The Colleges of the Fenway—Emmanuel College, Massachusetts College of Pharmacy and Allied Health Sciences, Simmons College, Wentworth Institute of Technology, and Wheelock College—agreed to share courses, programs, and services, while retaining the distinctive mission and character of each individual institution. Our primary goals were to enhance the educational experience of our students and to slow down the escalating costs of higher education.

With the public announcement of the collaborative in March 1996 came recognition from the media and local and national press, including two articles in *The Chronicle of Higher Education*. *The Boston Business Journal* called it "a bold move," and Boston mayor Thomas Menino called it "a wonderfully creative solution." Televised panel discussions followed, as did site visits from 30 college and university presidents from South America, recognizing the potential of the collaborative to become a groundbreaking model in higher education.

In this chapter, I shall outline the context and process of our coming together, the early successes and obstacles we faced, and the strategic issues we are addressing as we enter our third year. The Colleges of the Fenway collaborative is truly a work in progress. While several plans are yet to be implemented and new focal points continue to emerge, the presidents remain committed to the founding principles and purposes of the collaborative.

BACKGROUND

From the beginning, the five presidents recognized the imperative of affirming and retaining the distinctive mission of each individual college. We are well-established colleges, with distinguished histories, founding dates ranging from 1823 to 1919, and thousands of loyal alumnae/i.

Emmanuel College, founded in 1919 by the Sisters of Notre Dame de Namur, is a four-year Catholic, liberal arts college for women; the college also offers graduate and undergraduate degree programs to women and men adult learners. Massachusetts College of Pharmacy and Allied Health Sciences, founded in 1823, is the second oldest college of pharmacy in the United States and offers bachelor's degrees in pharmacy, chemistry, nuclear medicine technology, and other allied health programs, with graduate degrees in the pharmaceutical sciences. Simmons College, which celebrates its centennial in 1999, educates undergraduate women and graduate men and women for professional careers that encompass a liberal arts perspective. Wentworth Institute of Technology, a coeducational college founded in 1904, offers programs in architecture, design, engineering, technology and management of technology. Wheelock College, founded in 1888, is committed to improving the lives of children and families through undergraduate programs in education, social work, and child life.

Prior to the formal initiative of the Colleges of the Fenway, the colleges had a history of cooperation. Several colleges participated in the Fenway Library Consortium, Emmanuel and Simmons had cross-registered students for 25 years, and colleges had shared some facilities and programs over the years. This was the first time, however, that all five presidents had come together to shape a common vision for collaboration across all five institutions. We had the unique advantage of close proximity where students could walk between the most distant campuses in 10 minutes.

PRINCIPLES OF COLLABORATION

In March 1996, the Colleges of the Fenway adopted straightforward principles of collaboration to guide all activities:

> We believe that by working together we can enhance the student and faculty environments of our individual institutions while retaining the unique and special qualities of each of our schools. Moreover, we believe that through the economic benefits of collaboration we can slow down the escalating costs of higher education through the sharing of resources, the ending of costly duplication, and the advantages of joint purchasing. Through collaboration, our students and faculty will be able to share the best of both worlds: continuing to study, live, and teach in a small college environment while also enjoying the resources of a major academic environment (Colleges of the Fenway, 1996, March).

Collectively, in the spring of 1996, the Colleges of the Fenway enrolled 6,766 students, with 482 full-time faculty, 1,703 courses, and an annual operating budget of $160 million. Students now shared all the advantages of a small college environment as well as those of a larger university.

In conjunction with its principles of collaboration, the Colleges of the Fenway stated this goal: To expand and enrich the academic offerings available to students at any participating institution through open enrollment at all participating institutions without additional cost to the students. Cross-registration became an immediate priority for the colleges and one of the collaborative's early and greatest successes.

Cross-Registration

At the request of the presidents, in January 1996 the academic officers and registrars of the Colleges of the Fenway outlined an ambitious plan for cross-registration—ambitious because the goal was to implement registration among the five colleges in September 1996. An easy, convenient, student-centered process was envisioned; in fact, all agreed that a "no-hassle" process was essential for student participation. In February 1996, after several planning meetings, the academic officers and registrars proposed that, in less than one month, a single description of the Colleges of the Fenway be drafted and included in each college's course catalogue for 1996–97, that information sessions be held with each college's faculty, that publicity of the colleges' shared goals and plans be maximized, and that admissions directors develop information resources for current and prospective students that highlighted the benefits of the Colleges of the Fenway while avoiding recruitment conflicts. The colleges agreed on the following principles:

- ◆ The colleges would synchronize their academic calendars for September 1996.

- ◆ No tuition would be exchanged. Tuition would remain at the student's home institution.

- ◆ The registrars would create a unified schedule of courses which would be open to students in the Colleges of the Fenway, and they would specify courses that required permission by the host college's registrar.

- ◆ Faculty and administrators would receive communications about cross-registration to mitigate any glitches for students. Meetings would be held for faculty across the five colleges, including several meetings organized according to academic discipline.

- ◆ The registrars would coordinate deadlines for examinations and reporting of grades, and would monitor the cross-registration process, sharing statistical information for each semester.

The synchronization of academic calendars was, in fact, a major accomplishment since all the colleges had different calendars, including one that was on a trimester calendar. Even with significant preparation for cross-registration, administrators and faculty had many questions. Would students take advantage of the program? Would the import and export of students from one campus to another be balanced? Would a tuition-free exchange work? What would be the impact of male students taking courses at the women's undergraduate colleges? No one knew the answers to the questions, but the presidents of the five campuses were committed to going forward with cross-registration for the fall semester.

In September 1996, 221 students took classes through the Colleges of the Fenway inaugural cross-registration program. Since then, cross-registration has become a recognized and appreciated benefit to students. After four semesters, 965 cross-registrations have occurred, the import/export numbers have balanced reasonably, no tuition dollars have been exchanged, and in the summer 1998, for the first time, students were invited to cross-register for summer sessions. The cross-registration plan was action- and goal-oriented; the immediate benefit to students was tangible; and the stage was set for longer-term strategic academic planning.

Academic Initiatives

With the adoption of a single academic calendar and the details of cross-registration mastered, the colleges had an opportunity to consider more innovative academic initiatives. Ideas ranged from joint planning of academic programs to sharing faculty appointments across colleges. While faculty expressed enthusiasm for the expanded resources that cooperative programming offered, they were also skeptical that too much cooperation might be the precursor to downsizing, fearing that small departments could face merger or elimination. The academic deans took particular efforts to communicate frequently with faculty emphasizing the enhancement of academic programs which could result from faculty participation in collaborative efforts.

By the second year of the collaborative, several academic collaborative efforts were in place. They included team teaching and joint courses (Simmons and Wentworth), joint academic programs (media services among Emmanuel, Simmons, and Wheelock), a dual degree program in engineering (Emmanuel and Wentworth), shared faculty appointments (Wentworth and Simmons), and several programs in faculty development sponsored by one college and open to faculty from all Colleges of the Fenway. Not only do students benefit from the collaborative efforts of faculty, but faculty members have spoken of a reinvigorated spirit from their work with colleagues at other Colleges in the Fenway.

In academic year 1997–98, the Davis Educational Foundation awarded the Colleges of the Fenway a grant of $250,000 for minigrants for faculty representing at least two member colleges, to work together on curricula. This funding provided an additional incentive for faculty to work together.

In Spring 1998, nine projects proposed by faculty were selected for funding, and faculty from each of the five campuses benefited. The topics included shared media resources using digital technologies across campuses, media programs, online instruction for research and library use, health studies library materials collaborative project, training and implementation of a computer-based instruction development resource team, service-learning workshops, an environmental study of the Muddy River, and an interinstitutional program in women's studies. It was exciting to see faculty across the campuses engaged actively in pooling their expertise and enthusiasm, generating new resources for our academic community. Technology played a prominent role in many of the projects, underscoring its increasing influence on the delivery and content of the curriculum.

Student Activities

From the beginning of the collaborative, the presidents focused attention on students, with student satisfaction a major objective. In addition to the substantial benefit which cross-registration provided students, the directors and deans of student life also developed an exciting array of student activities across the five colleges. With orientation programs, block parties, shared leadership training conferences, theater productions, and numerous social events, the students had many opportunities to meet their peers across the five colleges. Participation rates at the planned events were high, and enthusiastic responses generated yet further collaboration.

One of the most successful programs was a joint career fair which was held in Spring 1997 and 1998. In Spring 1998, more than 90 companies representing a wide range of career opportunities for students came to campus to meet and interview the 400+ students who attended. This event also served as a celebration of the second anniversary of the founding of the Colleges of the Fenway. The presidents all spoke at the event and presented T-shirts and hats with the Colleges of the Fenway logo to students.

During the spring of 1998, students participated in a survey and in focus groups evaluating their experiences of the Colleges of the Fenway. They gave high marks to cross-registration and to the advantages of a small college environment in a university setting. Students identified areas they felt the Colleges of the Fenway could expand collaboration, such as shared health services, internships, and career planning, a common web site, and intramural athletics.

Cost Savings

The second goal of the collaborative is to slow down the escalating costs of higher education. In the early months, the presidents and chief financial officers recognized the potential for significant savings in student health insurance if the colleges contracted with one provider through a group account. A student health insurance committee was appointed and information was collected from all of the colleges concerning their current provider such as the rates/services obtained. A request for proposals was issued. Interested companies were required to provide a single bundled insurance rate, an analysis of each college's current rate, a rate comparison identifying the individual colleges' insurance experience and the estimated potential savings. Upon receipt of the proposals, the committee recommended a single contract with one of the responding insurance companies. Four of the Colleges of the Fenway opted to participate in the new plan and collectively saved more than $230,000 in one year. These savings were felt immediately by the students since they received as much as a $95 savings in their student health bill in the fall.

Another area identified for cost savings the first year was liability and risk insurance which followed a similar procedure to the student health program and resulted in savings for several colleges. Other areas which the chief financial officers explored for cost savings included food service contracts, payroll, and campus security.

Organization

The presidents of the Colleges of the Fenway have met regularly, at least once a month, and often more frequently, since the inception of the collaborative. The colleges' chief academic officers, chief financial officers, and deans of students also have met with each other on a monthly basis. Other administrators, such as directors of public relations, development, admissions, and registrars have met in subcommittees as needed. A steering committee of presidents and chief academic and financial officers has met four times a year to assure clear communication and to address issues of the collaborative.

In June 1996, the Colleges of the Fenway appointed a coordinator to support planning initiatives and assist with implementation of specific projects. Attending the meetings of the presidents over the past three years, the president of Medical, Academic, and Scientific Community Organization (MASCO) has played an active role in the development of the Colleges of the Fenway. MASCO is a charitable corporation established by its 14 member institutions to enhance the Longwood Medical and Academic Area for the public and its member institutions. MASCO provided the colleges with financial assistance for specific projects, staff support, and an office for the coordinator.

When we considered how we would organize ourselves, we reviewed the materials of other collaboratives, such as the Five Colleges, Inc., the Claremont Colleges, and the Universities of Cambridge and Oxford. We recognized similarities but noted that our location and affiliation gave us remarkable opportunities for collaboration. Through our membership in MASCO, we enjoyed the support of a larger organization and the first-hand experience from neighboring medical institutions on the obstacles and possibilities of collaboration. We were all smaller institutions in a city of larger universities, with proximate—in some cases, adjacent—campuses and a history of affiliation.

RESULTS OF THE FIRST TWO YEARS OF COLLABORATION

At the end of the second year of the collaborative, the Colleges of the Fenway had achieved the following:

+ Synchronized academic calendars

+ Conducted four successful cross-registration semesters

+ Planned and implemented successful orientation programs, student activities, student leadership conferences, and social events for students across the colleges

+ Purchased joint student health insurance resulting in $230,000 in savings

- Received funding for two grants from the Davis Foundation and from Fidelity Corporation

- Attracted positive media coverage of the initiative

- Published brochures for student recruitment and designed a logo

- Shared academic resources and engaged faculty in cross college meetings by academic discipline

- Commissioned an architectural firm to review facilities and to recommend campus improvements such as pedestrian pathways, College of the Fenway banners, and signage

During the first year, the Colleges of the Fenway addressed problems in communication with some trustees. In the second year, we held two meetings with representatives of the respective boards. We responded to the misuse of the term "merger" by several media reports to describe the collaborative. We addressed the negative reaction of some students and alumnae to men attending classes at the two women's colleges—Emmanuel and Simmons—which had been allowing men to enroll in some classes for the past two decades. We experienced several concerns with delays in efforts to collaborate in the area of technology. The many accomplishments of the first two years gave impetus to continue to address issues as they emerge.

ADMINISTRATIVE COLLABORATION

Throughout the first year, the Colleges of the Fenway considered ways to find financial support for assessing administrative functions to examine the feasibility of reducing costs. In Spring 1997, we received a grant from Fidelity Corporation for $75,000 which MASCO and the colleges matched. We contracted with a management consulting firm to study potential administrative collaborations and to identify best practices in administration. They began work in June 1997, investigating two key questions: Will sharing services save money? Will sharing services improve the quality of education? The firm interviewed senior and middle managers at each college, reviewed strategic plans and administrative department plans, and researched other models of cooperation. The consultants developed inventories of administrative functions and business processes and, based on such input, created conceptual models for shared services, including cost analyses of conceptual models against current operating costs.

The Technical Development Corporation (TDC) shared their findings regularly with the five presidents who worked to refine continuously those areas of greatest potential savings. For example, in the area of contract services, such as payroll, security, food services, and liability insurance, the presidents advised that the colleges themselves, with MASCO, address such cooperation noting that several colleges shared the same vendor. TDC then generated draft models for collaboration in the areas of:

♦ Financial services (including purchasing, accounting, inventory)
♦ Human resources
♦ Facilities management
♦ Students services
♦ Libraries and information technology

In the draft models, TDC identified areas where:

♦ Each college retains responsibility, control, and staff
♦ Colleges could share or align staff and responsibilities
♦ One staff services all colleges with appropriate campus representation

In late August 1998, the consultants submitted a business plan to the presidents for further discussion, including the collaborative models and a proposed governance model. Following these discussions, meetings were scheduled with trustees with the intention of making decisions on the proposed administrative collaborations, an important chapter in the development of the Colleges of the Fenway.

Information Technology

The presidents of the Colleges of the Fenway are keenly aware of the challenges we face in moving forward with models calling for increased collaboration. In all of our discussions, we have emphasized the need for sensitivity to maintaining the individual college's identity and to understanding the various campus cultures. We know in painstaking detail from our efforts to date that effective collaboration, even on seemingly simple issues such as food service, can require extraordinary effort.

Information technology (IT) is a prime example of the challenges we face in collaboration. Few areas have as much potential for slowing down the escalating costs of higher education through the sharing of resources and the ending of costly duplication than information technology. While opportunities for collaboration are numerous, they are also among the most complex to implement.

In the fall of 1996, the presidents appointed a subcommittee of information technology directors and asked the members to develop a strategic IT plan which would address the following questions:

♦ What are the academic technology needs of students and faculty?

♦ What technology is needed to facilitate all current administrative processes and to provide new and improved capabilities?

♦ How can the colleges manage, share, and optimize existing resources to realize savings?

The subcommittee recommended some short-term projects which would begin the transition from five independent IT environments to a collaborative environment. These projects included shared Internet services, Colleges of the Fenway identification card for access to dining halls and libraries, coordinated faculty and staff training, and consolidated purchasing of hardware and software. The benefits of collaboration were readily apparent, such as better trained users, more proficient staff, discounts through bulk purchasing, and increased access to the Internet. The obstacles were enormous: hardware and software incompatibilities, various degrees of "wiredness" on the campuses, wide ranges of differences in staff size and expertise, and various budgetary constraints.

To illustrate further the complexity of sharing IT, I will use my own college as an example. In May 1994, I attended the IBM Advanced Business Institute on Business Planning for Networking held at the Palisades Center. As a result of this institute and the meetings held during the program with IBM planning consultants and technical staff, I and the two trustees who had joined me for the program invited IBM to work with Emmanuel to develop a strategic plan. After extensive meetings with IBM consultants, and after presentations to the trustees to secure funding, Emmanuel inaugurated its IT program. In the summer of 1994, IBM oversaw the fiber optic networking of our campus beginning with the residence halls. Every "pillow" was wired for voice, video, and data, providing free access to email and the Internet. Throughout the fall semester, the classrooms and offices were wired. By January 1995, when we opened our new state-of-the-art IBM classroom with video conferencing capability, Phase I of our strategic IT plan was complete. Phase II continued the program by training staff and faculty, providing additional computer labs for students and accomplishing the goal of connecting Emmanuel to the world. We made a major investment in our future, an investment that continues to require substantial budgetary support each year.

Each college in the Colleges of the Fenway used a different process to develop its IT program. The work of TDC has provided an inventory of hardware and software in use and has noted the pressures on each college to upgrade staff and systems. The Colleges of the Fenway have the opportunity to make decisions to facilitate compatibility in the future and to engage in cost sharing in some areas. Since IT will provide the underpinning to future administrative collaboration, it is essential for the colleges to focus attention on collaboration in this complex area.

THE MOST IMPORTANT FACTOR: PRESIDENTIAL LEADERSHIP

The active role the presidents played in imagining, creating, and developing the collaborative is clearly the most important single factor in the successful launching of the Colleges of the Fenway. Those who study consortia corroborate the fact that presidential leadership and commitment are essential to the success of such ventures. From the beginning, the presidents have met with each other regularly. We took the risk that five very different institutions could come together on common ground to enhance the educational experience of our students and to reduce costs.

Presidents Marjorie Bakken of Wheelock College, Daniel Cheever of Simmons College, Charles Monahan of the Massachusetts College of Pharmacy and Allied Health Sciences, John Van Domelen of

Wentworth Institute of Technology, and I have mutual respect for each other and a growing understanding of the distinctive mission, character, personality, peculiarity, and culture of each college. Most of all, we trust each other and like working together. Our discussions are marked by candor. We do not agree on all matters, but we are willing to listen and support differing views. In fact, it is a rare and valuable opportunity we have as colleagues to share openly our concerns, frustrations, hopes, and challenges as presidents. One of the most cherished parts of our meetings is the place where we do just that: sharing without recording minutes.

Over the past few years, we have shared our vision for higher education in the future, and we are developing a collective vision for the Colleges of the Fenway. We have been and continue to be the catalysts, mediators, negotiators, and inspirers on our own campuses and in the broader community on behalf of the Colleges of the Fenway.

The trust, candor, and mutual respect which have marked our work to date will continue to provide a remarkable support as we continue our collaboration. The Colleges of the Fenway collaboration is a work in progress. With committed leaders, early successes, and supportiveness, our students and faculty have benefited from our collaboration. We are on our way to creating a groundbreaking model for collaboration in higher education.

REFERENCE

Colleges of the Fenway. (1996, March). *Principles of collaboration.* Boston, MA: Colleges of the Fenway.

7

Transforming Student Services

Robert B. Kvavik and Michael N. Handberg

Transformations take many shapes. They can be structural or functional, subtle or dramatic, with major or minor impacts on institutions. They can be radical and revolutionary, occurring with great rapidity in response to external pressures for change, or they can be evolutionary and stable. They can be driven from within the organization with broad participation and expectations for change by the membership, or they can be driven by a few individuals, often from the top-down, with varying levels of resistance to change. And they can be comprehensive or narrow and occur with great fanfare or quietly. All permutations of the above are possible.

This chapter focuses on the transformation of student services at the University of Minnesota and provides lessons for student services more broadly. We posit that the transformations at Minnesota are affecting both structures and functions in rapid, dramatic, and comprehensive ways with major impact and consequences for the university. Participation by staff is gradual and incremental at this time, but student participation is enormous and growing. The public response and acceptance of the transformations have been overwhelmingly positive.

TRANSFORMING STUDENT SERVICES

Two transformations are especially noteworthy and represent a sea change in how student service units support the university community. First, student services are undergoing a fundamental change moving beyond the traditional responsibilities of maintaining student records, financial aid administration, and student advocacy. They are becoming more tightly linked with the strategic, academic, and economic objectives of the institution.

Student services professionals, in partnership with academic officers, are placing greater emphasis on higher value activities, such as student retention and graduation rates, enrollment management, resource management and revenue generation, academic planning, marketing, and performance assessment, both for students and the institution. As a consequence, their internal value to the institution increases as they shift from a role of unfortunate public utility to a strategic contributor to the management and growth of the instructional programs of the university.

Second, centralized, producer-oriented services are giving way to decentralized, learner-oriented services. This shift includes numerous opportunities for self-help as well as access to information and services on the part of students and faculty with concomitant greater local authority and responsibility. Of the two transformations, this change is the most radical.

Increasingly services are being provided electronically rather than in a paper mode and without the intermediation of student services staff. Services are increasingly accessible at any time from any place. And student service professionals are becoming generalists who serve as facilitators and navigators in an information-rich environment that is shared by provider and client alike. In such an environment, the existing organizational structure and ways of doing business are subject to increasing scrutiny and are under enormous pressure to change.

THE NEED AND CONTEXT FOR CHANGE

At many—if not most—universities, student service units are classic models of Weberian bureaucracy. They are rule-oriented as is demonstrated by their publications: Financial aid handbooks and college catalogues elaborate upon an endless set of procedures and processes for determining eligibility for access to programs as well as resources. Decisions are based upon the formal and impartial application of a system of laws to specific cases. Within each unit, roles are hierarchical and highly specialized. Official business is conducted on the basis of written documents that are founded upon enactments of state and federal governments or board of trustees. Approved forms, rule books, and written records of transactions with students are the context of client-customer interaction.

In fairness to these units, all have had a major impact in making possible an equitable distribution of resources and access to opportunities in higher education. Today, however, they are perceived to be slow and unwieldy, inflexible and poorly coordinated, inefficient and costly. A worst-case scenario finds these units acting on the basis of different values, perspectives, and information sometimes with negative consequences for their clients. They are viewed by some as prone to defend their domains and jurisdictions, enlisting allies as needed. Rivalries and personalities are major obstacles to coordination and joint policymaking even with such minor matters as setting event deadlines. For example, financial aid deadlines sometimes contradict admissions and registration deadlines and vice versa to the detriment of student satisfaction with the institution.

Dolence and Norris (1995) have argued persuasively for the need to transform the sector's institutions to learner-oriented service providers. For them, the rule-oriented, bureaucratic decision-making process must give way to informed judgment with an ability to self-inform and self-correct. Instead of provider-driven services being offered at a set time and place, they must offer student- and faculty-driven services. Self-help and decentralization of information, services, authority, and responsibility are key.

One of the most powerful insights of Dolence and Norris is their recasting of the concept of productivity. They argue that cost savings, downsizing/rightsizing, and restructuring all miss the point. Enhancing productivity is the end game and learner needs must drive the concept of productivity. Variety, quality, timeliness, and responsiveness are central aspects of information age productivity. This contrasts with the bureaucratic model of productivity that is heavily oriented toward processes, procedural accuracy, and outputs, rather than outcomes. The unit's immediate goal (e.g., the number of students given the "right" award) blurs a concern for a larger institutional goal of timely completion and graduation rates. Financial aid as entitlement conflicts with financial aid as a tool to leverage resources for maximizing income, to manage the composition of an incoming class, and/or to reward performance.

Embedded in the discussion of productivity is the expectation that student service units add value to the institution beyond improving the quality and timeliness of traditional activities such as record keeping (Dolence & Norris, 1995). At most institutions, there is little expectation that the registrar and financial aid offices do more than register students for classes, report grades, schedule classrooms, print transcripts, and award aid in the form of scholarships, need-based grants, work study, and loans. Part of the problem is organizational; part is the student affairs legacy. There is nothing inherently wrong with locating these units within student affairs. This is a common arrangement. What is wrong is the broader institutional perception that, because these units are in student affairs, they serve only students and are marginally related to academic affairs (e.g., they admit students, they ship diplomas, they give students money, or they fine them for late payments or registration). They do things to and for students. It is also often the case that these units, the biggest in terms of budgets and staffing, have been marginalized in student affairs in favor of cocurricular student activities.

TRANSFORMATION AT THE UNIVERSITY OF MINNESOTA

As we have thought about reengineering student services and building new administrative systems at Minnesota, we realize that these units and their computer systems are fundamental to the management of our instructional programs—a $700 million per year enterprise. Far more than providing services to students, their activities are tied to the management of the curriculum and instruction, to generating and maximizing revenues for the institution (especially tuition), and to the retention and graduation of students. The challenge is to build an awareness of this reality.

At the same time, we need to be more aggressive in using the transactional data and the processes that generate these data (e.g., grade reports, faculty course assignments) in ways that add value. Can the process of registering for courses also be a process for assessing performance (e.g., time of completion) and for planning one's academic program? Can the process of reporting grades and assigning faculty to courses simultaneously generate information on instructional productivity and demand? Can we acknowledge the role of the admissions director, registrar, financial aid director, bursar, and their staff as key players in facilitating strategic academic decisions?

There is a very compelling reality internal to the organization that drives the need to transform student services in the ways outlined above: money. We estimate that it will take in excess of $20 million to make our student systems Year 2000 compliant, support a change to the semester calendar, and, at the same time, improve the quality of services to students. It would be hard to generate such a financial commitment if our objective was to preserve the status quo with little possible return on investment.

The University of Minnesota's student service units have been under enormous pressure for the last three years. As with most American universities operating mainframe legacy systems in support of student administration, our programs are not Year 2000 compliant and must be fixed or replaced. Several years ago, the legislature mandated a change from the quarter calendar to the semester calendar. A change would be hard to accomplish with existing built-in-house programs which have to be rewritten with arcane codes and poor documentation. And to make matters worse, these units did not enjoy the respect of their clients: students, staff, and faculty. One survey, to our surprise, indicated that as students moved from their freshman year to their senior year, their dissatisfaction increased. We interpret the findings to mean that adjusting to the bureaucracy got even more frustrating and complicated as one progressed toward graduation.

There is probably no college graduate who lacks examples of college bureaucracy at work. The colleges of the University of Minnesota have employed nine different grading systems (three today), one of which awarded an F+ to students. We can only surmise that the F+ recognized "failure with distinction." Some of our college bulletins dedicate the first one-third of their pages to rules rather than to descriptions of courses and programs. And lengthy as it is, these bulletins represent a condensed version of the full set of rules found in the financial aid handbook and the registration bulletin. The publishing costs are enormous. Students, from the time of registration to the time of enrollment, need several pounds of bulletins and guides as reference materials. Because there are no one-stop registration centers and because both academic units and central support service units want to regulate the registration process, an unfortunate student can walk several miles and cross the Mississippi River numerous times prior to completing registration—assuming everything goes right.

Developing a New Vision

It does not take a rocket scientist to realize that the old system was close to bankruptcy and that dramatic transformations were needed. We began by shifting admissions, financial aid, and registration to the office of the senior vice president for academic affairs, assigning new personnel to the management of the units and radically simplifying policies. We engaged Coopers & L.L.P. (now Pricewaterhouse Coopers) to help us formulate a new vision. Throughout the project, we have continued to refine this vision. Three figures (Figures 7.1, 7.2, and 7.3) demonstrate our vision.

Student transactions. Figure 7.1 depicts the way in which student transactions may be completed: automatically, self-initiated, by means of a generalist, or with the assistance of a highly trained specialist. The left triangle suggests that the vast majority of the transactions require help from student service specialists. The challenge is to turn the left triangle on its head.

The number of transactions managed by student service units is enormous. Hundreds of thousands of grades are reported and recorded, thousands of students are registered, several hundred million dollars of tuition and fees are collected, and an even larger amount of financial aid is awarded annually. Many of these transactions are done manually, on paper, at fixed times, and at fixed locations.

Fully 75% to 90% of all transactions currently done manually and on paper should be done electronically and without the intervention of an administrator. Moreover, these transactions should be linked strategically to minimize runaround. For example, dropping a course

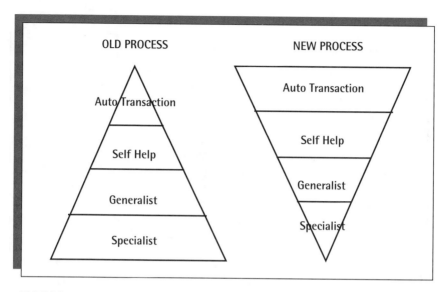

FIGURE 7.1   Transforming Student Service Processes

should automatically and simultaneously adjust financial aid, credit a student account, and notify a student of the academic and/or financial consequences of his or her decision.

Similarly, there are too few transactions that can be initiated directly by the student. The student must go to the appropriate office and complete a transaction with the assistance of a staff member. More egregious is not being able to complete these services at a single location and at a single time, but rather having to go to several locations—often with return visits—in order to complete a transaction or certification process. We believe that our processes can be redesigned in such a way that students can initiate the vast majority of the transactions and complete them with greater accuracy, in a timely fashion, when and where it is convenient for them. In the new environment, the vast majority of transactions must be either highly automated or self-initiated by the client via the web.

Self–certification.   Further improvements are possible, but these will involve a major change in business practices and culture. A large percentage of the transactions engaged in by student service units involve certification. Students are certified as admissible to colleges and majors, entry into courses, financial aid, and graduation. Can we create an environment that permits greater opportunities for self-

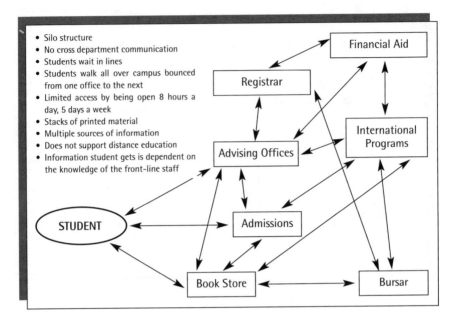

FIGURE 7.2   Traditional Delivery of Services to Students

certification? The University of California, Berkeley, for example, permits students to enter their own grades in the admissions process. It then reviews only the applications of students that are admitted. A study conducted at the University of Minnesota found that students taking courses without satisfying a prerequisite actually did better than students who had satisfied the requirement. We are of the opinion that students will not risk doing poorly in courses where they are underprepared and that they did better because they wanted to take the course. Despite such findings, we place numerous prerequisites on the courses we teach as our culture remains highly regulatory and is based on the belief that students will not make good decisions if left to their own devices. This approach to student management is antithetical to the vision we have articulated. Given the right tools, students can manage their own academic progress much more independently of the current advising system.

One-stop shopping.   Not all activities can be automated, and many require some assistance by trained advisors. Here the challenge is to cross-train staff so that they can answer a broader array of questions. This is the genesis of the concept of one-stop shopping. The generalist

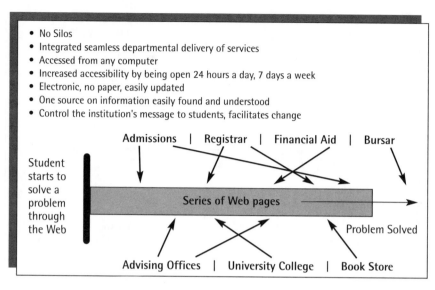

FIGURE 7.3   Web-Based Delivery of Services to Students

role challenges the current silo structure of student services which fosters decisions by specialists who control functional domains. We are of the opinion that student services has become overspecialized. Given the right kind of training and incentives for employees, our staff can answer a broader range of questions. This will result in a more user-friendly environment. Even so, there will always be a role for specialists (we will address these requirements in our discussion of the structure of the new student services office). In short, university service units must become client focused and seamless rather than be organized in silos (see Figures 7.2 and 7.3).

Systems and organizations must be designed to provide students, faculty, and staff with greater quantity, quality, and timely access to data. Those data should be integrated and support institutional personnel as well as strategic planning and decision-making. Service units must help build and support an environment where their clients are provided with knowledge and know-how to apply information to a given problem. Decision-making must be driven down into the organization with minimal intervention by central administrators (Figure 7.3).

The silo approach (Figure 7.2) must give way to a problem solving approach (Figure 7.3). In this model, the student extracts information

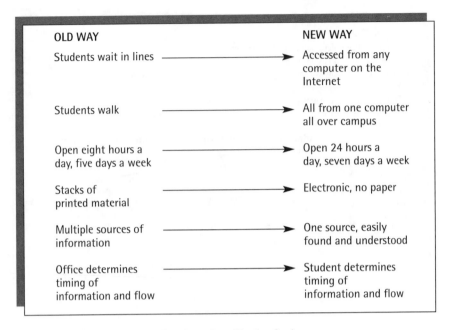

OLD WAY   **NEW WAY**

Students wait in lines ⟶ Accessed from any computer on the Internet

Students walk ⟶ All from one computer all over campus

Open eight hours a day, five days a week ⟶ Open 24 hours a day, seven days a week

Stacks of printed material ⟶ Electronic, no paper

Multiple sources of information ⟶ One source, easily found and understood

Office determines timing of information and flow ⟶ Student determines timing of information and flow

FIGURE 7.4   Outcomes of Transformation of Student Services

from a variety of university units as the information is needed. The problem being solved often transcends the tasks assigned to the individual units that provide data in several ways. First, registration is a seamless process that involves not only registration but also payment of tuition and fees as well as a draw-down of financial aid. Second, and perhaps more significant, the registration process is not only signing up for courses, but also a process of planning one's program and assessing one's performance to date. It is an opportunity to articulate expected outcomes such as personal academic goals.

The outcomes of the transformation are shown in Figure 7.4. Increasingly students control the time, pace, and place of registration. The process is electronic, instantaneous, and more accurate.

Planning and management.   Up until now, we have discussed ways to improve how transactions are handled. While these changes and their concomitant cost savings are significant, by themselves they do not fundamentally change the service paradigm, nor will they generate the kind of productivity and customer satisfaction we feel is needed in the future. They will not permit deans and department chairs to fully manage instructional and human resources. Nor do they permit students to take an increased control of their academic progress and performance. At a minimum, the systems must have three additional capacities: planning, performance assessment, and marketing.

We can best illustrate the importance of these added capacities with an example outside the realm of student services. Several years ago, the University of Minnesota purchased software to schedule classrooms that replaced a manual, labor-intensive system which had as its core technology 3" x 5" cards. What surprised us was that the cost savings from automated scheduling was initially and substantially overshadowed by savings made possible by the planning capacity of the scheduling software. We found that by increasing classroom utilization and occupancy rates and scheduling accordingly, fully 25% of the classroom inventory could be removed from service. Fundamental to the new student systems must be an enhanced capacity for planning.

Partnering for success. Concomitant with the building of an automatic and electronic registration system was the building of software tools to facilitate program planning and assessment by the student. The potential of the approach proved to be enormous, limited only by our imagination. That was the good news. The problem was the immense increase in the scope of the work we had undertaken and a lack of sufficient resources. As a consequence, the university looked for assistance from the private sector.

In December 1997, the University of Minnesota (U of M) and IBM announced a far-reaching agreement to develop a software product to support innovative advising and business processes that promises to fundamentally change how student services are provided at universities. The product of the U of M/IBM partnership will make it possible for students, parents, faculty, and staff to plan, assess performance, and make wise, productive decisions that will further both personal and institutional goals and objectives. Users of the product will be able to make decisions and take action in ways that were never before imagined with significant savings in time and increased productivity.

The U of M/IBM product provides powerful planning as well as time and resource management tools for students, faculty, and staff. Course, program, final exam, and career planning can improve timely degree completion. In addition, customized programs serve the academic and career goals of the student, financial aid planning (even while in high school with the parents as the client), faculty, and course resource planning.

Tools to assess performance will be part of the U of M/IBM product, as well. Students can determine academic progress toward their degree or a desired grade point average (GPA) by asking a host of "what if" or auditing questions (not unlike the performance tools in products such as Quicken). Administration can match faculty and course resources to student demand. Faculty can assess, in advance, the academic capability and interests of a class of students they are teaching. Finally, the U of M/IBM product provides a capacity to market programs, outsource book sales, and process loans.

IMPACT OF THE TRANSFORMATIONS

There will be many impacts from this transformation. The course planner and guide provides one example. By means of the course planner and guide, students have readily available to them a mass of information on the background, interests, and achievements of their instructors. Information ranges from the reputation of academic programs to the cost and availability of books.

What emerges is an integrated student system with powerful analytic and resource management tools which have major consequences on the way the university conducts several core businesses. First, we put in place a greatly enhanced instructional management system that makes it possible for deans and department chairs to take responsibility and be accountable for enrollments, manage instructional resources to better meet student demand, market courses and programs, and monitor and assess performance, including tuition revenues. Second, we radically change the advising relationships and responsibilities among students, faculty, and staff.

IMPLEMENTING THE VISION

We quickly realized that implementing the new vision required massive changes not only in business processes and technology, but also in the organization of student services and the skill sets of our employees. Figure 7.5 illustrates the old and new organization.

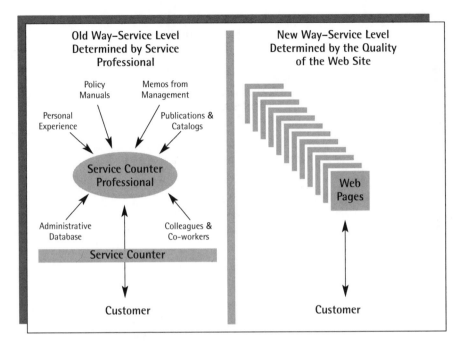

FIGURE 7.5 Comparison of Service Delivery Methods

Today, generalists or specialists serve behind counters and help students solve problems. The administrator is valued because he or she has digested a vast body of information needed by students to pursue an academic career. Our vision permits the student to bypass the desk by going directly to the electronic source of information and by creating software that serves as a guide to the extraction and application of the appropriate information. The student manages the data and uses it to solve problems without the active mediation of the administrator.

New Professional Roles

A practical consequence is the need to train advisors for roles in this new environment. Rather than serve behind a counter, they must redirect their efforts to the design and maintenance of the web site (Figure 7.6). Among the new roles we have envisioned under this model are information technology professional; content/service area professional; web communications professional; and high-level customer process professional.

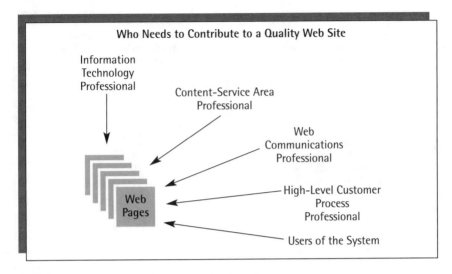

FIGURE 7.6   Staffing Requirements of the New System

Information technology professional.   Information technology professionals navigate the plethora of emerging Internet technologies and decide which of these technologies are of value in our environment. Their decisions inform the university's Internet-based technology strategy. In addition, the information technology (IT) professionals write code, manage data, and guide the entire team, helping them to understand what the new technology will allow them to do and the constraints it may impose on the system.

Content service professional.   Content service professionals are versed in the detail of the various functional areas served by the system. Included here are admissions, financial aid, bursar, and registration. In this role, the content service professional ensures that the team's applications meet the core business needs of the offices and institution. The specialists do not go away in this system. Rather, their energy is directed toward system design and performance rather than one-on-one counseling.

Web communications professional.   Web communications professionals set and maintain user-interface standards for the entire site. Institutions do students a disfavor by requiring them to learn new ways and methods of displaying information each time they move from page to page within the same web site. The web communication professional makes sure the site is consistent and user-friendly.

Customer process professional. The high-level customer process professionals integrate the services of the different back-end offices so that the site and the processes it serves effectively transcends its various parts. Rather than a sequential set of actions that moves the client through registration, securing financial aid, and paying tuition and fees, the client is able—through the vision and effort of the high-level customer process professional—to engage the various discrete tasks simultaneously. Transactions, planning, and performance assessment are now all part of the registration process. This individual works with all involved units to bring the ideas and creativity together into a coherent site design.

Role for end-users. The site must be tested and validated by the people who will use the system. Usability testing and involving end-users in the design process must be an integral part of the implementation process. Our experience suggests that it is never too early to bring this most important client group into the process.

Technology Requirements

The technology requirements of the new system can be daunting. Included here are both the central infrastructure to run the system and the equipment needed locally by users who access the new online services. To date, the university has wired the majority of its dorm rooms, developed a robust modem pool, and built a network of computer labs throughout campus. In addition, the university will require all students to own or to have ready access to a computer. The mainframe systems will be replaced by a new distributed computing system to support the new PeopleSoft™ systems that serve as the web back end.

CONCLUSION

Transforming student services must be driven by a vision, and it must have the active support of the institution's senior leadership. The institution must engage in substantial process reengineering and simplification of policies. It must be prepared to invest substantial financial resources in new technologies and in its staff. An enormous training effort is required because the transformation is, for all practical purposes, a change in institutional culture. There must be a communications plan that ties the many components together and makes the goals and implementation requirements clearly understood and supported through the institution.

The task of implementing this transformation is daunting but doable. If colleges and universities are to remain viable and competitive in the next decade, such transformations will be necessary.

REFERENCE

Dolence, M. G., & Norris, D. M. (1995). *Transforming higher education: A vision for learning in the 21st century.* Ann Arbor, MI: Society for College and University Planning.

8

Transforming Research Administration

James P. McKee, Sharon L. Kiser, and Russ Lea

INTRODUCTION

University research administration is undergoing a significant transformation catalyzed by the same issues that confront the university as a whole. The primary stresses are not about research, but about efficiency, effectiveness, and customer service. We are hopeful that the outcome of this transformation for research administration will be a shift from a rigid, bureaucratic enterprise to a flexible, responsive organization that can continually adapt to the needs of the institution and the external forces shaping the research enterprise.

The transformations that are taking place in university research administration are fundamental. Universities are promoting the integration of their research with local and regional economic development. Hybrid organizations are developing to address today's complex, multidisciplinary research problems. Bureaucratic processes and organizations are being restructured to emphasize service to researchers. Information technology is producing gains in productivity and enhancing the responsiveness of the organizations. Finally, research administrators are acquiring the new skills necessary to survive under these changing conditions.

Research administration is taking on a new character, requiring the continued support of the university leadership. This new character emphasizes strategic planning and service rather than monitoring transactions for compliance. To be effective, the new research administration needs executive-level support for flexibility in human resource development and deployment plus support for expanded research information systems which are part of an integrated university information strategy.

UNDERSTANDING RESEARCH AND RESEARCH ADMINISTRATION

Research administration can be broadly defined as the management of any activity related to research—excluding actually conducting the research. While the individual scientist provides direct management of a research project, research administrators are held responsible by university executives for ensuring that research supports the mission of the university and by sponsors for ensuring that their funds are being spent wisely.

Research administrators provide support services to the researcher throughout the lifecycle of a project. Some examples include:

◆ Identifying potential projects and funding sources

◆ Writing proposals and negotiating agreements

◆ Obtaining facilities and hiring personnel

◆ Managing project budgets

◆ Ensuring regulatory compliance

◆ Billing and receiving payment for services

◆ Reporting results

◆ Commercializing new technologies through patents, copyrights, and licenses

Increasingly, research administrators are involved in helping to educate the public and their representatives in government on the value of research in order to protect the funding their institutions receive.

In this chapter, the focus is on university research administration. Research administrators play a pivotal role in the research enterprise by providing a critical link between faculty and sponsors. Federal, state, and private sponsors have needs that are very different from the needs of the faculty and other research investigators. The research administrator provides a facilitation role to meet the needs of the university, the faculty, and the sponsor. As the needs of the university have changed and the funding priorities of sponsors have adjusted to the latest economic and societal trends, the issues that administrators have had to deal with have changed dramatically. Research administrators have had to adapt and evolve their organizations to keep up (Gunston & Keniston, 1994). Over the last 20 years the research and development expenditures of higher education institutions have increased from $3.4 billion in 1975 to $23 billion in 1996 (National Science Foundation, 1996). Just keeping up with the increased volume has put a strain on traditional research organizations, especially on the infrastructure needed to support this growth.

The Stress on Research Administration

Despite the rapid growth of university research during the 1980s, the system is experiencing significant stress (GUIRR, 1994). Some of the stresses on the research enterprise include:

- A lack of appreciation by the general public of the role of academic research within the mission of the university

- A lack of communication between those who do academic research and those who support them, both at the federal level and within their home institutions

- As academic research and those who perform it become increasingly removed from the other missions of the university, there is the risk of a loss of institutional integrity

- A growing divergence between the demands imposed on new faculty by the academic community and changing lifestyles, opportunities, and modes of research

- An erosion of the sense of partnership between the federal government and research universities

The source of these stresses can be both internal as well as external. Within the university, strategic initiatives to improve the university as

INTERNAL	EXTERNAL
University leadership establishes competitive performance goals for research growth	Reinvention efforts in federal agencies drive changes in university research administration
Increase in industry sponsored research brings new challenges	Public pressure for demonstrated outcomes from research investment
Cross-campus quality or reengineering efforts engulf research administration	Media attention on selected cases of apparent misconduct undermines public trust

FIGURE 8.1   Sources of Stress on University Research Administrators

a whole put pressure on the research area. Quality improvement and reengineering projects sweep across the campus and encompass the research organization. Faculty "customers" demand more service at a lower cost from research administration. The transition from primarily federal funding support to more industry support raises internal issues and challenges. Externally, media publicity directs taxpayer attention to mismanagement of funds or scientific misconduct eroding trust in research universities and threatening funding. Federal sponsors, facing tightening administrative budgets and personnel reductions, pass responsibility and accountability down to universities as part of the federal reinvention efforts.

UNIVERSITY COMPETITIVE GOALS IMPACT RESEARCH ADMINISTRATION

Success in reengineering can usually be traced back to strong executive leadership. Leaders set measures to focus the university's efforts on a competitive goal, such as improving the institution's ranking against peer universities.

Research is critical to universities as they plan their competitive strategies. The primary focus of most university research programs is not revenue but the critical nature of the relationship among the research, education, and public service missions of the university. Universities compete for students. They must also compete for and retain quality faculty who attract students. Since a strong research program attracts and helps retain faculty who want to maintain their professional standing among their peers, universities try to provide a supportive environment for research. Top-quality faculty and a robust learning environment created by advanced research labs attract top-quality students and meet the expectation of the public and parents for a comprehensive education. The faculty, students, and facilities, in turn, attract more funding through tuition and government sources. Faculty, students, and research are intertwined in institutional competitiveness.

For research administration, pressure from this competitiveness comes from multiple directions. The first challenge is achieving and managing growth. The university leadership holds the research administration organization accountable for providing an environment in which the research program supports a strategic goal—usually this implies achieving year-to-year growth in the research volume or a change in ranking relative to peer institutions. For universities that do little research this might mean starting a research program. Because so many institutions have research growth goals, competition for funding is intense. How many universities can fit in the NSF top 10? The challenge for research administrators in a mature research market is to differentiate themselves and displace their competitors or increase the size of the research market.

A typical measure used to compare competing research programs is the volume of funding for research. Each year the National Science Foundation (NSF) reports on the research and development expenditures of universities. Relative ranking on this report is closely monitored, particularly by the larger research universities. The latest published figures which show that the volume of research and development (R&D) has increased in higher education institutions from $3.4 billion in 1975 to $23 billion in 1996 (NSF, 1996). The National Institute of Health (NIH) publishes a similar list ranking academic medical centers. For research administrators, increased funding means processing more proposals, awards, and accounts. NIH data indicate that the number of competitive applications have more than doubled since 1970.

According to NSF, in 1995, the top 20 institutions accounted for 31% of the total R&D expenditures, receiving from $240 million to almost $800 million per year. Although research funding remains concentrated in the hands of larger research institutions, many more institutions are participating in research than 20 years ago. An increasing pressure is being applied to the research administration organization to plan and develop strategies that help the university maintain or increase its market share in the research environment. Sometimes this means developing new skills for marketing (e.g., marketing the strengths of the institution over peer institutions to gain market share) or creating new strategies that expand the market by attracting new sources of funding.

The stress of being held accountable for growth in research funding is compounded by the dilemma that research administrators do not control all the elements necessary to achieve the goal. Growing a research program is dependent on many activities outside of the control of research administration: the research capability and desire of existing faculty; the recruitment of new faculty; the focus of departmental priorities; the investment of institutional funds in facilities that support research; and salary structure, tenure, and promotion. For a research administrator, coordinating all these activities to support the research goal is a daunting task. Even more intimidating may be the task of convincing the faculty to support the new strategy.

Increasing Industry Funding

As a result of the effort to expand research dollars, universities have initiated strategies to attract research funds from industry. A report by the Government University Industry Research Roundtable (GUIRR) highlights the success of this new strategy.

> The broad structure of the US R&D system outlined above has been fairly stable in recent years. However, the period has seen some significant long-term trends. The percentage of federal R&D funds going for defense purposes has dropped from 69% in 1986 to less than 60% in 1992. This percentage can be expected to drop further in the future. Since 1985, academic R&D has expanded substantially, whereas R&D in industry and in government laboratories has grown less rapidly. The share of federal funds in academic R&D has declined over that period, from two-thirds of the total in the early 1980s to an estimated 57% today. This drop has been accompanied by an increase in funding from industry and from internal funds of universities and colleges (GUIRR, 1994).

According to the National Science Foundation, academic research plays a key role in enabling technological advances in the private sector. Studies show that 10% of the new products and processes developed by firms depend on recent academic research (NSF, 1996).

This change in emphasis to industry-sponsored research has led to new issues and challenges for researchers and research administrators, in part because the academic and corporate cultures are so different. There are many benefits of the increase in industry-sponsored research, such as faculty development, improved student learning and placement, and support through resources and facilities. There are also potential pitfalls such as reduced academic freedom to publish, tight constraints on the direction of research and delivery of results, loss of faculty to industry, and conflict with the traditional stovepipe organization and culture of universities (Waugaman, 1998). Research administrators have found that identifying, negotiating, and managing industry support for research takes new skills, more effort, and offers a host of challenges.

Cross-Campus Reeingineering

Like the transformation efforts in other areas of the university, research administrators have focused on the traditional quality themes of improving service to customers, reducing process times, and increasing productivity. Often these efforts come as a result of faculty pressure to reduce the administrative burdens that keep them from spending more time on their research.

As reengineering has emerged as a transformation strategy, a considerable number of research administration improvement efforts have switched from continuous quality improvement to reengineering. These efforts require considerable focus that takes attention away from other research administration tasks.

In many cases, research administration is swept up as part of an internal effort to reengineer the university's core processes: human resource development, financial management, and student services. Often these reengineering projects are intertwined with the replacement of the institution's core administrative information systems. For example, when the University of Virginia embarked on a sweeping reengineering effort across the campus, the first process to be overhauled was research administration. Research administration is a key participant in campus-wide efforts to revamp administrative services and systems at the University of Michigan, The Ohio State University, North Carolina State University, and Cornell University. These efforts have required considerable effort on the part of research administrators and have strained the already limited personnel resources. On a positive note, this may represent the first time that research administration has been given the opportunity to define their needs as a core part of the institution and not as a peripheral activity. The scope of these reengineering efforts and the changes envisioned are a constant source of anxiety and stress.

Public Pressure for Outcomes

When public funds are involved, there is pressure for accountability. "Support for science today is notably political, competitive, and demanding. What the populist tension really does is force advocates of scientific research to articulate a compelling public rationale for their preferences and then, like any beneficiary of public expenditures, be held accountable for the outcomes" (Gunston & Kenniston, 1994).

A 1993 report by the Committee on Science, Engineering, and Public Policy (CSEPP) outlined the struggle for public support of research.

> The intertwined economic, political, and social changes of recent years have had direct consequences for the public's support of science and technology. In the past, this support has rested largely on the assumption that science and technology would contribute to national objectives by helping to ensure security and by generating new products, services, and economic growth. Today, this assumption is being questioned. Primacy in science has not prevented the loss of international market share. Continued biomedical advances have failed to produce uniformly affordable health care. Environmental threats persist despite our greater ecological knowledge and analytical skills. Although science and technology are but two facets of these complex problems, the persistence of these problems has moved the relationship between science, technology, and society onto new and uncertain ground.

Research administrators must work with scientists to develop the compelling public rationale for scientific research. Traditional research administration has focused on insular bureaucratic functions, such as monitoring regulations to ensure that the institution meets its compliance obligations and on transaction assistance, such as developing proposals, making purchases, and reporting to sponsors. Having to focus on the public perception of university research is new for most research administrators. Gunston and Kenniston (1994) refer to the fragile contract that existed between politics and science, where the scientific community promised that in return for research funding, science would improve society. Because of societal changes, the research community now must work to build a new, stronger contract that reflects society's changing needs. The burden of negotiating this new contract falls to research administrators.

The recent focus on health care provides an example of both the positive and negative pressures on universities that result from a change in public priorities. In 1997, NIH received its largest budget increase in recent years reflecting the priority on resolving health issues. This increase is a positive sign of public support for research. In the private sector, additional funding for health care research is provided by the growing biotechnology industry. The increased funding comes with a price. Research administrators are under increasing pressure to demonstrate that the investment is justified by the outcomes. Taxpayers and shareholders have a need to see the connection between increased R&D spending in an area and specific results, such as treatments that yield tangible improvements in the control of a disease. Research administration organizations must supply increasing numbers of specialized reports characterizing the value of the research programs in which they and their sponsors are engaged.

In addition to new cures for disease, the public also expects research to result in reduced health care costs. For research administration, this impact is particularly burdensome in academic medical centers and teaching hospitals. Previously, academic medical centers used revenues from patient services or physician practice plans to cover salaries and other expenses associated with research activities. Like education and research in the university, medical research and patient care are intertwined in an academic medical center. The strong public focus on reducing the costs of health care and the expansion of managed care programs have dramatically reduced the funds available to academic health centers for research and the infrastructure needed to support research. Yet managed health care plans are pressured to provide access to experimental (research) procedures. This may help mitigate the cost pressures on research in hospitals if managed care plans accept a role in funding research. To help reverse this cost pressure in managed care, research administrators must be able to show the value that developing new procedures will have on the long-term costs to the public and on the profitability of the managed care provider. The lack of integrated computer systems (e.g., human resources, accounting, patient care, and research administration) puts significant pressure on research administrators as they try to meet these increasing demands for information about research and outcomes.

Media Attention on Apparent Misconduct

Public support of university research is jeopardized by high-profile cases of apparent research misconduct (e.g., Stanford University, the University of Minnesota, Thomas Jefferson University, New York University). The issues in these cases are complex and difficult to understand without a background in research administration. The media coverage of the Stanford incident focused on fraud and misrepresentation. In reality, the central issue was the computation of indirect costs.

Media representation does not always converge with the actual issues. "Some of these violations may be trivial fiscally, but they are material in effects on public trust" (Gunston & Keniston, 1994). A similar sentiment was expressed by Stanford President Gerhard Lasper when announcing the $1.2 million settlement. "As a normal business settlement, this is unremarkable. . . . yet this case is not normal. No sponsored research dispute at Stanford . . . ever received as much attention and scrutiny" (Lasper, 1994). Stanford claims to have spent over $37 million in consultant and lawyer fees analyzing 18,000 contracts and grants and studying internal systems and controls when defending its case.

Although the university was ultimately vindicated, President Lasper says, "As we put this matter behind us, we realize that Stanford did harvest some benefit from this episode. We did obtain a thorough outside review of our internal controls, and we tightened them and improved our systems." Reengineering proponents indicate that such drastic threats to an institution often motivate the transformation. For research administrators, the result of these high-profile compliance cases is a strong, reactive effort to prove to senior university officials that this will not happen to them. These cases have resulted in pressure on government sponsors to tighten their oversight of universities. Hard-won administrative flexibility, such as the NIH expansion of authorities and reductions in prior approval requirements, are threatened.

Federal Reinvention

The transformation in university research administration is being driven by a similar effort within the federal government. This federal transformation has both process and technology implications for university research administration. Many of the reinvention efforts rely on technology to enable revised processes or better services. Government purchasing processes have received early attention. University research is ostensibly a purchased service. The Access America report (http://gits.gov/htm/access.htm) summarized the current status of the reinvention efforts and made some specific points about the grants process.

> In FY1996, the federal government provided approximately $300 billion in grants to governments, universities, tribal governments, nonprofit organizations, and individuals. The grants process can be improved and speeded up using electronic commerce, and ten federal agencies have joined together to form the US Electronic Grant Project. . . . A comprehensive grants system will require the development and implementation of administrative modules which, through partnership, will enable agencies and customers to manage the entire grant business process. This process includes steps for grant solicitation, application, and award. The modules should integrate key "electronic grants" approaches currently under development into a government-wide grants business model that will provide a common interface for customers. Specifically, ties are needed to the payment reengineering efforts that are underway at the Department of the Treasury (http://gits.gov/htm/ecomm.htm).

The federal agencies involved in the US Electronic Grant Project have made significant strides in many areas of electronic commerce and, through the Federal Demonstration Project (FDP), many new ideas are rapidly moving forward. The National Science Foundation FAST-LANE project has been conducting electronic commerce in most areas of the grant process for several years. NIH is pilot testing electronic processes with the Federal Demonstration Partnership, planning limited production implementation in 1999. Since research administration organizations usually have limited operational budgets, electronic commerce has significant implications.

Many of the reinvention efforts begin by streamlining processes. In research administration, much of the accountability and responsibility for stewardship of the public's money is delegated to the university. Many of these reinvention efforts have eliminated duplicate checks and balances within the funding agency, placing full responsibility with the university and its auditors. This results in a perception that the administrative rules have been relaxed. While many of the rules have increased flexibility, the burden of judgment is now the responsibility of the university. Research administration organizations are devoting significant effort to ensuring that their processes and procedures are equal to the task. Because researchers perceive the sponsor rules as more relaxed, research administrators are having to establish their own authority in enforcing proper stewardship. In the past, the strength and authority for the research administrator were derived from sponsor directive.

In addition to the impact of the process changes, the infrastructure implications are significant. Sponsors are moving toward electronic transactions (e.g., accepting a proposal electronically), but universities have not matched this pace in their implementation of campus-based research administration systems. Some of this delay can be attributed to the lack of experience of research administrators with implementing institutional information systems. In many cases these efforts in research administration are stalled because the institution's support and funding are committed to replacing other core administrative systems or resolving specific issues such as the Year 2000 problem.

THE TRANSFORMATION OF RESEARCH ADMINISTRATION

Research administration is taking on a new character. This new character emphasizes strategic planning and service, rather than monitoring transactions for compliance. Five fundamental transformations are taking place in university research administration.

1) *Redirecting the focus* so that the research enterprise becomes an integral contributor to local and regional economic expansion

2) *Creating hybrid organizations* that span academic departments and institutions to address complex, multidisciplinary research problems

3) *Emphasizing service* to researchers by reducing bureaucracy and reorganizing to distribute authority and accountability to the unit level

4) *Integrating information technology* into all research administration processes to enhance responsiveness to researchers and sponsors, to improve the productivity of people and processes, and to reduce the administrative costs of the research enterprise

5) *Encouraging professional development* of research administrators, through training and certification, to better help faculty and sponsors over the entire life cycle of a project

Integrating Research with Economic Development

Research administrators are helping ensure that the university research enterprise is an integral asset in state and local economic expansion. University research has benefited from these efforts because economic development has increased the total volume of research funds. In addition, the commercialization of research efforts results in outcomes the public can understand and support. Corporate R&D support to academic institutions has grown more rapidly than support from other sources since 1980. In constant dollars, industry-financed academic R&D increased by an estimated 250% from 1980 to 1995. Industry's share grew from 3.9% to an estimated 6.9% during this period (NSF, 1996).

This process has caused friction within the university. There are several new requirements:

◆ New organizations that unite universities, government, and industry require careful planning.

◆ The cross-disciplinary nature of the effort requires facilitation to bridge the traditional departmental organization as well as promotion and tenure.

◆ The opportunity for spin-off, start-up companies has raised the specter of conflict of interest and misconduct.

♦ Technology transfer and licensing requires new skills of research administration personnel.

Research in universities has been viewed as a quest for new knowledge. Scientists, shunning external guidance, devise the direction and approach of their research. They believe independence in research is both desirable and necessary, hence the need to separate fundamental research from development. According to the Committee on Science, Engineering, and Public Policy, ". . . it has proved impossible to predict reliably which areas of science will ultimately contribute to important new technologies. . . ." The report notes specific discoveries that have improved the public welfare yet were discovered while investigating something entirely different. Perhaps the strength of the commitment to independence voiced by universities and scientists has led the public to view scientists as elitist.

Commercialization can change the public perception of research. "World War II dramatically altered the relationship between science, engineering, and government. The atomic bomb, radar, nylon, penicillin, electronic computers, and a host of other products demonstrated the power of fundamental research when combined with engineering skills" (CSEPP, 1993). Recognizing its role in stimulating the connection between the research and outcomes, the government actively encouraged commercialization of research.

The Advanced Technology Program (ATP) and the Technology Reinvestment Project (TRP) provided substantial funding directed toward research and development of new products that would benefit both the government and the public through commercialization of the dual-use technologies. These programs also encouraged companies to take existing federally developed and owned technologies and find new commercial uses for them. Research administrators helped faculty develop partnerships with industry to attract some of these funds to the university. There are now more than 70 federal cooperative technology programs involving at least ten agencies. In fiscal year 1994, federal agencies spent approximately $2.7 billion on cooperative technology programs (NSF, 1996).

Another government action that encouraged a transformation in research administration was the Patent Amendment Act of 1980. The act allowed universities to own patents resulting from federally sponsored research for the first time. Academic patenting has increased dramatically (NSF, 1996).

♦ Patents awarded to US academic institutions increased from 434 to 1,970 in the decade ending in 1996.

♦ The academic sector's share of all US patent awards rose to 3% in 1994 from 1% in 1980.

♦ In 1994, only three patent-use classes (all related to biomedical activity) accounted for 25% of all academic patents, compared to 7% in 1980.

♦ Ninety percent of all academic patents were awarded to the 100 largest research universities.

♦ Income from royalties and licensing agreements has increased steeply to approximately $500 million in 1996.

Part of this growth in academic patenting resulted from the creation of technology transfer offices. University research administrators developed or hired new skills to handle patent filing, marketing, and licensing of new technologies. New technology transfer offices hired lawyers who could understand the complexities of technology licensing and intellectual property protection so that research projects did not prevent the university from patenting the intellectual property. In addition to intellectual property rights, research administrators had to anticipate contractual restrictions that might be introduced by corporate partners seeking to prevent sensitive information from reaching their competitors. From the university standpoint, protectionistic clauses may result in constraints on the direction of research, the delivery of results, and the freedom to publish.

Research administrators must bridge the gap between corporate and academic interests. The different needs and goals of industry require research administrators to be flexible, to be able to rapidly reach agreements, and to carefully manage project progress, including the resolution of problems. Because of the potential divergence between corporate and academic goals in licensing, freedom to publish, and intellectual property, negotiating industry/academic agreements has proven to be a difficult, time-consuming task. It also requires highly skilled research administrators who can balance the desire for speed of execution with the caution necessary to protect the interests of the university.

In addition to the new patent legislation, the GUIRR New Alliances report (GUIRR, 1986) also credits initiatives, such as focused NSF-sponsored university-industry collaborative research programs and state economic development initiatives for encouraging these new partnerships. Investments in these alliances were based on the premise that these arrangements were good for business, helpful to universities, and in the public interest.

One of the new skills for research administrators is promotion of the value of research to the economy. California provides an example of this promotion effort. "The state provides core support for the university's missions of teaching, research, and public service. In return, the university brings in billions of dollars of non-state funding, reinvesting this money in California, primarily through research, which leads to new technologies, new products, and jobs. . . . This research is a driving force behind the California economy" (University of California Office of the President, 1996). The report cites some specific examples:

♦ The University of California (UC) has created over 400 formal partnerships with industrial partners for cooperative research and development worth almost $1 billion.

♦ In 1994–95, UC received annual royalties of $63.2 million from products developed by UC scientists.

♦ California is the world leader in biotechnology, due in large part to UC research.

♦ UC scientists founded three of the nation's top biotechnology companies: Genentech, Chiron Corporation, and Amgen.

♦ UC graduates about 42,000 students a year, 96% of them California residents. Having a skilled work force is a key incentive for companies to locate in California and to remain there.

Research administrators are developing skills in starting small businesses as the result of the federal government promoting the critical role of small business in economic development. The Small Business Innovation Development Act (1982) established the Small Business Innovation Research (SBIR) Program within the major federal R&D

agencies to increase government funding of research with commercialization potential in the small high-technology company sector. Each federal agency with an R&D budget of $100 million or more is required to set aside a certain percentage of that amount to finance the effort. The 1998 SBIR Program provides over $1 billion to small companies to encourage the commercialization of new technologies. University research administrators working with state economic development organizations have used these funds to encourage small business development of technologies that often started in a university research lab. Making connections between researchers and interested companies has become a full-time effort for some research administrators.

A successful example of connecting university research with small business development is the Ben Franklin Program in Pennsylvania which has positively influenced the state's economy. Through a combination of regional technology centers, small business incubators, and partnerships with universities, the program helps small companies in high technology fields commercialize new ideas. Since 1983 the program has created 1,270 new companies and over 24,000 new jobs of which more than 21,000 have been retained. In addition, it has attracted more than $1.2 billion dollars from state, private, and federal sources. Universities have benefited from the program through the receipt of research and development funding, broadening the learning experience for faculty and students, as well as developing new and lasting relationships (Werner, 1997).

Universities and state governments are exploiting the drawing power of universities as technology transfer agents to attract big businesses into the region. When Alabama was recruiting JVC and Mercedes-Benz to relocate, the university was an integral part of the package. The research administrators and executives at the University of Alabama created technology research centers to jointly focus on addressing the technology needs of these manufacturers. Special cultural and language programs were implemented to make employees and their families more comfortable and to provide for the needs of a diverse learning community within the region.

North Carolina State University (NCSU), expanding on the successful technology businesses of Research Triangle Park in North Carolina, has established the Centennial Campus. The Centennial

Campus is a new model for industry and university collaborative research: High technology businesses physically colocate in buildings on the campus with university programs that share a similar focus in their research. This symbiotic relationship is expected to help attract business to the area, increase the competitiveness of these businesses internationally, and establish a strong base of economic and political support for the university.

From these examples, it is clear that a new role has evolved for university research administrators: promotion of the value of their research programs in the local, national, and international economy. Realizing that federal funding could not expand the available research funds rapidly enough to meet their needs, universities have increased the available pool of funds for research by reestablishing themselves as the economic engine that generates the nation's wealth. Rather than competing for a share of finite government research funds, universities are taking a proactive approach by bringing new funds into the market and by stimulating the economy. The ancillary benefit is that commercialization is a tangible outcome that is visible to the public and provides justification for university research efforts.

CONCENTRATING RESEARCH IN NONACADEMIC HYBRID ORGANIZATIONS

Research administration is moving away from the traditional academic department structure to a cross-departmental organization which reflects today's complex, multidisciplinary problems. Some of this organizational change is the result of the increase in collaboration with industry. However, most is because today's scientific problems are highly complex and require a blend of disciplinary skills to solve. While these organizational changes were created to remedy complex problems, they also add stress within the university that must be managed by research administrators.

◆ Within academic institutions, for example, the nature of tenure and promotion discourages multidisciplinary work, reinforcing single-authored research publications, conducted within traditional disciplinary boundaries.

♦ Interdisciplinary programs are orphans within the fiscal bureaucracy of the university. These programs are at a further disadvantage since most of the university's planning efforts are based on the department-based fiscal structure. Thus, interdisciplinary programs play a less prominent role in the long-range planning of the university.

♦ At the federal level, rigid indirect cost recovery rules and regulations pertaining to the carryover and allocation of costs by scientists with multiple awards impede collaboration with colleagues in other departments (GUIRR, 1994).

Hybrid organizations, such as centers and institutes, have been developed through the cooperative efforts of research administrators, departments, and faculty to enable universities to address new, more complex research challenges. Usually the researchers in these organizations have both traditional single investigator research grants and multiple investigator grants through the hybrid organization. It is the sharing among various disciplines that allows the hybrid organization to accomplish its goal. The hybrid organization usually has a separate accounting for its efforts and an administrative staff dedicated to the work of the organization. This provides investigators with some flexible accounting options that are not available from a traditional single investigator award. It also provides dedicated, knowledgeable research administration staff to help develop proposals, negotiate awards, and manage projects. The faculty member is usually loosely affiliated with the hybrid organization and retains a traditional appointment with an academic department.

In 1989 and 1991, NSF funded the establishment of 25 Science and Technology Centers (STCs) which span a wide range of science and engineering fields. In 1996, the Committee on Science, Engineering, and Public Policy (CSEPP), under the National Academy of Sciences, undertook an evaluation of the STC program. "Many STCs provide a model for the creative interaction of scientists, engineers, and students in various disciplines and across academic, industry, and other institutional boundaries. . . . Most centers serve efficiently as two-way conduits between universities and their industrial partners. In general, they perform that function better than traditional departments do" (CSEPP, 1996).

This report points out "the success of the individual STCs depends critically on the presence of strong scientific and administrative leadership." Strong science, they found, was not enough. Research administrators serve as the bridge in these organizations, helping meet the diverse goals of the various constituents and resolving issues while the researchers focus on their research.

These hybrid organizations are usually supported by a combination of institutional, federal, state, local, and private funds, resulting in greater leverage for achieving results than an individual sponsor could obtain with a traditional single investigator agreement. Hybrid organizations have proven particularly useful for cooperative funding with industry where a single company could not afford to pay for all the research, but a group of companies could. In this case, the research administrator must play the role of marketeer, promoting the benefits to groups of companies. Part of the process involves structuring an agreement that avoids rivalry between the corporate partners, which might threaten the stability of the funding. The research administrator also must ensure that the results produced by the project meet the needs and expectations of all the partners. This is not always easy since the academy emphasizes discovery, while the business culture is focused on product development.

The National Textile Center (NTC) is an example of the value provided by hybrid organizations. Funded with federal and textile industry funds, the NTC involves six universities with strong textile academic programs and ties to the textile industry. The program was designed to consolidate the strengths of multiple universities to address the competitive needs of the US textile industry. The rationale focused on the fact that the textile industry is no longer a low-technology business; instead it is an intensely technological process that would benefit significantly from university research. At NCSU, one of the NTC sites, the entire textile process—from raw material to finished garment—can be run through textile machinery donated by the textile industry. Complex, high-technology processes such as computer-integrated manufacturing, computer-aided design and automated process control can be reproduced and studied in a complete production environment at the NTC.

The hybrid structure of the NTC is critical to managing large-scale projects where each project may have multiple funding sources. The projects combine the skills of researchers from many disciplines across several universities with other faculty from traditional academic disciplines (e.g., mechanical, industrial, and electrical engineering; graphic and fashion design; chemistry, math, and other scientific disciplines; as well as business management and marketing). Research administrators provide the coordination, logistics, and complex budgeting skills for hundreds of projects like these under the NTC. To ensure that the results are meeting the expectations of the sponsors, these administrators host visits and briefings for their government and industry partners.

Hybrid organizations enable universities to tackle research problems that could not have been solved through the traditional academic structure. To manage the complex sources of funds and accommodate the varying needs of multiple participants, research administrators in these organizations must develop new skills. Hence, compared to the traditional academic department, these hybrid organizations require new or upgraded administrative positions.

Emphasizing Service over Compliance

Another transformation in research administration is the shift in emphasis from compliance to service. The traditional research administration organization was a central office providing protection for the university. This central organization ensured that projects adhered to federal, state, and local regulations; contract requirements; and university policies. The penalty for noncompliance included poor audit reports, loss of future funding, and payback of funds already spent. Research administration organizations took this responsibility seriously, even though faculty often felt the oversight was overdone.

As universities grew their research base, the research administration organization stratified into two central offices. One, usually called sponsored projects or research development, often reports through the provost or chief academic officer with a focus on pre-award services to faculty and research growth. The other, sometimes called sponsored project accounting, reports through the administrative or financial organization and focuses on post-award compliance and stewardship of sponsors' funds. The transformation that is occurring on many campuses is a blending of the functions of these offices. The universities are applying a more balanced approach to regulation and compliance,

COMPLIANCE	SERVICE
Internal audits	Online searchable, databases of funding sources
Faculty and departmental compliance training	Summarized award terms and conditions for faculty
Prior approvals of purchases with research funds	Purchase cards with preset limits
Conflict of interest certifications	Reduced number of proposal approval signatures
Published roles and responsibilities	Assistance with proposal budget preparations

FIGURE 8.2   Compliance and Service Functions

reorganizing so that authority and accountability can be distributed closer to where the research work is performed.

When acting strictly as a compliance monitor, research administrators have been criticized for holding back the growth and flexibility of the research enterprise. Research administrators have reevaluated their roles within the university. While they continue to maintain the compliance role, they are emphasizing the service aspect more often. Some examples are listed in Figure 8.2.

Many of the initial transformation efforts focused on streamlining compliance so that the oversight was reduced, easing the burden on the researcher. This was designed to reduce the historic escalation of rules and regulations. Each time a problem occurred with a transaction, a compliance-oriented organization applied a new rule to that type of transaction. For example, the first time a purchase was found to be inappropriate for a grant, a new rule was established that required all grant purchases to be reviewed by the compliance organization. Over time these transaction rules have accumulated. Often, the original cause of the compliance need no longer exists. For example, sponsor restrictions on what can be purchased may have become more lenient, yet the rule requiring review of all purchases remains because the responsibility to review and remove rules is missing. For compliance-oriented organizations, the emphasis is on enforcement of existing rules or adding new ones. The philosophy is intolerance of error, regardless of the cost to the system. The accumulation of these rules slows the entire process. When customers of the process need faster turnaround, they establish shortcuts around the procedures.

	COMPLIANCE	SERVICE
Process	• More clearly define authority and responsibility • Carefully scrutinize high-risk, low-volume transactions • Define the meaning of signature • Post-audit	• Reduce cycle time by eliminating unnecessary oversight • Process low-risk, high-volume transactions quickly • Reduce signature steps • Eliminate pre-audit functions
Organization	• Central training and certification • Central lines of reporting	• Distribute authority • Increase productivity
Technology	• Build in rules • Apply procedures consistently	• Improve accessibility of information

FIGURE 8.3 Balancing Compliance and Service Functions

As research administration organizations have analyzed their processes, they found that these rules frustrated faculty and consumed substantial human resources. Taking a risk management perspective, research administrators could balance the cost to implement the rules with the risk of a violation occurring. Many research administration organizations that routinely reviewed every purchase made with research funds have eliminated this practice. At the University of California at Los Angeles (UCLA), administrators are notified when a purchase request is made, but the purchase automatically proceeds unless the administrator identifies a problem and intervenes. At other institutions, pre-audits occur only for purchases over an established threshold. An analysis of purchases often finds that 80–90% are under the threshold with few compliance violations being found. By treating high-volume, low-risk transactions differently, the majority of the transactions go through a streamlined process. Compliance oversight focuses only on low-volume, high-risk transactions.

For research administrators, reducing the overhead for compliance has not been enough. Additional efforts are focusing on process, organization, and technology to balance the elements of compliance and service provided by each.

Three primary changes are evident in these transformation efforts.

♦ Cycle time is shortened by reducing the approval steps in research administration processes.

♦ Delegation of authority and responsibility has moved research administration closer to their customers for both service and compliance.

♦ Technology is facilitating these changes by enabling a smaller group of administrators to handle a larger volume of proposals and projects.

Shorter Process Cycles

Cycle time should be influenced by its service and cost. Faculty cite turnaround time for proposal approvals, research subject protocol approvals, and new project start-up delays as significant frustrations, consuming both time and energy. Diverting attention to administrative details reduces time available for research. Long process times often reveal steps that do not add value, are out of sequence, or are unnecessary. A proposal with investigators from several departments might have to wind its way past the office of every department chair and several central offices before receiving approval, whether the proposal is for $10,000 or $10 million. By significantly reducing the approval steps, often to one or two signatures, this process can be shortened from days to hours.

This same approach is being applied to many processes in research administration, such as account setup for new projects, rebudgeting of funds, or purchasing. Enabling this reduction in approval steps comes from process improvement techniques. One of the keys is to handle the majority of transactions with a simple process, saving the more complicated process for the exceptions—the high-risk, low-volume transactions. Additionally, each review is analyzed for its value. If a signature is required only as part of a routine with little or no review, it's a candidate for elimination. The signature steps that remain should provide real value to the process through a careful review of the critical information required for that step.

A Hybrid Research Administration Organization

The idea of balanced compliance and service extends to the organization of research administration. Many universities that have reevaluated the traditional, centralized organizational model for research administration have rebuilt very distributed organizations with an emphasis on autonomy and authority at the departmental level. In other cases, universities have retained the benefits of a central organization grouping the academic, pre-award focus and the financial, post-award focus together in a combined central office. In most cases, the outcome is a hybrid centralized/distributed organization that offers some services that can be delivered more effectively through a consolidated office, such as billing, financial reporting, and subcontracting. Other services, such as proposal development and project financial management, are being distributed and managed in the units.

For a compliance organization like research administration, the critical issue is one of responsibility. In a distributed departmental model, there is some question whether the research administrators are independent enough to keep the institution's compliance requirements above the desires of the department chair or faculty. A central organization is more insulated from departmental pressure because the reporting structure ensures the lines of authority. However, a central model may not accommodate the desired level of service to faculty for a number of reasons: lack of knowledge about the department's activities, lack of trust by faculty who feel the central organization is remote with no common motivation to assist the department, and conflicting priorities in central administration.

A model that offers a blend of compliance and service is evolving, with growing support at many campuses. Based on initial work at Stanford, the model consists of Research Process Managers (RPMs) who report to the central research administration office, but who work and are housed in the departments they support. The RPMs are given extensive training and are certified at specific levels of expertise so that faculty and departments know the level of support they will receive. All RPMs are given tools, such as mobile phones, pagers, and laptop computers so that they can be immediately accessible to the faculty and departments that they serve. The RPMs have both pre- and post-award responsibilities. In the past these services were offered by people in two different central departments. The central reporting structure in this model ensures that the RPMs understand their compliance responsibilities and are accountable to the university, not an individual department. Because they work in departments with the researchers they serve, their mobility and certified expertise helps the faculty view the RPM as a department resource, responsive to their needs. The RPMs get to know their faculty and departments in much greater depth than before. Since the RPMs offer both pre- and post-award services, the faculty have a single point of contact for questions and answers—a significant benefit. Another component of the model that engenders trust is that the departments have input to the 360 degree evaluation of the RPM at appraisal time. This encourages the RPM to be as responsive as possible to the faculty and departments because their evaluation and remuneration depend on positive feedback from those they serve.

Several universities, such as Virginia Polytechnic Institute and State University and the University of Pennsylvania, are not making as dramatic a shift as the RPM model, but they are merging pre-award and post-award functions into a common office. These combined offices often report to one person. This enables faculty and departments to reach one office—sometimes a single person—for help no matter what the issue, pre- or post-award. This approach uses existing skills, combining them in a more service-oriented model, while retaining the compliance benefits of a central organization.

Compared to the Stanford RPM system, this latter approach requires less change. The Stanford model requires a significant investment in the curriculum for training and certification, mobile tools, and modifications to the employee evaluation model. In most distributed authority models, positions and salaries must be upgraded to attract and retain professionals who have the skill and personality to make the effort successful. This new blend of service and compliance may not require more people, but it will certainly require the development of higher-level skills, increased salaries, and a higher investment in technology.

Technology

Technology is the other significant transformation that offers the promise of balancing service and compliance. The Grant Application and Management System (GAMS), developed and implemented by a consortium of six universities, is a good example. Started at North Carolina State University, this system provides faculty and departments with a proposal development tool that allows them to develop proposals more quickly and get them approved online. While significantly reducing the effort required to prepare the administrative content of the proposal, often a frustrating exercise for faculty, the GAMS system provides consistent budgets and rule-driven processing that ensures more consistent compliance. NCSU's experience is that traditional proposals and budgets, prepared manually or with a faculty or departmental system, often contain a significant number of errors and must be returned for revision. GAMS proposals are consistently error free. Thus, the review and approval process can focus on real issues, rather than on mechanics and administrative details. At NCSU, this information system has been developed in parallel with process and organizational changes that reduce the paper-pusher mentality and administrative drag of the central office during proposal development and focuses instead on value added activities.

Reengineered Processes

The characteristics of this transformation in research administration—from a compliance orientation to one of service—are predicted by reengineering texts (Hammer & Champy, 1993).

- *Several jobs are combined into one.* The Stanford RPM performs the entire process and serves as the single point of contact for the customer.

- *Workers make decisions.* In the Stanford and other distributed authority models, signature authority for approving proposals is given to certified RPMs.

- *Processes have multiple versions.* To be flexible, organizations need multiple versions of the same process to handle different situations. For example, proposals and awards from standard sponsors like NIH or NSF grants are handled through a streamlined process at the unit level, but contracts and clinical trials are processed through a different, more complex version of the process.

- *Checks and controls are reduced; reconciliation is minimized.* The concept is one of risk management: Reengineered processes use controls only to the extent that they make economic sense, such as removing pre-audit controls on grant purchases and eliminating budget reviews at multiple steps.

INVESTING IN ELECTRONIC RESEARCH ADMINISTRATION

The National Science Foundation reports that almost all academic researchers have access to computers. Over 96% of science and engineering PhD faculty with research as their primary activity have access to a personal computer. Electronic communication has greatly enhanced scientific communication. Scientists, operating in virtual research teams in different institutions or even different countries, are transferring information about ongoing work electronically and making information available more rapidly through electronic journals.

Research administrators are applying information technology not just to improve their productivity but also to enhance the services provided to the university, departments, and faculty. This trend can be seen at federal agencies, as well. Much of the development of these electronic research administration systems is occurring through a collaborative, iterative process. Government agencies and universities are working together through the Federal Demonstration Partnership with a goal to reduce administrative overhead. The expected benefit of reduced overhead is that a greater proportion of funds will be spent on research. Electronic commerce is rapidly taking shape in research administration.

For universities, the core of research administration information support has come from the financial system. This is changing.

> In the 1970s, centralized computing architectures and the economics of computing influenced the evolution of a typically centralized financial management environment. The financial officer specified requirements to the administrative information systems office. . . . The needs of the financial office revolved around controlling financial processes, maintaining the general ledger, issuing vendor checks, etc. Rarely were such systems designed to meet the planning, monitoring, and controlling requirements posed, for example, by complex auxiliary operations or the contract-intensive academic programs found at research universities. Since the intended users of these systems were typically professionals in the accounting office who used them intensively and extensively, the demands and expectations for user friendliness were modest. The failure of many such systems to meet the planning and operational needs of institutional subunits in a user-friendly fashion has contributed to the proliferation of "shadow systems" in these subunits (Woodrow, 1998).

The proliferation of personal computers has encouraged people to solve their own information needs. As a result, shadow systems have become prevalent in research administration. Many financial managers have created their own financial systems using sophisticated spreadsheet programs. Departments, centers, and other hybrid organizational units who depend on external funding are anxious for a financial system adapted to their needs. Historically, the central information technology (IT) organization responded to the needs of the comptroller at the university, not departmental financial needs.

Unable to wait for support from the central IT organization, many research intensive departments and centers have invested in their own shadow systems to remain responsive to the needs of their faculty and sponsors. This investment includes shadow accounting systems, databases about investigators' capabilities, electronic services that deliver information about sponsor funding, and proposal development programs. In research administration, better information systems help administrators and researchers be more productive by eliminating or streamlining routine tasks. Better information helps research administrators and department chairs identify trends in research funding, allowing them to develop financial and staffing strategies.

Many campuses are replacing independent information systems and investing in integrated administrative systems that support all their core processes: human resources, financial management, and student services. Research administrators are involved in this core systems replacement effort, particularly in the financial area. Systems from PeopleSoft, Oracle, and SCT all reference grant management components. Until it is clear what functions will be supported by these systems, departments continue to run their own shadow systems.

The trend toward electronic research administration is not being driven solely by internal pressures for productivity or better information. The federal government's reinvention efforts under the Government Performance and Results Act have a significant influence. Implementation of Electronic Research Administration (ERA) systems by major federal sponsors such as NIH and NSF, and a drive toward electronic commerce across the government, has significant implications for the technology needs of university research administration.

The federal electronic commerce philosophy, described in Vice President Gore's introduction to the 1997 Access America report, applies to university research administration, as well (Gore, 1997).

Many federal agencies, led by the NIH and NSF, appear to be making significant strides in electronic commerce and ERA. Early work has been completed on a common data dictionary for grant proposal submissions led by a multiagency working group called the Electronic Commerce Committee. This effort produced an American National Standards Institute (ANSI) electronic data interchange (EDI) standard for electronic proposal submission. The Access America report presented by Vice President Gore in 1997 called for a working demonstration of a single federal electronic grant submission system by fall 1998.

Universities are linked to the federal reinvention effort in two ways. First, process changes occurring at the federal level have a significant impact on the processes required at the university. These new or revised university processes have information requirements. Second, the new federal electronic commerce systems will require comparable systems at the university with which to interact and exchange data. Faculty and university administrators are depending on the research organization to enable their institution to capitalize on electronic commerce. Research administrators must invest in technology and the skills to manage the system. This is a fundamental change for an organization that has traditionally relied on paper systems and received little support from the university's IT organizations.

For example, proposal development is a critical activity at universities. Much of the electronic commerce effort is focused in this area. With federal budget pressures and increasing competition for research funding, universities are encouraging faculty to submit more proposals. Many process changes and information systems have attempted to facilitate both proposal development as well as review and approval—processes that faculty often cite as a stressful experience. By making the proposal process easier, research administrators expect more faculty to submit proposals. Electronic proposal development systems enable researchers to build proposals in substantially less time than with the traditional paper forms. Once the information is in the database electronically, the proposal can be reviewed and approved online in much less time.

As a result of universities increasing proposal submissions, federal agencies must process the increased volume of proposals. Under the reinvention efforts these agencies are investing in proposal receipt and processing systems. According to the Access America report, "in FY 1996, the federal government provided approximately $300 billion in grants to governments, universities, tribal governments, nonprofit organizations, and individuals. The grants process can be improved and speeded up using electronic commerce, and ten federal agencies have joined together to form the US Electronic Grant Project. This will provide a 'one-stop shop' for federal grant applications using World Wide Web and EDI technologies" (http://gits.gov/htm/access.htm).

The university proposal systems need to be able to send their proposal information directly to the sponsoring agency's proposal receipt system. The key is identifying the information that must be exchanged. In the case of proposal submission this has been solved by the ANSI EDI standard. For universities that have to submit proposals to many different sponsors, the benefit of such a standard is that one system can produce proposals for many sponsors. For research administrators, managing the technologies associated with the electronic proposals has been difficult and time consuming.

To achieve the full benefit from investments in technology, universities and federal agencies must dedicate time and resources to electronic commerce. Even though electronic commerce promises tremendous value to universities and the sponsors they serve, research administrators are finding it difficult to obtain support. University IT organizations are concentrating on replacing other core systems. The full transformative power of the research administration process has yet to be realized by senior university administrators. Most of the current efforts are being led by the pre-award offices at universities without the full support and energy of the university leadership. Although research administrators are articulating both the benefits of the new systems as well as the potential competitive risk of being left behind, the transformation is not rapid enough. NIH is piloting their electronic proposal receiving system to be in limited production by 1999. NSF has already required use of its FASTLANE system for proposal submission on selected funding opportunities. Electronic commerce in research administration is becoming a reality.

A PROFESSION OF GENERALISTS

Research administrators are changing from specialists to generalists. While remaining specialists in research administration, they are broadening their role and skills to cover the entire research administration process. Previously research administrators became very adept in a single component of the process (e.g., pre-award proposal processing or contract negotiation) or a particular sponsor (e.g., NIH, foundations, or industry). Now research administrators are providing support throughout the entire process. In addition, research administrators are working together to distinguish their profession from other university administrative functions. Through professional societies, they are developing their own training and certification standards.

Research administrators have created professional organizations like the National Council of University Research Administrations (NCURA) and the Society of Research Administrators (SRA) to share information and best practices among their institutions and to monitor the latest regulatory changes. The focus of these efforts has been to support the development of research administrators as a critical resource within the university. Because of the knowledge and skills required, these organizations continue to be the primary source of professional development for research administrators.

NCURA and SRA collaborated in defining the capabilities required of research administrators. From this they developed a professional certification standard and designed a curriculum to train research administrators to the standard. Training and certification for research administrators covers all parts of the research administration process. This certification program is managed by the Research Administrators Certification Council which bestows the designation of Certified Research Administrator on those who meet its requirements. During NCURA and SRA meetings, attendees can accumulate continuing education points toward this certification (See http://www.ncura.edu/originfo/memberinfo/purposes.html and http://web.fie.com/cws/sra/mem.htm#C http://web.fie.com/cws/ sra/mem.htm#C.)

As more research administrators become generalists, the central research administration organization is changing. First, the central organization must manage the more complex distributed organization ensuring that the proper blend of service and compliance is maintained for both the institution and the sponsors. An effective training and certification process is critical to success of the distributed organization. This is becoming a responsibility of the central research administration office. The central experts in particular elements of research administration support the generalists. These specialists may have significantly more training (e.g., lawyers) or skills that are used infrequently within any single research unit (e.g., complex contract negotiation or technology licensing). Functions, such as invoicing, are centralized to economize transaction processing. Others, such as internal audit and the protection of research subjects, are centralized because their responsibility is more of a risk management function for the institution than service in the general research administration process.

CONCLUSION

"Science cannot live by science alone. Research needs education, just as education thrives when it is conducted in an atmosphere of inquiry and discovery" (Lane, 1996).

University research administration is undergoing a dramatic transformation as the academic research enterprise responds to the needs of society. While the underlying emphasis of research may change and the funding sources shift, the underlying rationale of research and education continues. The role of the research administrator is to understand the changing needs of sponsors and university researchers and to find a way to match the two. Research administration is shifting from a rigid bureaucracy to a flexible, responsive organization that can continually adapt to the needs of the institution and the external forces shaping the research enterprise.

The fundamental transformations demonstrate the tenacity with which research administrators strive to provide an environment for a robust research program:

♦ By making the academic research enterprise a vital link in the economy

♦ By promoting and managing new organizational structures that bring researchers together to address the complex, multidisciplinary, international research problems facing society today

+ By establishing new services that provide researchers more time for their investigations

+ By using information technology to enhance responsiveness, improve productivity, and reduce administrative costs of the research enterprise

+ By creating professional development opportunities

The challenge for research administrators is to continue to redefine themselves so that the value they provide is clearly recognized and acknowledged by the university, faculty, and sponsors.

REFERENCES

Access America. (1997). *National performance review.* (US) PRVP 42.2:AC 2. [0556-C]. Government Information Technology Services Board. [http://gits.gov/htm/access.htm.]

Barbett, S., & Korb, R. A. (1997, July). *Current funds revenues and expenditures of institutions of higher education: Fiscal years 1987 through 1995.* Washington, DC: US Department of Education, National Center for Education Statistics.

Caspa, H. (1997, Winter). The price of higher education. *NCURA Research Management Review, 9* (2), 29–32.

Committee on Science, Engineering, and Public Policy (CSEPP). (1993). *Science, technology, and the federal government: National goals for a new era.* Washington, DC: National Academy of Sciences.

Committee on Science, Engineering, and Public Policy (CSEPP). (1996). *An assessment of the National Science Foundation's science and technology centers program.* Washington, DC: National Academy of Sciences.

Denton, J., & Hunter, F. A. (1997, Spring). The multiple effects of influencing external funding productivity. *NCURA Research Management Review, 9* (1), 37–50.

Gore, A. (1997). Introduction. In *Access America. National performance review.* (US) PRVP 42.2:AC2. [0556-C]. Washington, DC: Government Information Technology Services Board. [http://gits.gov/htm/intro.htm.]

Government-University-Industry Research Roundtable. (1986). *New alliances and partnerships in American science and engineering.* Washington, DC: National Academy Press.

Government-University-Industry Research Roundtable. (1994, July). *Stresses on research and education at colleges and universities: Institutional and sponsoring agency responses.* Washington, DC: National Academy Press.

Grant, G. E. (1997, Spring) Is this your research administration? *SRA Journal, 28* (3&4), 35–37.

Gunston, D. H., & Keniston, K. (Eds.). (1994). *The fragile contract: University science and the federal government.* Cambridge, MA: MIT Press.

Hammer, M., & Champy, J. (1993). *Reengineering the corporation: A manifesto for business revolution.* New York, NY: HarperCollins.

Horowitz, F. D. (1997, Winter). For want of a crystal ball. *NCURA Research Management Review, 9* (2), 33–39.

Jonas, S., Katz, R. N., Martinson, L., Plympton, M. F., Relyea, S. W., Rennie, E. D., Rudy, J. A., & Walsh, J. F. (1997). *Campus financial systems for the future.* Washington, DC: National Association of College and University Business Officers and CAUSE. [http://www.cause.org/pub/fis/ch1/1b.html.]

Lane, N. (1996). *Science and engineering indicators. NSF report.* Washington, DC: National Science Foundation. [http://www.nsf.gov/sbe/srs/seind96/ovquotes.htm.]

Langenberg, D. N. (1997, Winter). The past as prologue: What the future holds for research universities. *NCURA Research Management Review, 9* (2), 41–46.

Lasper, G. (1994, October 18). *Statement on resolution of outstanding disputes between Stanford and the government on indirect cost issues.* Palo Alto, CA: Stanford University.

National Institutes of Health. (1997, May). *NIH era and reinvention status report.* Washington, DC: National Institutes of Health. [http://www.nih.gov/grants/reinvention/statusreport0597.htm#I.]

National Science Foundation (NSF). (1996). *1996 research and development indicators.* Washington, DC: National Science Foundation.

University of California Office of the President. (1996). *UC means business: The economic impact of the University of California.* Oakland, CA: University of California Regents.

Waugaman, P. (1998, April 6). *Down the slippery slope: When faculty get involved in technology commercialization.* Technology Transfer and Management, Inc. Biloxi, MS: SRA Southern Section Meeting.

Werner, J. (1997, October 7). *Ben Franklin Partnership Program: Leveraging state and federal research and technology incentive programs.* Presentation to the Society of Research Administrators. Atlanta, GA.

Woodrow, R. J. (1998). *Management for research in US universities.* Washington, DC: NACUBO.

*[*All company names or products are trademarks or registered trademarks of their respective companies.]*

9

Transforming Human Resources in Higher Education

Thomas R. Connolly

Now I saw, though too late, the folly of beginning a work before we count the cost and before we judge rightly of our own strength to go through with it.

Robinson Crusoe

QUESTIONS TO ANSWER SO WE CAN "JUDGE RIGHTLY"

What do you really want to do and why? The answer is paramount for us to understand. The issues driving colleges and universities to transform human resources (HR) are what we must know before we can "judge rightly of our own strength to go through with it."

Is cost the major issue? Cost can derive from two sources: organizational cost and process cost. How many HR staff members does it take to perform the functions of HR? How does that compare to your competitors'? How much do you pay for benefits? How much do they pay? How many times must data be entered for a new employee? Do these data get entered by a staff member in one office, then passed over to benefits for keying again, then transferred to payroll for rekeying yet another time, with each functional area entering data into their own segment of a legacy HR system?

Is the improvement of processes most important? As one Ivy League president recently said, "This hiring process is driving me crazy. It takes too long and I don't see quality candidates." Can employees easily make changes in their personal data or benefits choices? Do forms require multiple approvals for data that only employees need to own?

Is there a positive alignment among the mission and long-range goals of the university, the annual objectives of departments, and the performance measurements of employees? Do the goals of the university translate to objectives—for schools, for departments, for individuals? And do employees get measured on how well they perform against these objectives? Better yet, do they get rewarded when they achieve their objectives?

Is the transformation you are about to begin driven by technology? Can you get at the information you need? Can your "customers" get at information they need to make decisions for the university? Does your system work? Or has it been cobbled together over time, modified by new regulatory requirements and reporting needs, built by in-house staff with too few resources? Has the system reached the point where it cannot give you what want, when you need it?

Is your organization now being asked to perform a different role? Are you being challenged to move from business transactions into activities which add more value or involve partners? Are deans asking you to help stop the revolving door, understand why people are leaving, help hire the right people quickly when someone leaves, and make certain that the right pay, training, and environment are in place to make your institution a great place to work?

These are the questions we must answer so we can "judge rightly." They have to do with process, organization, and technology.

Process is the work of the college or university: It is what we do. Processes have beginnings and ends. Their steps add value to the overall process. If hiring begins with a position opening and ends with successfully hiring the right person, it also has a series of value-adding steps along the way that help speed the process and ensure that the right candidates are identified. Organization and technology are enablers of the process. Form follows function.

Organization is the structure, roles, and accountabilities for the people who complete the process work. Process extends the boundaries of the HR organization. It is no longer functional. It is cross-organizational and cross-functional. It begins with a department manager who needs to hire an employee, goes into the school's finance organization to ensure that the position is classified and budgeted, moves through human resources to posting, applicant tracking, candidate interviewing, and affirmative action. After an offer is accepted, the correct information is entered into benefits, payroll, and the human resources information system (HRIS). The HR organization is being challenged to develop new ways to support processes that are customer—rather than compliance—driven.

Technology is the information enabler, just as organization is the people enabler. Technology is bounded by attributes, such as ease of use, data entry at the point of origination, and speed. It is technology that allows a manager to post a job opening on a local system or the Internet. It is technology that allows applicants to submit applications online and HR departments to convert applicant data into hiring data without rekeying. And it is technology that lets employees enter their time worked online, forward it to their supervisor who approves it electronically after which it is automatically transferred to the HR/payroll system.

Process, organization, and technology must be understood in the context of the overall university, returning us to the question of alignment. What are the goals of the university? In what context is the university operating? How does it stack up competitively in higher education? What are its strategies? Process, organization, and technology are integral to each other. They must align and, when being transformed, must be enabled by change management—the glue that helps higher management communicate to employees what is happening and why. Universities can achieve maximum performance when all elements of the management framework are integrated and effectively targeted toward meeting the strategic requirements of the institution (Figure 9.1).

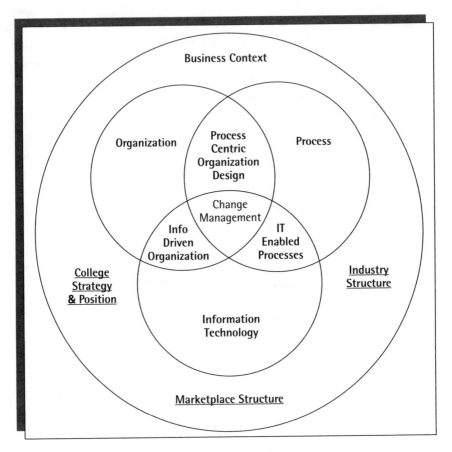

FIGURE 9.1 Integrated Elements of the Management Framework

A DEEPER LOOK

A fully developed human resources process supports the context of the college or university: It is enabled by an organizational design that minimizes transaction costs while maximizing communication. Information technology supports the needs of the customers of the process, providing ease of access to required information. Key in any transformation is change management which involves an awareness of how ready the organization—and the executive leadership—is for substantial change, along with targeted communications and training which are required to support the change (Figure 9.2). Peter Drucker writes that in the next 50 years, schools and universities will change more than they have in the past 300 years (Drucker, 1995). He states,

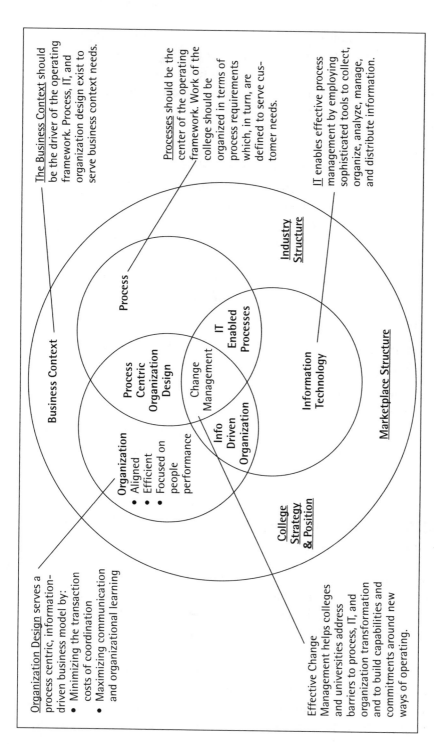

The Business Context should be the driver of the operating framework. Process, IT, and organization design exist to serve business context needs.

Processes should be the center of the operating framework. Work of the college should be organized in terms of process requirements which, in turn, are defined to serve customer needs.

IT enables effective process management by employing sophisticated tools to collect, organize, analyze, manage, and distribute information.

Organization Design serves a process centric, information-driven business model by:
- Minimizing the transaction costs of coordination
- Maximizing communication and organizational learning

Effective Change Management helps colleges and universities address barriers to process, IT, and organization transformation and to build capabilities and commitments around new ways of operating.

Business Context

Process

Industry Structure

Process Centric Organization Design

Change Management

IT Enabled Processes

Organization
- Aligned
- Efficient
- Focused on people performance

Info Driven Organization

Information Technology

Marketplace Structure

College Strategy & Position

FIGURE 9.2   Process-Centered Design and Technology-Enabled Processes "every organization has to build the management of change into its very structure . . . this means every organization has to prepare for the abandonment of everything it does." Human resources transformation occurs when the information-driven organization is enabled by process-centric organization design and information technology-enabled processes.

So, when we understand what we are about as a college or university, what the institution needs HR to help with, and where there are gaps, then we can begin the transformation. One final caveat: Transformation does not always start in the same place or for the same reasons. The preceding description would be the logical, classical way of beginning. We do not work in a perfectly logical world, so we do not always begin at the beginning. In fact, we do not always need to begin at the beginning. The answers to transforming human resources in higher education come from four questions:

1) What works well and what doesn't work well in HR today?

2) What are the best practices in HR in higher education and elsewhere?

3) Is there a vision of how HR processes should be performed? How they should be enabled?

4) How can we change the processes to perform the way the college or university needs and get line management buy-in to implement the changes?

WHAT WORKS WELL AND WHAT DOESN'T WORK WELL IN HR TODAY

Most of what we see in human resources functions today has evolved over 40 to 50 years. The role of HR has changed dramatically due to the new partnering role senior management sees for HR and the way people work today (Connolly, 1995). This paradigm shift is outlined in Figure 9.3.

HR finds itself at the confluence of change. Systems that are not able to provide information to management do not work well. Central university systems that schools and departments do not trust as having correct data or from which they cannot get information cause

FROM	To
Advisors—who tell	Partners—who consult/coach/participate
Policy and practice advice	Principles based decisions
Individual case management	Organizational and team effectiveness
Continuous employment	Competency identification/skills strategy
Resource balancing	Labor cost management
Management responsibilities	Personal accountability
University training programs	Continuous learning
Culture of stability	Culture of change

FIGURE 9.3   Paradigm Shift from Advisor to Partner

these units to keep shadow systems that duplicate information stored in the central system. Fault is not the issue here. This is simply what has happened in most institutions. Today's HR software is typically ten to 15 years old. There are generally five or six packages, some purchased, some home-grown, that when viewed as a whole constitute the HR and payroll system. These packages are not integrated, so data have to be entered multiple times. Once data are in, removal is difficult, requiring near genius to write the macros for specific reports.

Processes fare no better. They are encumbered by labyrinthine steps, approvals, and paperwork. These processes grew up over time. If the university had difficult financial times you can often see the effect in the sedimentary layers of financial approvals. If new regulatory steps were legislated, you see it in the number of participants involved in the process. Mixed with this are the coping steps inserted in the process to deal with the special needs of certain schools. However, once part of the process, they are required of all who use the process.

The human resources function must deal with staffing to perform transactional work, answering employee benefits questions and resolving payroll deduction problems, even when payroll is handled by finance. The HR staff is being challenged to improve the quantity and quality of hires. They are frequently asked to make do with the current university practice, rather than being sought out as a partner to develop a strategy to reduce attrition, improve base pay, and move to a rewards system that enhances motivation and retention. This is in spite of the fact that compensation surveys show HR staff pay at the lower end of the spectrum.

These challenges are only somewhat different than what is found in the private sector. Dave Ulrich, a professor at the University of Michigan, states that senior management must recognize and support the new role of partner that it is asking HR to undertake (Ulrich, 1998). Ulrich states that "HR's activities appear to be—and often are—disconnected from the real work of an organization." He sees a four-part role for HR:

1. To become a partner with executive management to move planning along
2. To become an expert in the way it is organized and the way it executes work, efficiently and effectively
3. To become a champion for employees representing them to senior management
4. To be an agent of continuous transformation

An emerging organizational model for HR was described after a study of 17 global corporations (Connolly, 1997). In this model, HR is seen to be moving in the following directions:

- To strategically recentralize—providing greater control from the center of the organization and providing uniform approaches regarding critical HR activities
- To move to scale-driven economics—consolidating routine HR administrative tasks into an HR service center
- To line delivery of HR services—the expectation that line managers are accountable for people and supported by HR systems that deliver information

What works well and what doesn't work well has to do with time, money, and expectations. Increasingly, we have found managers need more information and need it faster. Oftentimes, the processes and systems of HR cannot deliver it. We are seeing colleges and universities adopt management techniques for their business processes, reducing bureaucracy, making processes more efficient and responsive, and improving the effectiveness of communication and cooperation. Senior managers at universities have more pressure on them from more stakeholders than ever before: Parents want lower cost, students want more flexibility in class schedules, faculty want better facilities and more competitive pay, schools want more autonomy and less centralized control, alumni want a higher standing for their alma mater, and the board wants financial accountability within the bounds of annual revenue and without reducing the endowment.

Yes, expectations are rising for HR: They are in the center of the cauldron, the spot that generates the highest boiling point. However, many things work well in HR today. Invariably, what universities tell us works best is the HR team. More and more institutions are addressing these challenges and beginning the transformation. Colleges and universities are putting up web pages that detail policy and process reengineering highlights, providing descriptions of new technology platforms (e.g., PeopleSoft or Oracle) that are being installed and new roles and responsibilities for HR staffs.

WHAT ARE THE BEST HR PRACTICES?

Best practices are best defined by process since so much of human resources is functionally driven. Conversely, a number of process solutions can be supported by common organization and technology improvements; these best practices are best summarized by organization and technology enablement. We have performed many reengineering engagements both in higher education and in the private sector and are seeing commonality among these best practices. At the moment, the move toward these best practices is more rapid in higher education than in other sectors. This is fostered by the more open sharing of information in higher education through information available on the web and the chronicling of best practices by organizations such as EDUCAUSE. While initial development of best practices grew out of the quality movement of the 70s and gained momentum with the Baldridge Award criteria in the 80s, higher education and private industry find themselves at a similar crossroads: The world has changed. Market force, cost reduction, and revenue generation pressures are intense; organizations have flattened; people work in networks and over networks; and technology has dramatically improved.

The human resources process, when viewed at an enterprise level, generally looks like the enterprise model displayed in Figure 9.4. HR processes are made up of a series of subprocesses, each of which has its own series of steps required to complete the subprocess. For each

Manage Employee Relations Management	Select & Hire	Train	Access & Recognize	Benefits	Process & Payroll Time	Separate	Manage Employee Data	Position
Provide advice and counsel	Identify current/future needs	Conduct new employee orientation	Manage performance	Identify requirements	Add employee to payroll	Separate employees	Collect employee data	Establish position
Manage and disseminate HR info	Source candidates/ including job posting	Develop training requirements	Assess employee competence	Develop proposal	Process changes to payroll		Update employee data	Develop & manage budget
Manage the grievance process	Hire the right people	Define delivery method	Reward accomplish-ment	Negotiate services	Process time/ attendance		Prepare employee data reports	Position control
Manage discipline	Select people for future	Provide the right training at the right time	Manage compensation	Communicate & educate	Distribute payroll		Provide link to payroll process	
	Place people in open positions	Consider future needs in individual development		Administer health & welfare plans	Payroll accounting			
				Administer retirement plans	Delete employee from payroll			
				Reporting & analysis				

FIGURE 9.4   Enterprise-wide Human Resources Process

subprocess we have researched best practices—those innovations that add value to the institution. A best practice also can constitute a particular way of managing people that has a positive impact on customer satisfaction, employee satisfaction, and/or financial results. They may be better termed innovative practices from the viewpoint of the observer: Someone else's best practice may not apply or add value to your institution, but it may provide you with guidance which allows you to develop a best practice for your institution. The appendix contains best practices culled from research in both higher education and private industry.

THE CHANGING ROLES OF HR

In leading organizations, human resources departments have shed the traditional stereotype of lots of administrative duties and transaction processing with little strategic work and cursory involvement in hiring, retaining, and motivating. The emerging role is of a knowledgeable business partner, a catalyst for change and a risk taker, which balances employee and institutional interests (Connolly & Mastranunzio, 1995). HR is playing a less prominent role in the administrative domain. No longer is the emphasis on control tasks and transaction processing. HR is using technology to streamline and automate administrative tasks and to provide more value-added work as a strategic partner.

Major responsibilities include:

♦ Building HR staff capabilities and skills to move toward a consultative business partner model

♦ More strategic thinking coupled with a shift of people responsibilities from HR to line management (e.g., HR is reducing individual case management and moving towards strategic planning, organizational alignment, and structure)

♦ External financial and process benchmarking to measure effectiveness

♦ Organizational development

   Cross-functional personnel development resulting from the flattening of organizations

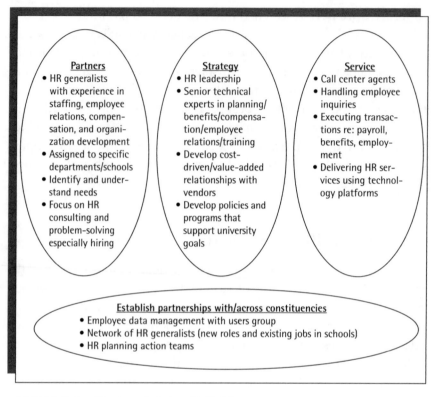

FIGURE 9.5   Structure of a Partnership Model

- ◆ Becoming a culture change catalyst for organization and behavior transformation
- ◆ Succession planning
- ◆ Career development planning
- ◆ Building a multicultural, diverse infrastructure with flexible work environments and policies
- ◆ Designing HR systems to implement and support business strategies
- ◆ Developing labor cost containment strategies

Figure 9.5 outlines how the new HR organization might be structured as it moves toward a partnership model, strategically designing programs and delivering better service. This new organization model was developed by one university to address all of the major service and support issues by partnering to understand customer needs, develop-

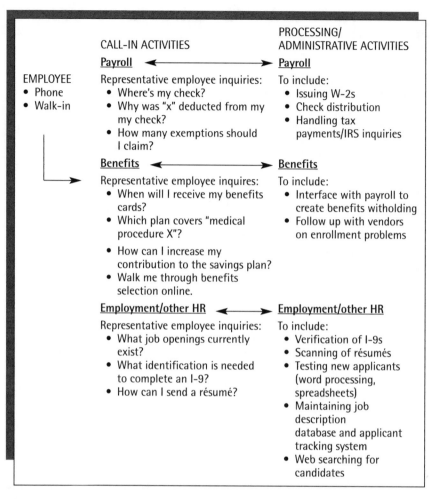

FIGURE 9.6　Service Function Responsibilities

ing expert solutions, and making information easily accessible. Figures 9.6 and 9.7 provide additional detail behind some of the concepts in this new organizational model.

Figure 9.6 shows that the units and jobs comprising the service function would have dual responsibilities: handling employee queries via a call-center approach and executing some specialized HR/payroll functions. The service center is critical in this new HR organizational model because it handles not only transaction processing but also answers phone inquiries about policy, practice, and programs. HR's new partnership model is described further (Figure 9.7), suggesting

Senior line management
- For strategy development
- For organizational alignment

HR/Payroll/IT
- For integrated services delivery

Partner (generalists)
- Reach out to schools
  Understand needs
  Translate to actions

Partner association
- HR generalists across the university come together as an association of professional colleagues—central and schools
  Education and training
  Best practices exchange
  Teamwork/task force—across organizations

Benefits specialists
- Vendor relationship management
  For best practices
  Competitive costs
  Service delivery management

User group of HRIT professionals
- For need identification and customer satisfaction
  EDM (Employee Data Management), payroll, benefits, schools, IT & HR leaders

Employee Relations (ER)
- Proactive partnerships with union leadership
  Creative program development and communications to improve worker productivity and job satisfaction

FIGURE 9.7   Human Resources Functions in a Partnership Model

that a new skill set is required compared to the traditional advice and counsel skills that are most common today.

HR employee data management principles that view end users as customers constitute best practices. Previously, shadow systems were seen as bootlegged and undermining the data integrity and goals of central HR systems. Today's HR systems architecture captures common data elements used university-wide and supplies information back to schools. This includes providing local systems with common information on all employees. The colleges/schools/departments can then merge it with specific data (e.g., state medical school certification for teaching doctors or budgeted positions by department). This approach saves the rekeying of data, eliminating system redundancies, and allows organizations to focus on value-adding analysis rather than building duplicate databases, locally.

HR INFORMATION TECHNOLOGY (HRIT) BEST PRACTICES

The best approaches in identifying technology needs to support HR processes are those that highlight user needs. Central administration Human Resources Information Technology (HRIT) requirements are explicit, and most software packages are designed for central input. What makes the design depicted in Figure 9.8 unique is its focus on the customer. It identifies, by process, user needs broken into five categories. Human resources information must be entered at the point of origin, be easily viewed and updated by manager and employees, and be supported by an efficient, integrated system. This outline is particularly effective since it helps the IT staff identify the infrastructure and skills needed to give life to this new technology.

VISION FOR HR

We see many organizations developing visions of what is possible for HR processes. The best are those that are customized to the organization. While a university might assimilate many of the best practices they have discovered, those that do best in developing a vision are the ones that use customers' needs and concerns to drive the vision. The customers are the users of the HR processes—the managers and employees of the university. In an earlier article (Connolly, 1997), I discussed world-class organizations implementing many of the same innovative practices. What made it innovative was the way in which the practice was tailored and implemented to suit the culture of these global organizations.

As an example, what follows is one university's vision of how human resources processes should function in order to help the university realize its mission by improving the efficiency and interconnectedness of payroll and human resources processes, organization, and technology.

- ◆ Processes must be streamlined to reduce the number of approval levels and increase accountability. They must be clear and well communicated while being user friendly and cost efficient.

- ◆ The organization must be structured to understand customer needs. It must be specialized to develop expert solutions. It must

Human Resources Processes

USER NEEDS	Plan	Mgr ER	Hire	Train	Assess	Compensate	Benefits	Payroll	Separate	Mgr Emp Data
DATA ENTRY AT POINT OF ORIGINATION	• HR forms online • Linked to manager tables		• Résumé application online	• Registration for classes	• Performance plan online	• Salary increases by managers online	• Benefits enrollment/ deductions by employee online	• Time and attendance reporting	• Manager initiates online	• Integrated system • Single entry
ELECTRONIC WORK FLOW		• Resource planning linked to financial planning	• Applicant tracking • Link to AA under utilized jobs	• Feedback on training application	• Assessment online					• Ability of users to track progress of process element
ABILITY TO UPDATE	• Succession planning			• Skills data bank		• Salary plan online	• Benefits deductions changes online	• Salary and benefits changes linked		• Manager/ employee can update
ABILITY TO VIEW QUERY		• Manager/ employee can view work history	• Job description data bank	• Online catalog of courses • Training online	• Appraisal distribution					• Employee can view records • Manager can obtain reports
SEARCH FOR INFORMATION	• Policies • Who to call • FAQs • Benefits	• Labor contracts • Web benchmark of best HR practices	• Web access to résumé banks	• Web connection for people knowledge			• Web pages of benefits vendors			• Web home page and intranet development

FIGURE 9.8   Customer-Focused HRIT Design

be service oriented to deliver information in a user-friendly manner.

- ◆ The technology must allow the user to enter data at the point of origin and have access to update and view information online; it must integrate benefits, payroll, and personnel information in a seamless way that also allows for data flow between central and local systems.

Many visions are expressed as models. They tend to be a positive way for a redesign team express a concept. Edwin Land, the founder of Polaroid, used to say, "Any problem that can be stated, can be solved." Once the team can state the problem, developing a mental model is a good bridge to the solution. It helps a team "see" the solution. Visions are necessary when solving a problem. They help the team see the ultimate objective. Without a vision it would be like putting a football team on the field and removing the end zones. Where are we going and how are we going to get there? The vision is the beginning of the answer. Once the problem of where we are going is stated, it can be solved.

ENSURING IMPLEMENTATION

Any reengineering effort needs a disciplined methodology (i.e., the approach to be used in stating and solving the problem). The university usually selects a team (eight to ten people) with some representation of the HR/payroll functions. The team's charge is to develop a more efficient and effective set of processes for the university. They may begin by identifying the strengths and weaknesses of the current processes. They gather suggestions for improvement. The methodology is best led by a consultant to help keep the team on track and to keep institutional bias (oftentimes for the status quo) to a minimum. Reinvention occurs once all the facts have been gathered and the underlying problems have been identified. The key to change is in the details of implementation—in the planning and execution. Strong sponsorship and leadership from university executives is paramount to foster change. Leadership and buy-in from line management are essential if change is to occur. Communication and training for all affected employees is essential if change is to result. The reengineering team must develop a compelling case for change that encourages all participants to get on board: There must be something in it for everyone. Among the benefits are savings for finance, senior management, and departments; improved service for the customers of the process; a process flow that is logical and time saving with minimal bureaucracy for users of the process; and better information for decision makers.

One institution argued that rather than facilitating results, existing HR/payroll processes at the university often become obstacles to success. They said:

- We are not competitive in recruiting the best people.
- We do not support collaboration.
- We do not encourage, recognize, or reward excellent performance.
- We do not provide high-quality services to students, faculty, or staff.
- We do not operate cost-effectively.
- We do not communicate in ways that are clear, timely, and consistent.
- We do not engender confidence in our ability to manage well.
- We do not value our staff as individuals.

Entrapment in these dysfunctional processes contributes to:

- High levels of frustration
- Inability to reach our potential
- Misapplication of resources, both human and financial
- Circumvention and contravention of the processes

They stated that the improved human resources and payroll functions recommended by the team would place the university in a stronger position. The university would benefit from:

- Better trained personnel
- Better recruitment and retention of talented people
- Increased productivity
- Reduced hidden costs formerly caused by redundancy and ineffectiveness

- Correct, up-to-date, and readily available payroll and personnel data
- Meaningful communications throughout the university
- Employees who are confident of the administration's ability to manage
- A service-driven environment
- Better compliance with legal and university requirements
- A better quality of working life for faculty, staff, and students

Another segment of any good case for change comes in the form of complexity reduction. Figure 9.9 illustrates how one university showed the dramatic impact their process redesign would have on both cost and complexity. (The participants are the number of people involved from start to finish in the process, and the steps are the number of hand-offs required along the way.) In a case like this, the argument is overwhelming. Cost and complexity for the processes are reduced by 40%. Even though the figure is impressive, it is just one component of the overall case to be made for change.

PROCESS	OLD PROCESS Participants + Steps = Complexity			NEW PROCESS Participants + Steps = Complexity			% Complexity Reduction	% Cost Reduction
Manage Positions	6	17	23	4	8	12	48%	38%
Manage EE Data	8	8	17	3	5	8	53%	75%
Select & Hire	10	34	44	6	24	30	32%	22%
Payroll	10	27	37	3	10	13	30%	38%
Benefits	11	36	47	6	16	22	53%	66%
Assess & Recognize	8	17	25	5	14	19	24%	6%
Average	9	23	32	4	13	17	40%	41%

FIGURE 9.9   Reductions in Process Complexity and Cost

SUMMARY

Early communication and a compelling case for change are critical to the success of HR initiatives as is a detailed implementation plan. The hard work will begin when the design of the new processes is turned over to process owners. We are seeing universities develop detailed project plans, with timetables prioritized by what is doable first, second, and third. Redesign of HR and payroll processes is occurring in many universities. Redesign is gaining favor as an approach to reduce costs, improve service, and provide management and employees with information in an increasingly information-driven workplace.

"'Deaning' is the form of administrative servitude with which I am most familiar," writes Henry Rosovsky in his book, *The University: An Owner's Manual* (Rosovsky, 1990). Two pieces of advice from Mr. Rosovsky stand out. The first one is "cultivate the art of asking for money; your career may depend on it." While he is referring to the fundraising requirements that come with the job of administering, clearly the administrators who are driving HR process change at the university must be aware that to make money you must spend money. One university recently spent $300,000 in one-time investments to improve its processes. The return was $2.5 million in documented annual savings. In another university, $5 million in annual savings was identified by the university's reengineering team. The investment required to achieve that level of savings amounted to a one-time cost of $5 million and annual costs of $500,000. In this case, the investments required to bring about change did not occur because leadership had not cultivated a disciplined approach for making strategic investments in critical administrative processes.

Mr. Rosovsky's second piece of advice has to do with the seven principles he outlines for reliable performance in governing the university. His fourth principle states, "Those with knowledge are entitled to a greater say." The role of human resources is changing so dramatically that it will perform one of the most critical functions of the university in the future: helping the university define and retain its knowledge base. In the new partnership model, the HR staff must see themselves as a key enabler of knowledge attainment and management. This role begins with understanding the core competencies required to support the mission of the college or university, the skills base on hand, and the training required to develop core competence. This role requires developing an empowered work force, free to search for information on either the Internet or the intranet. It requires the HR staff to build key partnerships to understand what is required and an HR staff that deploys itself in a new organizational model to help build and grow the university's intellectual capital. HR will have a greater say in the affairs and development of the university as it demonstrates it is a knowledgeable partner who understands the needs of the university and is involved in executing strategies to carry out its mission.

REFERENCES

Connolly, T. R. (1995). Human resources capabilities change management plan. Unpublished, p. 8.

Connolly, T. R. (1997, June). Transforming human resources. *Management Review,* 10–16.

Connolly, T. R., & Mastranunzio, J. (1995). Global challenges require new HR capabilities. Unpublished.

Drucker, P. (1995). *Managing in a time of great change.* Dutton, NY: Truman Talley Books.

Rosovsky, H. (1990). *The university: An owner's manual.* New York, NY: Norton.

Ulrich, D. (1998, January/February). A new mandate for human resources. *Harvard University Business Review, 76* (1), 124–134.

APPENDIX: BEST PRACTICES IN HR

General Practices

- ◆ Strategic staffing, selection, and alternative work force arrangements
- ◆ Performance measurement
- ◆ Alternative rewards and employee recognition
- ◆ Employee training and capability building
- ◆ Leadership development
- ◆ Cultural change fostered by a strong employee communication program
- ◆ Effective planning requiring high-level consensus and commitment to people and management practices that support the institution's goals

For example, the Massachusetts Institute of Technology (MIT) has identified eight areas to support the needs of MIT and employees in its HR redesign: 1) HR practices applicable to teams; 2) job design and classification; 3) hiring procedures; 4) compensation; 5) employee recognition and rewards; 6) effective performance evaluation, 7) assessment, development, and training; and 8) strategic planning.

Employee Relations

- ◆ Online access to policies and procedures (University of Illinois, Stanford University, University of Michigan, Boston College)
- ◆ Employee assistance programs to help employees deal with personal issues, such as drug or alcohol dependency, financial problems, family crisis, etc. (Cornell University)
- ◆ Tracking systems for grievance activity
- ◆ Formation of stronger partnerships with union leadership

Selection and Hiring

- ◆ Online application forms and résumé builders (Duke University, Northwestern University)

- Electronic job posting system (Pennsylvania State University, Columbia University)

- Use of the web to post vacancies and to find qualified candidates (University of Texas)

- Implementation of applicant tracking systems with scanning of résumés (MIT, Stanford University, Pennsylvania State University, University of Miami)

- In-house temporary hiring services (Stanford University)

- Redesign of the hiring process from the approval of the initial request through the enrollment of the person in benefits and payroll (Harvard University)

Training

- Core competencies required for organizational success are identified.

- Training is skill and competency based.

- Understanding the university's mission is stressed.

- A common technology platform of training is identified for all employees. This includes training in the use of common systems hardware, common systems applications, such as email and groupware and PC-based applications such as word processors, spreadsheets, and graphics packages.

- Learning accountability is stressed, and employees are trained in self-management skills.

    Virtual learning resource centers are being created, based on both intranets and the Internet.

    Intellectual capital (IC) systems are being created for all employees to share.

- Training outcomes are tied to strategic university, school, and department initiatives.

- Line management is involved in the design of course content and delivery, providing feedback to the training department on the value of the training employees received. Specific examples include:

    Automated training and development tracking system (University of Miami).

    Web-based orientation and staff training (Stanford University)

- Multimedia learning center to provide technical training (MIT and University of Miami).
- Increased focus on training first-line supervisors (University of Pennsylvania).
- High-level administration officers involvement in new employee orientation programs (University of Pennsylvania).
- Leadership development program offered to administrators (University of Miami).

Performance Assessment and 360 Degree Feedback

- Simplified assessment tools and simplified rating scheme
  Emphasize teamwork with 360 degree feedback (peer/manager/employee) (Seton Hall University)
- De-emphasize ratings and evaluation—emphasize skill development
- Include employees as active participants
- Focus on the process, not the form
- Alignment of individual objectives with department, school, and university goals and objectives
- Supervisors behave as performance coaches, managers as advisors
- Performance management systems are aligned with team environments
- Individual development plans are tied to performance requirements; training plans are developed to offer just-in-time skills
- Bonuses, alternative rewards, and employee recognition programs are developed

Specific detailed examples by institution include:

- All employees receive an annual merit review (MIT).
- The president's objectives become a part of each employee's performance plan (Seton Hall University)
- Simplified performance appraisals that measure performance against goals are established jointly by managers and employees (University of Vermont, University of Illinois, MIT, University of California at San Diego, Seton Hall University)

+ Linking performance to pay (University of California at San Diego)

Compensation

+ The alignment of objectives and achievement rewards with strategic direction (includes all employees)
+ Broad banding (i.e., creating broader salary bands and broader job descriptions with fewer titles) (Stanford University, MIT, University of Pennsylvania, University of Minnesota, Duke University, Tufts University)
+ Pay tied to performance
+ Greater prevalence of variable pay and bonuses (MIT)
+ Competency-based pay (i.e., moving away from what people do to how they do it). Instead of valuing jobs against a set of rigid factors, individuals are paid for their contributions to the organization's success

Benefits

+ Online benefits modeling and selection (Northwestern University)
+ Organizations are developing access to vendor web sites (benefits, retirement accounts) (Harvard University)
+ Employee assistance programs (Cornell University, University of Miami)
+ Outsourcing of Consolidated Omnibus Budget Reconciliation Act (COBRA) processing (Harvard University, MIT)
+ Flexible benefits/spending
+ Small number of plans for better management and buying power

Payroll

+ The alignment of payroll and human resource systems to provide a comprehensive database of employee information (University of Northern Arizona, Ohio State University, Princeton University, Pennsylvania State University, Harvard University, Tufts University)

♦ Direct deposit and electronic pay stub for all employees (exceptions are made available)

♦ Automating time and attendance records

Some examples by institution:

♦ Online time collection system (Pennsylvania State University, University of Vermont, University of Pennsylvania)

♦ Online input of information by departments to HR system (Johns Hopkins University, University of Pennsylvania)

♦ Imaging projects to eliminate paper employee files (University of Miami, Pennsylvania State University)

♦ Redesign of payroll stub for mailer format (Pennsylvania State University)

♦ Use of web technology to reduce paper forms (Pennsylvania State University, University of Minnesota, Harvard University, MIT, University of Vermont, Stanford University, Cornell University, University of Pennsylvania, Princeton University, University of Miami)

♦ Implementing an integrated system solution with a web front-end (Harvard University)

♦ Data warehouse to facilitate query and analysis of employee data (MIT)

♦ Outsource payroll (Wesleyan University)

♦ Online payroll manual (Stanford University, University of Vermont)

Managing Employee Data

♦ Online data entry at the point of origin (University of Minnesota, The Ohio State University, Northwestern University)

♦ Integration of HR/Payroll/Benefits systems (The Ohio State University, University of Vermont, Pennsylvania State University, University of Chicago, Tufts University)

♦ Employee/manager self-service access (University of Minnesota, The Ohio State University, University of Vermont)

HR Organization Structure

+ Integrate benefit operations, such as counseling/customer service groups, which are currently split between finance and HR (Harvard University)

+ HR generalists become responsible for serving department management rather than employees (MIT, Princeton University)

Other Best Practices

+ "What happens when you retire" web pages (Harvard University)

+ Pre-retirement planning

+ Use of outplacement services

+ Exit interviews to get feedback, assess attrition (retention), and to provide benefits counseling

10

Agora: Building the Campus of the Future—Today

Bernard W. Gleason and William J. Fleming

INTRODUCTION

"**A**gora" was the marketplace of ancient Greece. Today, Agora is the electronic gathering place of modern Boston College. The Greek marketplace served for much more than the exchange of goods and services. People gathered there to share ideas, engage in discourse, and catch up on political happenings. It had social, cultural, and political characteristics as well as economic and business functions. In creating Agora, the university has purposefully sought to translate the spirit of its ancient counterpart into an electronic gathering place for the community of Boston College. Agora focuses on action and self-service, but it also promotes student-faculty relations; strengthens services; and gives distant members (alumni, parents) a greater sense of belonging to the university community.

The inspiration behind Agora stems from many different sources, but above all else its creation reflects a distinct view of next-generation technologies in service to higher education. When the core design team first met during the summer of 1997, it quickly concluded that no single application or suite of applications could meet its objectives.

218

Instead, the team realized that it needed to articulate a distinct navigational framework within which both existing and emerging technologies could deliver desired services to community members. Those services would appear within a consistent, graphical, and predictable computing and communications environment. Agora embodies that navigational architecture.

> The emerging generation of web sites will be fundamentally different from what exists today. The technological mysteries of working in an electronic world will be gone. Instead, a highly intuitive and customer friendly graphical environment will free users to act directly and for themselves. Intelligent profiles will translate customers' credentials into personalized suites of services and direct them to their attention. The new web will engage the user with targeted information; simple and consistent navigational elements; and secure, integrated, and interactive applications (Gleason, 1997).

By the end of the spring semester 1998, certain core features of Agora had taken shape in a working prototype. The model was network based, it organized services by "customer neighborhoods," it delivered just-in-time information and action-oriented services via "customer profiles," and provided for a single log-on process, a consistent user interface, and uniform navigational principles. The initial suite of services delivered for the opening of the fall semester 1998 are described in this chapter. What became readily apparent, however, is that Agora is a developmental journey, not an application destination. Its services and capabilities will continue to evolve until the next, next-generation of web-based intranet sites emerges.

ORIGINS

Business Process Redesign

The Agora development team had consulted extensively with community members who were engaged in a multiyear, campus-wide effort to alter dramatically the existing business processes and organizational structures of the university. Self-service by end users stood as a core component of the new, high-level models that had begun to take shape. "Self-service" can often mean more low-level work by more people, but, in this case, it represented an imperative to remove as many barriers as possible between a desired action and execution of that action.

The business process redesign and information technology teams concluded that the desktop would be the entryway to all services and transactions. To maximize ease of use and to minimize training and support, the interface would be web-based, and all services would reside in an intranet environment. Functions would appear as personalized self-service items. Information and action items would be organized for, and directed to, the individual who had logged into Agora, thus making it appear that the environment had been designed specifically for that person. As an intranet and web-based service, Agora would provide users access from anywhere, at any time.

In a traditional, organizationally based information environment, getting a question answered or originating an action usually requires knowing which office to call or visit. The temptation has been all but irresistible to translate this hierarchical and functional approach into an intranet environment. That certainly was the case at Boston College. A network-centric approach to information and action, however, permits service provision to cut horizontally through an organization's structure and deliver one-stop shopping functions. The user does not need to know, for example, that it is the registrar's office that handles parking permits and not the police department, only that she or he needs a parking permit.

Under those conditions, do-it-yourself origination becomes a practical, efficient, and effective means of conducting business. There is no need to pass routine work off to other people for processing. This leads to a significant reduction in time and effort associated with common action requests. That, in turn, represents both an opportunity to reduce costs and to increase the ability of otherwise talented clerical and administrative staff to pursue higher-level responsibilities.

Boston College had implemented an almost paperless purchasing environment in the late 1980s with its "U-Buy" series. With one stroke, sending check requisition forms and purchase orders around campus became a thing of the past. Still, people who had responsibility for approving or taking other actions on purchasing requests had to remember to log into the system to see if there were any actions pending for them. What was needed was an automatic notification and

SHORTCOMINGS OF CURRENT ENVIRONMENT	NEW NAVIGATIONAL MODEL
Navigational free-for-all	Consistent navigational elements
Inconsistent and confusing interfaces	Uniform interface design across all elements
Based on departmental hierarchies	Directed services for customer "neighborhoods"
User unknown	Customized for users and groups
Just retrieve "stuff"	Direct action and communication
Limited security	Single, secure log on
Limited transactional processing	Interactive
Surf for information	Information delivered when needed

FIGURE 10.1 Traditional Web Shortcomings vs. Agora Navigational Model

alert system that would prompt people individually according to events happening elsewhere on campus. Users would automatically receive notification, for example, that they needed to take a certain action. But they would also receive notification when an action they requested was completed. This would permit the university to take another major step toward a paperless and cashless workplace. All paper forms would be eliminated, and all reports would be delivered electronically.

Common Web Shortcomings

The new design requirements implied an entirely different approach to the university's web-based information services environment. The existing, information-oriented web pages had served a valuable purpose in their first years but now revealed serious shortcomings. Many of these seem typical of web sites throughout the Internet, especially at academic institutions. Some of the key shortcomings we identified appear in Figure 10.1.

Part of the difficulty stemmed directly from the "silo" approach to information services. The existing web pages reflected a departmental hierarchy. If customers wanted to access benefits information, they went to the human resources page. If they wanted to know how to use voice mail, they had to know to go to information technology's web page. If they wanted some course information, they had to go to the registrar's area. Find the department that handles the information, and you will find the information sought. The worst connotations of surfing the intranet lie with wandering around, just retrieving stuff. This is no different from telephoning around from one department to another trying to solve a problem or trotting from office to office in search of effective assistance.

While departments certainly often did a fine job of organizing and presenting information for web-based access, the localized approach led to a multitude of individuals of varying talent doing the interface design work. Many of these efforts were quite good, though some were not. Regardless of quality, because the pages reflected personal approaches, taken together they represented a navigational free-for-all environment. Users could not rely on a consistent means for navigating sites. The variations in web page designs collectively lacked integrating elements; they instead constituted a mishmash of inconsistent interfaces, even though when viewed individually some were high-quality designs.

Two somewhat more subtle problems slowly emerged. The user had no identity within the system. All information was presented for mass access in the expectation that some people would find value in it. This treated everyone, both on- and off-campus, as though they were all alike with the same needs and desires. Without a requirement that customers identify themselves to the web environment, services could not be personalized or targeted. Moreover, without provisions for authentication, encryption, and authorization the web site could not provide transaction-based business services to the community.

New Intranet Principles

When the Agora navigation team considered the process reports and the evident shortcomings of the university's existing web environment, some new principles for an intranet architecture emerged. First and foremost the fundamental "feeling" of an intranet versus an Internet site is quite different. By design, Internets are meant to be attractive and captivating. They say, "Come look at me. Come on in and stay awhile. Look around, you'll find interesting and useful things here. Come back soon, and come back often." Internet sites want you to stay there.

Intranets have exactly the opposite mission. Their sense is: "What do you want? What are you doing here? Fine. Here. Now go back to work." They should be this way because their primary mission is to support the business needs of the organization. Their emphasis should not be on exploring and lounging, but on action and communication. Intranets should focus on speed, efficiency, and effectiveness. They should quickly and easily take the user to the desired action. Nine out of ten times, the user is accessing an intranet for a specific purpose. We needed to avoid doing anything with Agora's design that would inhibit fulfilling that purpose.

Within every organization of any significant size there are bound to be multiple audiences that can be grouped. For example, people who work in financial and budgetary areas form a logical group. The error, however, is including only those who work in departments that are designated as having financial responsibilities. Such a group should also include individuals anywhere in the organization with budgetary responsibilities. To reflect Agora's intent of carrying the university's traditional sense of community into the electronic environment, these audiences are termed "neighborhoods."

Although we tend to view most users by their primary function or interest, they actually have "multiple personalities." That is, they have a primary role they play within the organization but may also have secondary roles that once in a while they need to fulfill. An administrator, for example, could also be the parent of a student. That person would most likely use the intranet for administrative purposes, but, once in a while, will want to use it as a parent.

One of the greatest difficulties of Internet usage is that it so often assumes we are all the same person. Services are not customized according to who we are from either a collective or a personal perspective. Intranets need to be customizable for personalized usage within the objectives of the intranet. Only in this fashion is it possible to offer a large range of services but keep access, execution, and communication fast and effective.

The entire site needed to be modeled in high-level terms to avoid the trap of having a particular application drive how the intranet service itself was presented or functioned. For Agora we identified a navigational model with some very ambitious characteristics. Not all of the design points could be implemented immediately, but, taken together, they represent a suite of objectives to guide the model's development over time.

Navigation needed to be simple and persistent. There would be only one navigational method for the entire site and it would always be present on the screen. Users would need no more than two clicks of the mouse to get what they needed. No navigation elements would appear in the content area of the screen except for internal hyperlinks. Other than a brief explanation of how the model works, there would be no help function because help would be unnecessary. Help related to services would appear within context. Fancy graphics that tend to slow down web site response times would not be allowed, especially in the content area where speed is most essential to action.

FEATURES

Part of the reason for placing priority on a navigational framework before considering specific applications is to create an action-oriented environment from the customer's perspective. At first, the neighborhoods represented large groups of people with common functional interests (faculty, staff, students, parents, and alumni). This permits both organizing services in groups that are most likely wanted or needed by a "neighborhood" while not having to clutter the services menus with items that are really only pertinent to other clusters of users. Within each neighborhood, services can be customized according to individuals, time of year, and the like.

To maintain navigational consistency, everything is grouped within processes and subprocesses. As far as possible the labels at the highest levels—the processes—are made consistent across neighborhoods. For example, "request action" might appear on all neighborhood menus but what is under that designation would change according to the user's role (student vs. faculty) and function (purchase order approver vs. originator). In addition, people can arrive at the same point of action from multiple approaches. The "communications" process might have an entry for email and voice-mail distribution lists which would lead a faculty member to a course listing and an option to automatically generate a voice-mail distribution list for the students enrolled in a particular course. On the other hand, a process called "manage courses" could lead to a listing of the courses a faculty member currently teaches. There, an option would appear for automatically creating a voice-mail distribution list for a particular course.

The navigational framework envisioned by the Agora model required a more integrated approach to service delivery than existed previously. It also required a more active method for anticipating user needs and interests rather than placing information in a dormant state, just waiting for the user to show up. Agora met these architectural objectives through a number of mechanisms, including a single point of entry, customer profiles, customized service delivery, an action orientation, just-in-time information delivery, and integrated communication services.

Single Point of Entry

The starting point for resolving many of the service access issues discussed earlier lies with affording users a single point of entry versus an array of mysterious URLs or server path strings. The answer to the all-too-familiar "Who do I call?" question, translated into a web environment, is "Agora"—always and no matter what the subject. The common alternative, relying on users to bookmark isolated web pages, is not satisfactory. Bookmarking streamlines access to favorite sites, and Agora's users can certainly do that, but bookmarking by itself also has some unfortunate consequences that the Agora navigational model addresses.

Simply bookmarking tends to shift the burden for organizing information services to the local desktop, which is rather inefficient. Almost by definition, the bookmarked route makes it more difficult for end users to learn about new, perhaps related, services that might be of benefit to them. Linking directly to the specific action bypasses all other information. Instead, Agora adds value to the standard browser process of bookmarking in two ways. First, the user who has not logged into the Agora is unobtrusively redirected to the "entrance" where a quick series of checks is performed. Second, the Agora navigational model groups related services together, often in the form of checklists. Any new services would thus appear within the navigational confines of the linked page.

One key to this approach lies with universal access and identification. To enter Agora, the customer must be a citizen, which means the user must have an authorized ID number or username and PIN. In addition, the person must have a certain level of equipment, operating

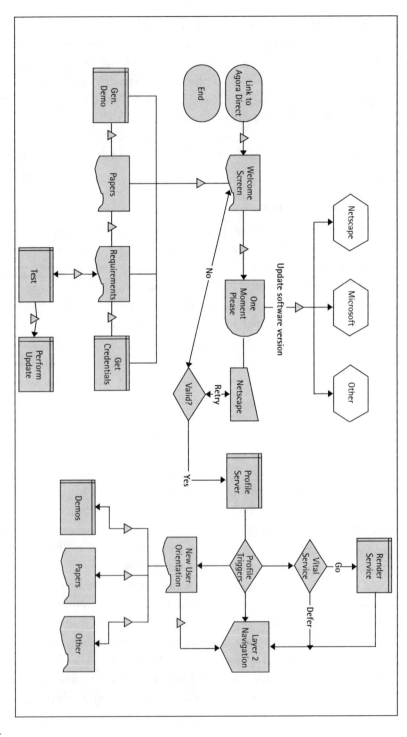

FIGURE 10.2 Process Flow for Entering Agora

system, and application software. Simultaneous with verifying the customer's credentials, the system automatically retrieves a host of personalized services. It also checks to see if there are any important notifications or alerts pending for that person.

To help visualize how features like the single point of entry might work, we mocked up some sample flow models. Figure 10.2 shows the access flow from the entrance to Agora through a successful login and startup screen. The diagram reads from left to right. A user clicks on a link for Agora, or one of its services, from a web-browser page. The "Welcome" screen is meant as a general greeting for people unfamiliar with the service and affords opportunities to see a demonstration, read about Agora, check to see if their system is compatible, or get credentials assigned to them if they are not a university employee or student.

People who are familiar with the service can, of course, simply set a bookmark in their browser to go directly to the login screen or some favorite service. No matter which route is taken, the session request is automatically redirected to an application that tests to see if the user has the correct version of all requirements. If not, they are offered an opportunity to link off to an internal or external site, as appropriate, to get their software updated. Once their credentials have been verified, the process flow continues to a central "profile server."

Customer Profiles

Most of us have become all too familiar with companies using electronically gathered information about ourselves to inform their marketing and sales efforts. The evidence of the effectiveness of this approach shows up daily in our paper and email slots. Given this reality, it is somewhat surprising that more effort has not been expended to apply these same principles to our organizational environments. We "know" quite a bit about our own personnel. Housed within the confines of one application or another, for example, is information about our age, position, title, salary, office, residential address, insurer, benefits, courses being taken, whether we have children in school, parking permits, courses taught, account responsibilities, etc.

In the late 1980s, Boston College created a position-based security system to facilitate easier access to our mainframe information systems. Later, we converted from a paper-based purchasing system to an all-electronic one and used the security system's features to control access and to automatically route requests to the right people for processing. This same approach was subsequently extended to our adaptation of automated teller machines as information dispensers.

With Agora, this approach has been moved into a networked environment via the implementation of a relational database that acts as a profile server. The basic information it uses originates with the position-based security system, but the new environment permits several important enhancements. All Agora citizens have services that reflect their roles and responsibilities within the community. These focus on the individual, not on his/her organizational affiliation. For example, budgetary services are available not only to workers in the budget office or to people with account management responsibilities, but to parents with students and faculty seeking research funding as well.

In addition, certain fields in the profile server reflect a customer's affiliation with one or more Agora neighborhoods. These are collections of services customized for collective or broadly shared interests. For example, a faculty member who is also the parent of a student most often enters Agora for academic purposes, but once in a while needs to access services focused on parental interests. The profile server is aware of the two roles, and the user is able to transfer from faculty-oriented items to parent-focused services with a simple click of the mouse button. The interface and navigational elements do not change.

Customers are able to use a simple checklist to modify certain aspects of their profiles. They can indicate, for example, which information they wish to receive or not receive. Some information will be mandatory and thus not "de-selectable" for delivery. For example, employees, by the nature of their position, may be required to know that a new purchase order approval is pending. On the other hand, the same customer may elect not to receive an automatic notification when the purchase cycle is complete.

Actions that occur within the Agora environment can set triggers in the profile server to launch automatic alerts when a customer enters or exits Agora. This is shown on the right side of Figure 10.2. The diagram assumes that the person who has entered Agora has an important item of business pending (e.g., a purchase order is waiting for their approval). The customer is automatically notified of this fact and is offered an opportunity to deal with it now or wait until later.

The profile server also can detect if this is a first-time user and offer the customer a chance to see sample demonstrations of how to conduct his or her affairs within Agora, read about what's coming in the near future, or take advantage of other types of orientation materials. Only first-time users see these options upon login. Otherwise, the line from login to the first neighborhood screen is direct and very quick.

The single point of entry and profile server features of the Agora model combine to permit customized service delivery. Community members typically have to search for the information they need (if they even know they need it) or seek out a method for getting something done. The Agora inverts this typical relationship by having information and action seek out the appropriate customer. Using characteristics from a customer's profile, a database manages the instant construction of customer-aware web pages. These are delivered to the Agora citizen at the moment he or she enters the electronic community. What is not present at the entrance is extraneous information and links.

Action Orientation

The goal of eliminating the circulation of paper forms around an organization is years old within the information technology community. Applications that offer electronic forms management have existed for a long time as well. Still, tens of thousands of paper forms migrate around campus annually.

The core issue has been how to integrate electronic forms handling with other enterprise information systems to truly automate the flow of work, not just the appearance of the form. The Agora model enables doing just that because of its other features (e.g., profile servers and access control) and because it requires helper applications to comply with open, Internet standards. Its workflow engine adds other critical capabilities, such as high-level editing. This permits the system to control the integrity of information provided by the user (name, address consistency) and permits data to be automatically entered in response to certain key entries (e.g., providing an ID number).

In addition, the Agora environment provides for dynamic forms. Traditional web forms are static which, in an enterprise-wide web site, would inevitably lead to extensive effort being extended to keep the old forms current and to create new ones as circumstances change. Agora's forms are created on demand, automatically eliminating administrative problems. Because the forms generator is connected to a relational database and a universal script for handling forms submissions, the Agora approach also brings a great deal of high-level editing into the process. Fields are automatically initialized with appropriate information as they are created in response to a link selected by the user. If the user, for example, went into Agora to file a vacation request, the current version of the appropriate form would be created and delivered to the user's desktop with personal information already filled in.

The forms themselves contain dynamically created menus as well. This makes it unnecessary to create multiple static forms for similar processes to differentiate between groups of customers (e.g., students vs. faculty or alumni vs. administrative staff). Their content and available choices change as certain fields are completed. For example, a prospective student who fills in an "intended major" field as business would see a different list of requirements and faculty from someone who declared history as the probable major. Finally, the Agora model makes a lot of work truly automatic in that the workflow engine transmits information, sets notification triggers, and processes data (e.g., encumbering an account for the cost of an item being purchased) without human intervention.

One of the most important objectives of Agora is to clear a straight path between the user and a desired action. Doing so, however, opens up two major issues: 1) how to get the customer informed that there are other, related services available that they might like to access; and 2) how to quickly lead a user through a series of related actions so that they can take care of several "to-dos" at once. There are multiple occasions when one or the other of these two issues arises. A new employee provides a good example.

When a manager hires a new employee, he or she is naturally focused on getting the best person for the position. After a decision is made, attention may turn to anticipating the arrival of much needed assistance for a department's efforts, but it often does not turn to the more mundane aspects of hiring someone. Where will they sit? Is there already an active phone there? Is the phone's class of service appropriate? Is a computer needed? Office supplies? Security clearance? The same thing is true from the new employee's perspective whose focus is usually on the new job, not on asking about parking, identification badges, cafeterias, getting used to a new voice-mail system, and so on.

To address these conditions, we invented the concept of checklists. A new hire would automatically be presented with a new employee checklist upon logging into Agora. It would contain information about and links to action forms concerning the details of being a new employee. A supervisor would be able to call up a new hire checklist with similar information on it. For example, a new computer needed? Check here. Link to request form. The checklist tracks the progress of each item and triggers reminders on the profile server if, for example, taking action on setting a 401k retirement plan components is overdue.

Perhaps more important, the capabilities of the Agora workflow engine encourage rethinking an entire business process before beginning work on automating that process. There are numerous examples of individual actions that many employees and students have to perform annually. The new employee checklist mentioned earlier is one. The many mundane and academic "to-dos" that newly entered students have to complete are another example.

Our business process redesign teams have developed the notion of service renewals which automatically group action items that people used to have to handle individually, often through separate offices, into a single collection that can be dealt with all at once. In the summer of 1998, before Agora was released for general use, the university tested the renewal of services concept in paper form. Via the completion of a single form, employees could authorize money to be placed in an optional meal plan, request a new university ID card, and request a parking sticker for next year. To get an EagleOne card, the employee attached a standard portrait photograph to the form. The photo was digitized for the ID card, and the card was mailed back to the employee. Parking stickers were also mailed back to the requestors. Three trips to three separate offices became no trips to any offices and a single mail-in form.

Figure 10.3 shows another kind of checklist that Agora makes possible. In this example, an employee named "Lara Croft" wishes to take some time off. Agora presents her with a checklist that offers a direct link to the appropriate request form but which also contains links for related items. Lara will notice that she can change her voice-mail

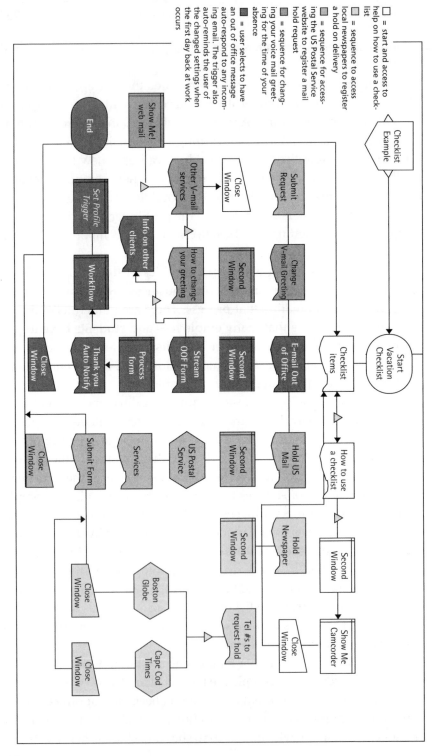

□ = start and access to help on how to use a checklist

□ = sequence to access local newspapers to register a hold on delivery

▨ = sequence for accessing the US Postal Service website to register a mail hold request

▨ = sequence for changing your voice mail greeting for the time of your absence

■ = user selects to have an out of office message auto-respond to any incoming email. The trigger also auto-reminds the user of the changed settings when the first day back at work occurs

FIGURE 10.3   Sample Agora Checklist: Vacation Request

232

greeting to inform callers how long she will be out of the office. She can set an automatic response in her email account that will send a message to all correspondents indicating she is on vacation. If Lara will be gone for a week or more, she may also link off to the US Postal Service site to submit a hold mail form or, via another set of links, get the telephone numbers of local newspapers to request a hold on delivery.

In the process of filling out the time-off request form (not shown on Figure 10.3), Lara can click on links to see how much vacation time she currently has or to view a calendar to verify the dates in question. Because she has purchase approval responsibilities, she can also activate a trigger that will cause any purchase orders that come through while she is gone to automatically show up in her alternate approver's in-box. A second trigger is automatically set to return the routing of purchase orders to normal on the date she returns to the office. Once the request form has been submitted, Lara can track its status through her Agora out box. The information includes what steps remain in the process and how long each step has taken. This is one form of just-in-time information that the Agora navigational model offers.

JUST-IN-TIME-INFORMATION

We have all become familiar with the information overload problems of modern society. The explosive rise of electronic information that has accompanied the Internet's growth has only exacerbated the issues. The core problem is less one of sorting and organizing information to make it more useful than it is one of receiving the right information at the right time. Instances abound in every organizational environment of people sending out policy changes, for example, to broad audiences to "inform" everyone of what has happened. Weeks or months pass and then someone attempts to do something and complains they did not know the policy had changed.

The problem is that many recipients either dismiss the news as unrelated to them (at the moment) or have long since forgotten the news. What is needed instead are mechanisms to deliver information exactly at the moment it is needed; to deliver it just-in-time for it to be used. As evidenced in some of our previous discussions, the Agora navigational model accomplishes this by associating action-related information with execution of the action in question. Agora also automates the intended effect of some information (e.g., a certain procedure has changed or includes new options) by building forms as an action is executed. The changes are evident and explained, if necessary, in context.

Still, there remains the question of finding the desired action quickly. The central elements of the Agora navigational framework do a lot to simplify and expedite the path from login to desired action. Nevertheless, as the number of actions covered by Agora grows (ideally, to every possible action) keeping the path simple and direct will become ever more difficult. Our solution was to invent a unique kind of search engine. We created "How do I . . . ?" as an action-oriented mechanism for locating both information about something the customer wanted to accomplish and the electronic form(s) for doing it.

"How do I . . . ?" establishes a controlled natural language environment. It has two changeable drop-down lists to complete the sentence, one for the verb and one for the object. The user thus selects an action verb from a list (e.g., "order"). That causes a second drop-down list to appear with all the possible objects for the desired action, ordering. The objects might include books, airplane tickets, office furniture, a new ID card, food for an event. Behind this interface is a database table that tracks the appropriate verb/object associations.

The table also contains information on actions not yet implemented within the Agora electronic environment. In that case, the user receives instructions related to the traditional way the action in question is done. Other fields help to control the amount of possibilities by only providing results that make sense for the user's neighborhood. Students, for example, would not see "my benefits" as an object for the verb "change" since that action is pertinent only to employees.

Providing information just-in-time thus permits the university to intelligently target who should receive which information and when. With that capability, Agora eliminates unnecessary paper-based notifications. Grade reports do not have to be sent out in the mail. Instead, the day after grades are due for a particular course, the students enrolled in that course will be auto-notified upon entering Agora that the grades are out. A link will carry them to the appropriate report page. In a similar way, reports for staff and faculty that are currently printed out can be delivered electronically to the appropriate end users. In fact, people can select the exact information they need for delivery rather than receive a large printout, which they traditionally page through to find the bits they actually need.

Integrated Communications

Although the focus of Agora is a web-based intranet environment, participation in the electronic community is not the exclusive domain of browsers and computers. Both voice and data are integrated into the Agora model. Certain services can be accessed either by a web browser or by telephone (e.g., registering for classes) or by ATM-style machines that dispense information. Other services use voice or data as a primary access with the other providing supplementary service.

Students and staff, for example, obviously use telephones to access their voice-mail, but they can also listen to their voice-mail via a web page. The added value of the latter approach is that customers can see a listing of originating phone numbers for new messages and access them nonsequentially. For example, they can choose to listen to message number six first because they note the originating telephone number to be the office of their dean.

One of the most important communications capabilities of Agora is its ability to generate messages and mail lists automatically. Voice-mail distribution lists are the most problematic. A touchtone phone is a poor interface for entering data such as voice-mail lists contain. The user has to enter everyone's phone number to build the list. If a mistake is made, the process often must be started over. If membership in the list changes, a new list has to be built. That assumes that the originator is even aware that a change has taken place.

This clumsy process may not be a serious problem for short lists of known office associates, for example, but building and maintaining such a list for a class of 25–30 students is very difficult; doing it for 100 or more is practically impossible. Within the Agora environment, faculty can simply select the option of creating an email or voice-mail distribution list for a particular class. The system autogenerates the list based on current course enrollment information from the registration system. Whenever a student adds or drops the course, the list is automatically updated.

Site Management

Many of the features of Agora have obvious levels of benefit for community members. Less obvious, but almost more important, is what takes place behind the user's view of the services. From the outset, Agora's developers placed major emphasis on site management as a critical factor for delivering dramatically better services while avoiding staff and operating expense increases. The degree of automation associated with many of the features already discussed suggests how we were able to do this.

Most forms on the web operate via scripts which execute certain functions when a "submit" button is pressed. This is perfectly fine, but as a site grows in complexity, managing its look and feel, changes in how forms or scripts should behave, alterations in navigational elements and the like become steadily more complex. With a static approach, creating new elements also means a great deal of tedious, repetitive coding or scripting and an increased need to monitor how pages look and feel.

To avoid those types of problems, a distinct authoring tool was developed to automatically control Agora's environment variables. A universal script controls the environment and any need to access data, for example, on our administrative mainframe system. Environment variables like the Agora banner are automatically inserted in a page at the proper location with the proper parameters set. What this means is that if a change takes place in graphical elements, color, or menu styles, it only needs to be done once. All pages are then automatically brought up to date because the element is provided from a single source and the page is built dynamically.

What that in turn means is that we have separated work on the main navigational architecture from authoring services and new web pages. Developing a new web page involves no more authoring skill than many community members already have. The page developer need not worry about navigation, main graphical elements, or how information is retrieved. Thus, knowledgeable community members can learn quickly the few unique features of using this system and concentrate on creating otherwise standard web pages to offer ever increasing services to their constituencies. Equally important, highly skilled Information Technology personnel can concentrate on complex

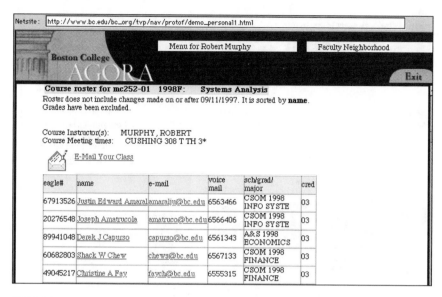

FIGURE 10.4   Automated Class Lists

university-wide technology issues rather than spend a lot of time on low-level site maintenance or simple web page development work.

Examples of First Services

By its very nature, the Agora navigational environment is constantly evolving. Not all of the desired services could be implemented immediately. Some required technology changes that were in the works to come to market. Others first required organizational changes within the university. Still, the initial suite of services that accompanied Agora's implementation in the fall of 1998 illustrate well many of the principles discussed above. The examples assume the Agora citizen is a faculty member who is also a department chair with budgetary responsibilities.

Figure 10.4 is a screen shot of the course management process for a particular faculty member. The profile server knew that he was a faculty member and when he clicked on "Course Management," automatically retrieved his current courses. In this case, he chose to view the roster for a particular computer science course sorted by name and without grades. Figure 10.5 shows what happens if he clicks on the name for a particular student in the course. He could have viewed his roster by pictures rather than by student names. This is a popular

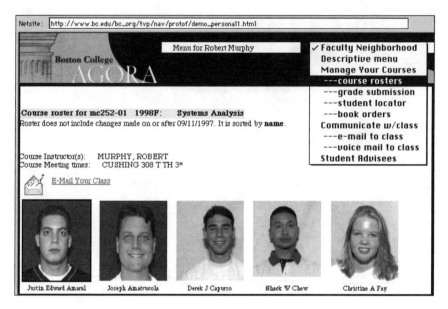

FIGURE 10.5   Picture-Based Class Lists

service that permits faculty to become familiar with students' faces before the first class meets. (It also permits them to retrieve a new student's name if they remember what she or he looks like.)

Email and voice-mail distribution lists per class are autogenerated if those menu items are selected. Besides the obvious convenience of not having to construct their own lists manually, the faculty is also guaranteed of the lists' accuracy. The Agora environment automatically updates the entries because the originating data comes from the registration system. As students drop and add courses, their names are removed or added to the appropriate distribution lists.

Traditionally, grades are hand recorded, sent, or delivered to the registrar's office, entered in the administrative system by office personnel, and then processed. Handwriting grades and then rekeying them for thousands of students runs a risk of clerical error and adds hours of intensive work (and therefore costs) to the process. It also results in several days of students constantly dialing into a voice response unit application to see if grades have been posted or logging into the administrative system to perform the same check. Since the students are usually off campus by this time, connecting to the admin-

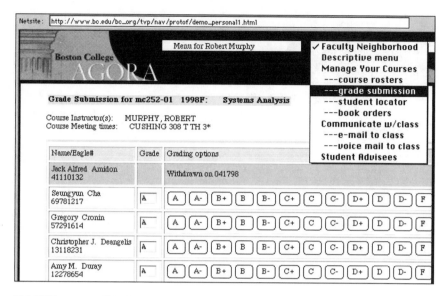

FIGURE 10.6   Submitting Grades via Agora

istrative system means that repeated demand is placed on our dial-in access services.

Figure 10.6 offers a screen shot of the new grade submission form. Faculty submit grades via the Agora environment with a simple click of the mouse button. The workflow engine operating behind the scenes automatically transmits the grades for processing. Triggers are also set to autonotify the students in the course that their grades have been posted. They then can retrieve their grades by logging into the Agora environment or by using a telephone to log into a voice response unit.

Having completed his grade submissions for the semester, Professor Murphy switches roles with the click of the mouse button and enters the administrative neighborhood as computer science department chair. Figure 10.7 shows a fictitious operating budget for his department. Because all expenditures—including purchases—are processed electronically, the budget is updated daily. Note that he has the option of downloading the current state of affairs as either an Excel spreadsheet or a Word document in case he wants to work with the numbers offline or incorporate certain information in another document.

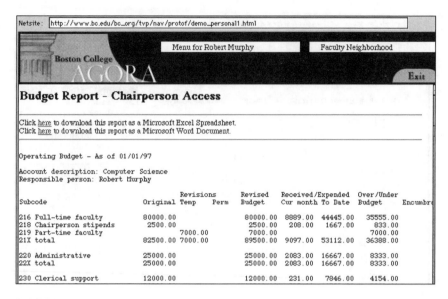

FIGURE 10.7   Departmental Budgets

THE AGORA JOURNEY

The initial suite of services released in fall 1998 were not just academically oriented. Administrative staff and students benefited by being able to view and change personal information via the web, for example. In the months ahead, a rich workflow engine would be added and a system for truly automating notifications needed to be implemented. Still, with Agora's inauguration a uniform, highly intuitive, and customer-friendly navigational environment had been created that freed people to act directly and for themselves.

Although the technology behind Agora and the services it offers may be exciting, we should not lose sight of why we developed this navigational architecture. Agora was designed to support the ambitious goals of a university-wide business process reengineering effort. Begun in the summer of 1996, the effort sought to reexamine and reformulate every major business process in the university. The objectives were to dramatically reduce administrative cost; significantly increase the quality of services rendered to students, parents, and alumni; and simultaneously rechannel millions of dollars in current administrative and operational expenditures toward a new instructional and research improvement agenda.

With Agora's deployment, we have implemented an enterprise-wide and innovative application of information technology that is leading to important changes in human behavior. How people work with each other and how they conduct the administrative affairs of the university has changed forever. Community members used to have to seek out certain offices, individuals, or paper forms, often during the relatively restricted hours of normal business operations, to get their work done. Now they are able to act directly for themselves in a far quicker and more effective manner. The constraints of location, time of day, and ignorance of procedure are removed.

These kinds of changes are rapidly generating a more productive administrative workforce as well. Increased productivity means reduced costs of operation. The university is saving millions of dollars in administrative expense in the process. This has permitted the transfer of several million dollars to academic priorities.

By dramatically changing the administrative environment, Agora has also permitted the talented employees of the university to concentrate on higher-level pursuits. By creating new processes for handling such things as student services and departmental support, the design teams have created opportunities for employees to change positions. While such change can certainly be unsettling, in reality many employees welcome the opportunity to learn new things and to engage in more meaningful work than mundane administrative tasks often require. Simply put, the work environment has become more pleasant and more rewarding for employees.

Agora permits teams of employees to exercise their imaginations and creative powers to invent new services for the environment. The navigational architecture behind Agora freed them from the implicit barriers to change that technology so often seems to represent to people outside of information systems staff offices. Boston College created a new standard for both the conduct of administration in colleges and universities and the enterprise-wide use of technology. In doing so, we feel that we have also created a friendly challenge for our higher education colleagues to strive for similarly dramatic changes at their home institutions.

For us, the challenge is to meet the expectations that the inauguration of Agora in the fall of 1998 created. In one sense, fomenting the growth of an electronic community is no different from the traditional meaning of building community: It is forever a work-in-progress because the community itself keeps changing and adapting to change. What Agora did was to present Boston College with an environment within which growth and change could occur, and continue occurring, while the university concentrated on charting the direction change ought to take. The Agora journey has begun, but it has only begun. Its destination is in the community's hands.

REFERENCE

Gleason, B. W. (1997, December 8). *Campus of the future draft reports.* Boston College. Unpublished.

PART III

Sustaining Change

11

Partnership for Performance: The Balanced Scorecard Put to the Test at the University of California

Kristine A. Hafner

In the early 1990s, the state of California was in the midst of a deep recession, which imposed steep budget cuts and a new era of fiscal constraint on the state's higher education institutions. Adding to the escalating pressures on our colleges and universities were demands from the legislature to curb mounting education costs, to deliver more value for taxpayers' investment, to increase productivity, and to eliminate the fat in administrative bureaucracies. Prompted by a transition in leadership, the University of California (UC) engaged in a comprehensive reevaluation of the role of business administration and operations in sustaining excellence into the 21st century. The administrative management systems that had supported the rise of the University of California to preeminence among worldwide research universities were no longer suited to the demands of the 1990s and beyond. Future administrative functions would, by necessity, become more innovative, consumer-oriented, streamlined, and decentralized. They would demonstrate accountability by delivering consistently high degrees of productivity and service quality for fixed or decreasing cost to the university.

A PERFORMANCE ARCHITECTURE TO ADDRESS ACCOUNTABILITY

One of the University of California's initiatives to transform its administrative culture targeted organizational accountability—the need for UC campuses, departments, and business units to continuously assess and strive to improve their performance. The university's management and control systems had been built over time to address the phenomenal growth in size and complexity of the nine-campus UC system, to standardize policies and procedures, to ensure compliance, and to minimize risk and exposure. The underlying need for effective controls is as pressing today as it has ever been. It is the nature and implementation of these controls, however, that imposes formidable obstacles to evolving into an innovative, efficient, and service-oriented operation. The university has recognized, at the root of the problem, the need to shift the emphasis in UC's control systems from those that are primarily procedural in nature (i.e., rules, regulations, policies, and restrictions) to controls that can play a diagnostic role (i.e., goal setting, performance measurement, and evaluation). This change in focus to a management style of self-evaluation will also encourage and stimulate a dialogue about institutional priorities, culminating in new levels of organizational effectiveness.

In 1994, the university committed to developing a performance "architecture" which would add diagnostics and performance measures to the current system of internal controls for managing its business. A performance architecture would enable business administration and operations departments to:

♦ Focus on the future

♦ Set strategic goals and performance objectives

♦ Track progress over time in achieving these goals through a meaningful set of performance metrics

Managing this way would offset the need for multiple layers of reviews, approvals, signatures, checks, and audits. Decision-makers would have at their disposal timely, accurate, relevant performance information to assess their business functions and processes, to compare themselves to others both inside and outside higher education, to diagnose problems, and, most importantly, to make the kinds of changes and improvements required to support the teaching, research, and public service mission of the University of California into the next century.

Unfortunately, the University of California could not rely on its traditional planning processes to build this new performance architecture. As is the case with most higher education institutions, the budget process has traditionally driven the planning process at UC. It has also dominated critical measures. The budget review process forces the institution to look back in time, at past mandates, workloads, staffing levels, and programs. Formulating the budget for the next year or biennium takes past performance as a baseline and projects it into the future. Institutional or departmental plans focus primarily on financial operations, budgets, people resource allocations, and funding strategies. Strong performance is described as staying within budget (i.e., spending no more—and no less—than the allocated budget). Moreover, traditional financial measures tell management nothing about how and how well the policies, processes, and practices of the institution are working. With a legislature and board of regents demanding evidence of good business management and increased administrative efficiency and productivity, traditional financial measures of past performance do little to convince the skeptics. In fact, they often serve primarily to defend institutional growth, program expansion, or budget increases (Rush, 1994). Traditional models for measuring higher education performance also are constrained by departmental boundaries, which encourages unit managers to be concerned only with their portion of a process that may span multiple work groups or units within the institution. Allowing the budget process to drive performance measures does not take into account the critical outside perspectives of customers and stakeholders as well as the dimensions of performance that are meaningful to them, such as time, cost, and quality of service. Finally, there is no opportunity to tie individual performance objectives and performance evaluation processes to institutional performance.

Private sector organizations recognized long ago that financial indicators alone do not offer the navigational information they need. They know that a measurement system is a critical communication vehicle and that it needs to address a number of different dimensions of performance. They understand that performance measures must link directly to vision and strategy. They have learned that reams of data do not constitute a good measurement system; rather, data must be gathered in support of specific goals and objectives. They have learned the hard way to listen to the voice of their customers and employees and to design their products and services to meet customer needs in order to remain competitive. They know that internal efficiency, productivity, and product/service quality are keys to success and that their ability to attract and retain motivated, highly skilled employees is critical to sustaining a competitive advantage.

THE BALANCED SCORECARD: PUTTING THE FUTURE IN FOCUS

Acknowledging that, while it is not a business, the University of California can benefit from innovative business practices, the UC selected the balanced scorecard to shape its performance architecture. With consulting assistance from IBM, UC administrative leadership launched an initiative called Partnership for Performance. The UC Partnership for Performance today refers to the collaborative performance management efforts of the University of California office of the president, the nine UC campuses, and the three national laboratories managed by the university under contract to the United States Department of Energy.

The balanced scorecard model for measuring performance was originally developed by Robert Kaplan and David Norton (1992, 1993, 1996). "Balanced" points to the need to view and calibrate strategy and performance from multiple perspectives. The "scorecard" notion communicates the need for a simple, concise, measurement framework for managers to consult in both strategic and operational decision-making.

Kaplan and Norton's work addressed the barriers to implementing strategy found in the short-term, financial indicators around

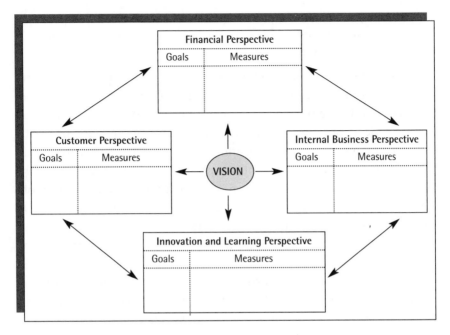

which traditional management systems are designed. Complementing financial measures in the balanced scorecard are measures of customer satisfaction, internal operational efficiency/effectiveness, and the organization's innovation and continuous improvement activities (Figure 11.1). The balanced scorecard focuses an organization's goals and performance measures on the attainment of its future vision. Goals are roadmaps to achieving the vision, and measures are indicators of progress in achieving the goals. Measures pull the entire organization toward the vision, toward the kind of organization that it is trying to become in order to succeed over time.

Think of the balanced scorecard as the dials and indicators in an airplane cockpit. For the complex task of navigating and flying an airplane, pilots need detailed information about many aspects of the flight. They need information about fuel, air speed, altitude, bearing, destination, and other indicators that summarize the current and predicted environment. Reliance on one instrument can be fatal.

Similarly, the complexity of managing an organization today requires that managers be able to view performance in several areas simultaneously (Kaplan & Norton, 1992).

When adapted to the administrative, service-oriented practices of both the UC campuses and the office of the president, each dimension of performance in the balanced scorecard would provide valuable management decision-making information to division and departmental business managers. In an environment that is extraordinarily decentralized and consensual in nature, performance measures offer the opportunity to develop a common "organizational language" to motivate action and change. They also address an important message to external stakeholders that the University of California sets clear directions for itself, both at the individual campus and at the university-wide level.

The University of California consists of nine distinctly different campuses (Berkeley, Davis, Irvine, Los Angeles, Riverside, San Diego, San Francisco, Santa Barbara, and Santa Cruz) governed by a single board of regents. The university's commitment to developing a performance architecture presented the opportunity to address institutional performance both at the university-wide business area level (e.g., environment health and safety functions across the nine campuses) and at the individual campus level (e.g., all business units within the business administration division at a UC campus). The university-wide Partnership for Performance was created to implement the balanced scorecard performance architecture through participation and collaboration among all nine campuses. In addition, several individual campuses (e.g., UC San Diego and UC Davis) have adopted the balanced scorecard for managing their administrative operations at the campus level.

By design, Partnership for Performance faced an enormous challenge: to engage nine institutions, each proud of and invested in its uniqueness, and, in many ways, competing with the others, in an exercise designed to identify common goals and performance measures. This challenge is compounded by a pervasive concern that sharing and comparing performance data among the nine institutions will result in negative repercussions at both the campus- and system-wide levels. While we have made progress in overcoming these obstacles, we rely on the ongoing support, commitment, and involvement of university senior management to emphasize the business improvement value of performance measurement. As a result, our administrative managers increasingly recognize the value of the effort.

While corporations originally viewed the balanced scorecard as a strategic performance measurement model, it has contributed to a new strategic management system in many organizations that have integrated it into the fabric of their decision-making. Each perspective in the balanced scorecard is a lens through which to view performance. When looked at in total, the balanced scorecard's goals and measures should communicate what is really important to the department in question. They also function as a set of levers which can be used to adjust and maintain the balance among those factors critical to the department's success. All four balanced scorecard perspectives have given our business units new information and insights into their operations.

How Do Customers See Us?

UC administration is increasingly comfortable with the notion of the "customer." There is growing acceptance that university administration must understand and address the wants, needs, and requirements of those it serves. Taking the customer view means focusing on responsiveness, timeliness, and product and service quality and cost—from the customer point of view. For revenue-generating operations such as campus bookstores, parking facilities, and dining and catering services, it also means retaining and expanding the existing customer base. We assess our performance from the perspectives of both customers who receive the services (students, faculty, staff, alumni, etc.), as well as the stakeholders who judge our effectiveness and have a direct impact or effect on our success or failure (legislators, regents, donors, grant agencies, etc.). Identifying key customers and stakeholders and understanding their requirements is a first step in designing customer-focused measures. Partnership for Performance developed a set of customer satisfaction survey tools which have been employed by the business area teams to gather information in such areas as importance/performance of key services in the eyes of the customer, customer needs and requirements that are not being addressed, and customer perception of the value and effectiveness of services being provided.

At What Must We Excel?

Internal operational measures focus inward into the internal workings of the business area, on those processes and activities that deliver critical services to both internal and external customers. These are the measures that tell the story of timely and accurate travel expense reimbursement, effective recruiting and hiring, quick turnaround on employee inquiries into retirement benefits, and efficient hazardous waste disposal programs. Internal business process measures address such things as productivity, accuracy, cycle time, core competencies, and effective use of people and information resources. In their simplest form, these indicators cast productivity in terms of ratios of resources to outputs (e.g., number of payroll transactions per central payroll office FTE). In their more complex form, they require process analysis techniques that identify and quantify the steps and critical resources required by a business process.

How Do We Look to Our Key Stakeholders and Resource Providers?

Traditional financial indicators retain an important role in the university's balanced scorecard initiatives. A set of key financial ratios assess the financial health of the UC institution as a whole. These are "top of the pyramid" measures, such as net operating ratio, facilities condition, reinvestment rate, research funding competitiveness, and debt capacity. At the operational level, financial goals and measures focus on the cost/quality of the service equation and on cost reduction or cost avoidance strategies within specific business areas. Revenue generation goals and measures enter the mix for auxiliary service areas, such as parking and bookstores.

Can We Continue to Improve and Create Value?

This category of the balanced scorecard addresses the organization's ability to sustain high performance levels over time. Here, we examine the more subjective factors that contribute to high performance, such as workplace climate, employee morale, skill alignment, professional development strategies, and effective use of technology. At the University of California, business areas increasingly recognize the value of assessing these factors as they contribute to business unit or department performance. No one underestimates, however, the challenge of identifying the most effective methods of performing this kind of culture tapping. Both individual campuses and the university-wide Partnership for Performance initiative have developed survey tools to assess organizational climate at the work group, department, division, or institution level. These surveys focus on such factors as leadership and management styles, decision-making, teamwork, morale, communications, training and skills, motivation and rewards, and attitudes toward change. When combined with focus groups and other employee input techniques, these surveys can identify trouble areas in need of management focus and attention.

The balanced scorecard has proven effective in resolving the inability of traditional management systems to link long-term strategy to short-term actions. At the University of California, it has served as a catalyst for developing and translating a university-wide vision for administration, for communicating goals and strategies and linking them throughout the organizational hierarchies, for integrating performance measurement into business planning, and for providing a forum for the ongoing transfer of knowledge among our institutions. Most importantly, performance measures are helping us establish and support a continuous process of self-evaluation and correction at all levels of the organization. Their role is to provide feedback about areas needing attention on a university-wide level and to support our managers' efforts to direct energy and resources to improvement efforts.

BUILDING CONSENSUS AROUND THE VISION AND STRATEGY FOR UC ADMINISTRATION

While many of the UC campuses have articulated their vision and goals for how campus administration can best support the teaching, research, and public service mission of the institution, the nine-campus University of California system had not developed a vision and strategic goals for administration as a whole. Partnership for Performance initially brought together the campus vice chancellors of administration and the senior business and finance executives in the office of the president to develop and align their vision and goals for the university administration (see Figure 11.2 below). This strategic

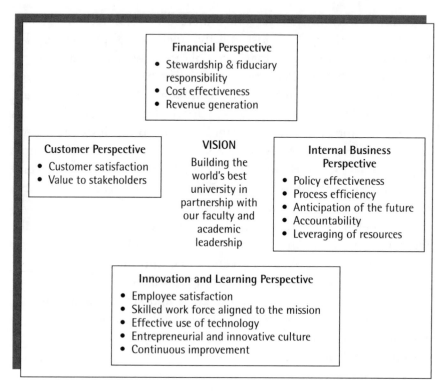

FIGURE 11.2   Summary of University of California Vision and Goals for Business Administration and Operations

view is still in focus today because it is broad, general, and directional enough to weather the test of time, and because the goals are translatable into more specific goals for each administrative business area. The fact that senior administrative managers from all the UC campuses participated in their creation made these goals a compass for business area managers and a catalyst for university-wide collaboration.

The pivotal role of the university's senior administrative management team did not end with the development of the vision and university-wide goals for business administration and operations. They have continued to act as a steering group over the life of the effort, providing ongoing direction, prioritization, problem solving, encouragement, and motivation for staff to participate. Their visible endorsement and support of Partnership for Performance has provided the necessary impetus when new business area teams are launched or when the challenge of reaching consensus among nine institutions appeared to be an insurmountable obstacle to the campus business managers.

LINKING THE VISION TO DEPARTMENTAL PERFORMANCE VIA STRATEGIC GOALS AND MEASURES

A performance architecture allows UC managers to communicate their strategy up and down the organization and eventually to link it to departmental and individual performance objectives. The university chose five key business areas to pilot the development of common balanced scorecard measures for the nine campuses. These are the core administrative functions: human resources, facilities management, environment health and safety, information technology, and financial operations. The senior managers responsible for each activity area formed the Partnership for Performance team and began by translating the university-wide goals into strategic goals specific to their area. For example, one financial goal is to "ensure UC financial integrity and demonstrate fiduciary responsibility for capital and financial assets throughout the system." When translating this goal into facilities management, the UC facilities managers looked to budget systems, internal controls, and accounting systems for performance indicators for financial integrity. They focused on their stewardship role as witnessed by the condition of facilities, responsible maintenance expenditures, and adequacy of maintenance budget allocations. Facilities performance measures which support this goal include:

- ◆ Annual facilities operations, maintenance, and physical plant expenditures as a percentage of current replacement value
- ◆ Deferred maintenance backlog ($) as a percent of current replacement value
- ◆ Facilities renewal requirements ($) as a percent of current replacement value

Likewise, the environment health and safety directors from the nine campuses mapped the strategic goals for UC administration into their business area. The UC business administration and operations financial goal is, "We deliver our services in an efficient, cost-effective manner. The value we create exceeds the cost of creating it." For Environment, Health, and Safety Financial (EH&S) the stated goal is, "EH&S programs and services are delivered in a cost-effective manner that contributes value to the campus." EH&S measures in support of this goal include:

♦ Total hazardous chemical waste cost per kilogram of hazardous chemical waste managed

♦ Radiation safety cost per authorized user and radiation worker

♦ Biological/medical waste cost per kilogram of biological/medical waste managed

Each of the performance measurement teams created a set of goals for their business area, arranged in the balanced scorecard categories to ensure that performance can be assessed from multiple perspectives. With the goals outlined, the teams selected key measures of performance to assess their progress over time in achieving each goal. These measures give them the ability to assess and track their unit's performance and to compare it to the performance of their UC peer institutions. Some measures are directed at assessing progress and diagnosing problems and obstacles while others highlight end results. The teams defined each measure clearly to ensure an "apples-to-apples" comparison from campus to campus. In addition, the data-gathering strategy was laid out, down to the location of the data elements, the frequency of data collection, and the format for reporting the data.

CREATING A PERFORMANCE MEASUREMENT CULTURE

When the university launched Partnership for Performance, the area business managers on the nine campuses were the logical points of departure. While these groups (e.g., human resources directors) meet periodically to share information and collaborate on common operational or policy issues, they do not typically engage in collective strategic planning. Those teams that have been most successful in defining common goals and performance measures have benefited from a champion and leader from within the team. A structured approach, training in performance measurement, and facilitated team work sessions have also helped to keep the focus and momentum.

The size, complexity, and decentralized nature of the University of California also required a strategy for sharing performance management information and for engaging campus leadership in an ongoing dialogue on the topic. The UC has benefited greatly from the performance measurement expertise of the UC-managed national laboratories (Los Alamos, Lawrence Livermore, and Lawrence Berkeley). Due to their pioneering work with the Department of Energy to transform their operations from contract compliance to performance management, the national laboratories have received national recognition as "best in class."

A university-wide "think tank," the Performance Champions group, meets quarterly as a forum for this regular dialogue and exchange on the many aspects of organizational performance measurement and management. The group, which includes our measurement team leaders and a broad range of campus and office of the president advocates, reviews measurement team initiatives and best practices, explores trends and models in use in other industries, provides important guidance and direction to Partnership for Performance, and functions as a conduit of information to their respective campuses. Partnership for Performance has also created a web site (http://www.ucop.edu/ucophome/businit) to disseminate a broad range of information throughout the university: UC vision, mission, values, and goals for business administration and operations; the balanced scorecard approach and objectives; work in progress by the measurement teams; downloadable customer satisfaction and organizational climate surveys; presentation materials; status reports; links to campus initiatives, and white papers on performance measurement-related topics.

STRATEGIC BUSINESS PLANNING USING THE BALANCED SCORECARD

Two UC campuses, UC Davis and UC San Diego, in particular, have adopted the balanced scorecard as a strategic business planning tool for business administration. UC San Diego (UCSD) has received national recognition for its leadership in successfully adapting it to the internal management of the business affairs division, which is responsible for a diverse set of business services, including campus computing; police; transportation; dining services; campus financial operations; facilities management; human resources; and environment, health, and safety programs. The four quadrants of the balanced scorecard guide the business planning within each department, and a division-wide process for gathering critical performance data provides systematic, consistent information for review by the division management team at annual planning retreats. Customer satisfaction surveys are administered annually to faculty, staff, and students as customers of the division's primary services. Financial and productivity metrics are tracked longitudinally for each business area. An organizational climate survey, administered annually to administrative management and staff, provides feedback on a broad range of workforce climate issues. The entire management team reviews the performance measurement data, business area by business area, providing a system view of the division's performance and an opportunity for dialogue and collaboration across business area boundaries. The data enables the management team to assess the impact of prior events and strategies on the performance outcomes of each unit and to identify focus areas for the coming year.

The UCSD business affairs division now has the ability to trend six years of data in many areas, which offers new insights into the longer-term impacts of the management team's focus and strategy. Several factors have contributed to the success of the UCSD business affairs team:

♦ Strong support and involvement by the vice chancellor and the business area managers

♦ A clear set of strategic goals for the division

♦ Direct linkage of the measurement data to the business planning and budget process

♦ Broad communication and sharing of performance information via the UCSD web site

♦ Investment in the resources required to ensure that the performance measurement data is collected and analyzed on a systematic basis

Now in its fifth year, UCSD's balanced scorecard program demonstrates that performance improves when it is effectively and routinely measured, analyzed, and addressed. But more importantly, the balanced scorecard approach provides an institution with a roadmap on where it should focus its energies, priorities, and resources in addressing administrative support services. So often, in the absence of relevant and timely information, campus leaders will call for change when a single incident occurs, believing it is indicative of a chronic problem. Or a chronic problem may go unnoticed for years until a crisis occurs. The balanced scorecard establishes an objective framework for continually assessing the effectiveness of campus administrative services using real data from customers, peer institutions, and the people providing the services (Relyea, 1998).

PERFORMANCE MANAGEMENT AS A LEARNING EXERCISE

The rapid growth of the University of California has forced each of our institutions to grapple with tough decisions about how to create and sustain an environment equipped to handle this growth with no additional administrative resources. A performance architecture creates a common language for the nine campuses to assess the effectiveness of their programs and services, and ultimately, to learn from each other. The UC campuses are a natural cohort group to discuss and compare business practices and to leverage the benefits of being part of a larger system. Previous efforts to participate in national higher education performance benchmarking have not been successful, in part, because UC campuses did not always find the right mix of cohort institutions for meaningful comparisons and because the measures often did not relate to campus or business area strategic goals. While our campuses look for ways to compare themselves to other institutions, this exercise requires a foundation of common practices, processes, definitions, and denominators that ultimately provide information that can lead to actions and results.

Partnership for Performance teams began with a clean slate and identified goal-oriented performance measures for their specific UC cohort group. Giving the managers responsibility for developing the business area goals and measures has been a critical success factor for Partnership for Performance. Several teams have invited non-UC institutions to collaborate with them in comparing performance and have incorporated relevant industry benchmarks at their discretion. The facilities management team, for example, invited the Stanford, CalTech, and University of Southern California (USC) facilities managers to join the performance measurement team, thus naturally extending the cohort group to California-based private institutions.

The real value of measuring performance in a comparative way is to view it in context, to understand what it reveals and why, and to use this as a springboard to sharing good practices from one campus to another. In addition to sharing performance data, the environment health and safety directors share risk and program self-assessment models. Payroll managers are deploying a common customer satisfaction survey of departmental users to provide them feedback to develop payroll process improvement strategies. Travel managers participated in a national travel management best practices study with companies doing business globally and incorporated these findings into their collective recommendations for improving travel reservations, booking, and expense reimbursement processes university-wide. Facilities managers compare campus strategies for building and landscape maintenance services, reviewing approaches and costs in relation to individual campus priorities.

This kind of dialogue and sharing among the managers about individual campus operations eventually led to decisions to take collective action to improve service cost and quality across the UC system. When the environment, health, and safety directors realized that there were significant discrepancies in their costs of hazardous waste disposal, they collaborated on a system-wide rebid of these services, which resulted in an average 25% savings per campus. Facilities managers collaborated with capital budget and planning, design, and construction counterparts to quantify the university's facilities renewal needs, and to arrive at a common working definition of "current replacement value." The UC partnered with the California State University system to reduce utility costs by $16 million over a four-year period.

At the University of California, administrative management and staff in every business area are directing their energy toward bridging the gap between our current performance and future potential. We are changing the way we manage many of our business functions. The

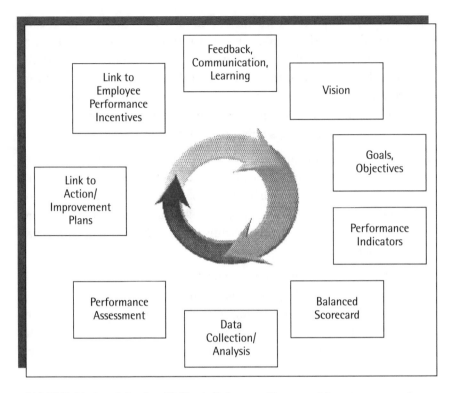

FIGURE 11.3   University of California Performance Management Process

balanced scorecard has helped sharpen our focus and better align our day-to-day activities with longer term strategies. In the process, we are also building trust, better collaboration and dialogue, higher levels of active employee participation in shaping the future of our operations, and a culture of evidence, where performance information is woven into the fabric of our administrative management philosophy. The wisdom of *The Farmers' Almanac* dictates: "A halo has to fall only a few inches to become a noose." Paying attention to measures of success is our best survival mechanism.

BUILDING A BALANCED SCORECARD: HOW TO MAKE IT WORK

While there is no single formula for building a successful balanced scorecard, there are several necessary steps and precautions for higher education institutions to take.

1) Define the scope of the business area for which the balanced score-card will be used: its mission, core products and services, and primary customers. Identify the business units responsible for delivering these products and services, and involve them in the effort, even if they are located in other parts of the organizational structure. Engage the management with direct responsibility for the functions and processes being measured.

2) Involve the senior management of the institution/department by first presenting the balanced scorecard concept and articulating the benefits of a vision-driven approach to performance measurement. Define a continuing sponsorship role for the senior management team that will span the duration of the creation of the balanced scorecard.

3) Engage the senior management of the institution or department in the process of creating the vision and strategic goals which provide the necessary context for assessing performance. Balance the institution's typical requirement for broad participation, consultation, and consensus with the need to identify future direction and strategy.

4) Seek input from key stakeholders and customers during the process of building the balanced scorecard to ensure that the view that emerges reflects their needs and expectations for performance.

5) Involve department management in both developing long-term goals for their departmental operations and selecting the measures of performance to track progress in attaining these goals over time. Recognize that empowering business unit managers to identify the right performance indicators for their business area is key to gaining their support and buy-in. Provide training in strategic thinking and in developing performance measures to all team members.

6) Identify what kinds of measures are appropriate for different levels of reporting. At the board of trustees/regents level of reporting, at a maximum, three to four indicators of performance in each balanced scorecard category suffice to communicate the message. The operational level requires more information and greater detail. Measures proposed during the building of the balanced scorecard should therefore be sorted, weighted, and priori-

tized. For every performance measure selected, you should know what information will be produced, why it is valuable, and to whom. Ultimately, you need to know what actions you can take based on this information. To start with, focus on the few critical measures that will tell you what you most need to know. Then, expand and refine your measures over time.

7) Define clear ownership of the process of maintaining the scorecard as well as collecting and analyzing the data. In the university world of "shadow" computer systems, duplicate databases, and inconsistent/incompatible data, the task of linking the measures to databases and information systems, is a challenging one. This becomes easier when the data sources for measurements are clearly identified.

8) Clearly communicate the role of the scorecard in managing the unit, department, or institution. Understand that, taken out of context, measurement information can not only be misinterpreted, it can be misused. In a complex environment such as UC, institutional and business-unit level outcomes vary because of differences in campus locations, resources, and goals, among other factors, all of which are outside management control. Punishing lack of performance will undercut the value of a performance measurement initiative. Performance shortfalls must be treated not as problems, but as opportunities. Above all, it is important to recognize and reward business managers' involvement in the process—as much for the value of the measurement information it provides as for the cultural change that the process effects within the institution. Make the balanced scorecard framework widely available, keep it visible, reference it often, and encourage the development of second-level metrics in operational units or decentralized parts of the organization to drive the performance measurement message as deep as possible into the culture of the institution. Ultimately, each employee's performance plan should reflect institutional goals and objectives.

9) Review the balanced scorecard periodically and ask the following kinds of questions:

Are we measuring the right things?

Does the cost of gathering the data exceed the value we receive?

Is performance measurement changing the way we do business? Are we making better decisions as a result?

How can we improve our measures to get the information we most need?

Revisit the department's vision, goals, and measures as needed to ensure that they present an accurate view of your focus and future direction. This feedback and review process allows you to monitor short-term results and to benefit from real-time learning. Make sure that your performance measures are not encouraging the kind of counterproductive behavior that has plagued some for-profit companies and most recently the Internal Revenue Service—managing the numbers rather than fixing the underlying problems.

REFERENCES

Kaplan, R. S., & Norton, D. P. (1992, January/February). The balanced scorecard: Measures that drive performance. *Harvard Business Review.*

Kaplan, R. S., & Norton, D. P. (1993, September/October). Putting the balanced scorecard to work. *Harvard Business Review.*

Kaplan, R. S., & Norton, D. P. (1996, January/February). Using the balanced scorecard as a strategic management system. *Harvard Business Review.*

Relyea, S. W. (1998, June). From gutter balls to strikes: UCSD's balanced scorecard program. *NACUBO Business Officer.*

Rush, S. (1994). Benchmarking: How good is good? *Measuring institutional performance in higher education.* Princeton, NJ: Peterson's Guides.

12

Why Some Enterprise Improvement Models Have More Lasting Effects than Others

Wendell C. Brase

THE NAIVE SIDE OF PROCESS IMPROVEMENT

Many process improvement systems are behaviorally naive—heavy on the rhetoric of teamwork, empowerment, new paradigms, and accountability—but lacking insight into workplace belief systems, values, motivations, and disincentives that underlie the behaviors targeted for change. Some management change models are precise and detailed about process redesign methods but vague and conceptual about behavioral dynamics. Sometimes they express behavioral expectations through new jargon or preachy admonitions, both readily construed by employees as "you're not doing it right." These actually thwart lasting change, although people may wisely adopt the new parlance rather than appear out-of-step with the change program. Such models are unsophisticated about how to stimulate fundamental, sustainable change in the way an enterprise does its business.

Too Many Good Ideas

The decade extending from about 1985–1995 saw a plethora of popular management books that advocated a variety of strategies and dogmas. Managers were urged to promote teamwork through reward systems and new organization forms, to pay for performance, to train managers and staff at all levels in total quality principles, to deploy cross-functional teams to reengineer core business processes, to return to value-based management fundamentals, to adopt the Baldridge criteria, to enable various forms of employee empowerment, to foster and reward continuous improvement, to implement balanced scorecards, to derive and use customer-driven performance measures, to benchmark these measures, and to employ all these strategies while downsizing, outsourcing, simplifying, and producing just-in-time results. No manager could employ all these strategies without a large staff and an ample budget. Some management improvement programs that advocated simplification, streamlining, clarity, and accountability became obese, rigid, and even bureaucratic, violating their own fundamental precepts. The streamlining agenda needed a dose of its own medicine, although most enterprise improvement programs did not contemplate that improvements might need to be applied to the program methodology itself.

To make matters worse, conscientious managers had little objective information to enable them to choose from an array of rapidly promulgated ideas. Most management new ideas were backed by little verifiable data demonstrating their efficacy. Many ideas were superbly presented not only in print but also by consultants who polished and added pricey legitimacy. Most new methods were promoted without attacking other strategies, but with a dogmatism that implied the superiority of new theories over their antecedents and competing models. Anecdotal evidence was used to extol new methods of organizing, managing, and rewarding people, buoyed by rising (warranted) optimism about the productivity and international competitiveness of American industries. However, the individual manager had insufficient evidence about the relative effectiveness of various improvement programs to enable an informed decision about where best to invest limited time. Which tools would lead most efficiently and assuredly to improved enterprise performance?

In fact, many of the enterprise improvement programs that surfaced (or resurfaced) in the past decade are unvalidated models. They may sound sensible and appear to yield measurable effects, but limited evidence links, in terms of systematic cause and effect, management actions believed to be effective with desired group behaviors (such as teamwork, collaboration, and information sharing), or with overall organizational performance.

THE IRVINE MANAGEMENT CHANGE MODEL

The University of California, Irvine "Model for Sustaining Administrative Improvement" (http://www.abs.uci.edu/depts/vcabs/toc .html) was similarly unvalidated. This award-winning program, which was recognized by the National Association of College & University Business Officers (Higher Education Awards Program first prize, 1996), by *USA Today* (1998 Quality Cup Award), and by a 1997 CAUSE (association for managing information resources in higher education) Best Practices Award, produced numerous process improvements and productivity results. However, no statistical evidence demonstrated that the program's normative elements correlated with desired organizational performance or with long-term change in the administrative culture—an articulated, overarching goal.

As a program dedicated to sustained, rather than episodic, improvement, UC Irvine's Model for Sustaining Administrative Improvement contained strong, value-based behavioral components. These elements were considered necessary to change the patterns of a bureaucracy, through altering the dynamic of values, expectations, rewards, disincentives, and belief systems that define and perpetuate the administrative culture of the institution.

The Irvine model contains strong normative elements in three areas:

1) **Teamwork principles:** increasingly needed as administrative organizations become more "matrixed," the organization becomes less hierarchical and more networked and process improvement becomes increasingly cross-functional and necessary.

2) **Simplification goals and principles:** to create explicit counter-pressure against the inherent tendencies of a bureaucracy to continually add more systems, program variants, controls, specialized policies, and layers of complexity.

3) **Effectiveness principles:** an interrelated set of normative quality criteria—centered around accountability and performance values—that differs sharply from prior shared beliefs, conventional wisdom, and bureaucratic patterns.

These principles play key roles in the Irvine model, as they are intentionally crafted to alter values and status quo behaviors that have become comfortable. Bureaucracies' internal dynamics create strong drives to preserve or return to status quo conditions in the face of change. These dynamics, rooted in rule-making and enforcement behavior, are typically entrenched because status quo practices embedded in policy allow accountability and responsibility to be comfortably fragmented in ways that are safe. Such a system is stable and predictable in its behavior yet inefficient when conditions shift and unresponsive when change is needed.

Individual, Group, and Supervisor Performance Expectations

The Irvine Model for Sustaining Administrative Improvement expressed normative behaviors for individuals, teams, and supervisors. Teamwork, simplification, and effectiveness principles and values were taught in workshops, folded into the performance evaluation process, incorporated into stated organizational goals, rewarded through incentive compensation, acknowledged through publicity and internal recognition, operationalized through delegated authorities, measured in numerous ways, and embodied in charts of guidelines that were posted in the workplace. Systems, policies, and practices that ran counter to the model's normative elements were dismantled or changed.

Since an administrative culture derives, in part, from workplace values, beliefs, expectations, and rewards that are embedded in human resources policies and practices, human resources programs were addressed early, as a foundation element in the model. For example, classification policies pertaining to management positions had rewarded bigger budgets, hierarchical layering, organizational complexity, and bureaucratic rigidity. Analysis also revealed that some managers were reluctant to pursue downsizing, restructuring, or outsourcing due to classification disincentives or concern about the university's track record in reemploying displaced staff. Finally, performance evaluation did not reinforce team behavior, innovation, and process streamlining to the extent needed for consistent support of campus administrative improvement goals. Therefore, as foundational elements—due to their precursor role—a reemployment program was instituted to enhance placement opportunities for laid-off staff, a size-neutral position classification system was introduced (removing such factors as number of staff, size of budget, and number of reporting levels below a position under consideration), and the performance evaluation form and incentive award program were revised to emphasize process improvement, innovation, and teamwork.

The Irvine Model for Sustaining Administrative Improvement included goals for reduction in the number of administrative systems and system variants, productivity targets in four service departments, goals for benchmarking and importing exemplary practices, and customer-driven performance measures. Implementing the model required process improvement projects ranging from cross-functional reengineering to widespread process streamlining throughout the organization. Teamwork, whether team-based problem solving or team behavior in terms of everyday cooperation, was essential.

The envisioned organizational effectiveness was value-based—rooted in shared values characterized by particular desired patterns.

◆ No one is rewarded for (intentionally) looking good at the expense of another. Team players are committed to each others' success; in a teamwork culture this value is understood.

◆ Teamwork requires willingness on the part of individuals to enter into interdependencies involving risk, which requires a foundation of trust. Supervisory practices, rewards, recognitions, and performance measurement systems must not undermine interdependencies or trust between individuals.

◆ Innovation requires open debate about many "wrong" ideas. Complex process redesign starts with creative chaos and early mistakes in order to avoid late-stage errors. Management must make it comfortable to be wrong at the beginning of problem solving.

- Teams, rather than individuals, are empowered to solve problems (rather than merely advise a manager's solution).

- Respect for facts, data, and objective analysis is essential to foster teamwork. People are more willing to create interdependencies involving trust and vulnerability when they feel that facts and neutral data are valued.

- A less authoritarian hierarchy reduces the risk exposure of competent individuals, enabling them to enter into interdependencies because their ideas can be expressed through fewer layers that might involve filtering or inadvertent distortion. Misunderstandings can be corrected more readily in a less hierarchical organization.

- Interpersonal problems are resolved effectively—limiting the degree to which they undermine teamwork by distorting perceptions of others' motives, which can easily occur when stakeholders struggle with change.

- Innovation, continuous improvement, and a willingness to question and improve upon the status quo are valued by supervisors and coworkers.

These values and desired dynamics were operationalized into 11 normative workplace patterns that could be stated as simple performance expectations, fostered through training (included as performance criteria in evaluation tools and reward systems), and measured through employee surveys.

1) People who seek better methods are respected and rewarded.

2) People experience a climate of mutual respect in the workplace.

3) Groups value member suggestions, including ones that are initially "wrong."

4) Coworkers produce ideas that help solve problems when they surface.

5) Problems with the way the group does its work are faced and addressed.

6) Members can criticize the way the work group functions without penalty.

7) People can discuss problems without fear of looking stupid to coworkers.

8) Interpersonal conflicts are addressed and resolved in the work group.

9) Differences of opinion about how to get the job done are discussed openly.

10) Differences of opinion about how to get the job done are resolved using facts.

11) Everyone shares responsibility for the results of group tasks, not just the supervisor of a few key participants.

DO MANAGEMENT BEHAVIORS AFFECT TEAMWORK AND COOPERATION?

A number of supervisory behaviors and values were articulated in the model because they were expected to reinforce the desired organizational performance. Again, these were expressed as performance expectations and incorporated into performance evaluations, reward criteria, management development workshops, and stated objectives.

Although these performance expectations were considered worthwhile on their own merits, it was important to discover whether they reinforce teamwork, problem solving and organizational effectiveness—either individually or in combination. And if the latter is evident, how well do envisioned supervisory qualities work together as a coherent, mutually reinforcing set?

In order to research this question, employees were surveyed across the entire administrative services organization of the University of California, Irvine. They evaluated their work groups in terms of the patterns, behaviors, and values highlighted above, and evaluated their supervisors in terms of 45 traits and behaviors. This survey was administered twice within 18 months, and questions that generated apparent confusion and spurious results were either clarified or eliminated between the first and second administration. The survey, which carried the neutral title "Survey of Management and Organizational Patterns" in order to reduce any Hawthorne Effect responses had it been called a "climate survey," yielded a 70% response rate through management encouragement to participate. (See chapter appendix for a copy of the survey.)

SUPERVISORY EFFECTIVENESS MODEL

Analysis of the survey responses revealed very strong correlations between many supervisory behaviors and self-assessed organizational effectiveness and with desired group patterns of open communications, trust, and collaborative problem solving. Further analysis using canonical correlation methodologies (with the assistance of the UC Irvine Center for Statistical Consulting) suggested a multistage causal model of the following structure.

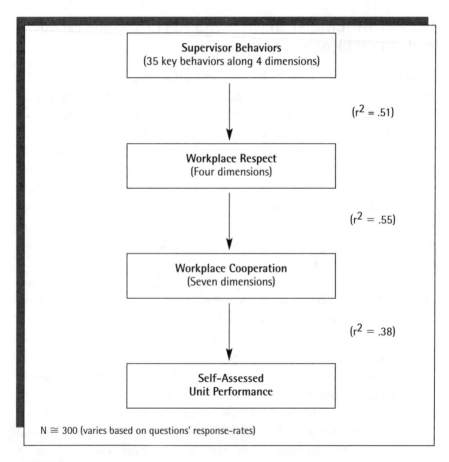

FIGURE 12.1

Supervisor Behaviors

The 35 supervisor behaviors that evidenced strength in this model fell into four distinct groupings:

1) *Ethically and emotionally consistent*
   - Supervisors model behavior they expect from others
   - Communicate honestly with employees
   - Keep promises and commitments to employees
   - Make important decisions based on the organization's best interests
   - Act in ways that build employees' respect
   - Act ethically even if personal sacrifice is required
   - Base their actions on a consistent set of principles
   - Earn most employees' trust
   - Control their tempers under pressure
   - Are emotionally predictable as experienced by employees

2) *Supervisors communicate respect for employees*
   - Supervisors communicate clear expectations
   - Trust subordinates' judgment
   - Take time to listen and understand employee views
   - Help employees understand "the bigger picture"
   - Show respect when communicating
   - Care about employees as individuals
   - Involve employees in developing objectives, performance measures, and plans
   - Do not gain advantage by holding back information
   - Do not make employees feel stupid when they disagree

3) *Supervisors accept responsibility and act on it*
   - Supervisors take steps to improve bad interpersonal relationships
   - Accept constructive criticism without becoming defensive

- ◆ Reward the best performers
- ◆ Make good decisions despite incomplete information
- ◆ Admit mistakes and move on
- ◆ Separate vital tasks from less important ones
- ◆ Do the most important tasks first
- ◆ Accept responsibility if things go wrong, rather than blame others

4) *Supervisors are open-minded, team players*

- ◆ Supervisors work well with their peers (are seen as team players)
- ◆ Support equal opportunity
- ◆ Seek a range of views when solving problems
- ◆ Value perspectives from people of diverse backgrounds
- ◆ Tend to find win-win solutions
- ◆ Encourage employees to surface problems
- ◆ Will praise an effort that was promising even if it failed
- ◆ Do not make some people look good at others' expense

Workplace Respect

The workplace respect measures included:

- ◆ People who seek better ways of doing things are respected and rewarded
- ◆ Members can criticize the way the work group functions without penalty
- ◆ People can discuss problems without fear of looking stupid to coworkers
- ◆ People experience a climate of mutual respect in the workplace

Workplace Cooperation

The workplace cooperation cluster of interrelated patterns comprised:

- ◆ Groups value member suggestions, including ones that are initially "wrong"

- Coworkers produce ideas that help solve problems when they surface

- Problems with the way the group does its work are faced and addressed

- Interpersonal conflicts are resolved in the work group

- Differences of opinion about how to get the job done are discussed openly

- Differences of opinion about how to get the job done are resolved using facts

- Everyone shares responsibility for the results of group tasks (not just the supervisor or a few key participants)

Self-Assessed Unit Performance

Finally, self-assessed unit performance refers to employees' responses to the question:

How effective is your unit, in terms of quality and productivity, compared to its potential?

- We perform at 90–100% of our full potential—consistently

- We perform at 70–90% of our potential—usually very good

- We perform at 50–70% of our potential—average or somewhat better

- We perform at less than 50% of our potential—below average

The Value of Coherence within Factor Groups

The groupings of Supervisor Behaviors, Workplace Respect, and Workplace Cooperation variables are tightly clustered, with strong intercorrelations (typically $r > .70$) linking many factors together. These tightly correlated clusters suggest that employees view these variables as part of a coherent experience.

Consistency and coherence are essential attributes of any management change model that aims to change an administrative culture. When people sense even the slightest inconsistency in the new rules of the game, they retreat to the safety of status quo behaviors. Coherence calls for a complete, fully integrated set of goals, foundations, and tools that together strike a balance between technical and behavioral dimensions. Coherence in a management change model means that no essential pieces are missing and that all components of the model—symbols, premises, implicit values, rewards, communications, and improvement tools, and protocols—are painstakingly consistent, with no mixed messages. The strong intercorrelations within the model's factor groupings provide evidence of both consistency and coherence.

How to Interpret This Model

The management change model shown in Figure 12.1 is remarkably simple, and its interpretation is therefore straightforward. Although canonical correlation analysis does not enable the assignment of causal arrows, they are hypothesized as follows: Management behaviors provide the foundation (or lack thereof) for workplace respect; this cluster of measures is, in turn, the precursor to workplace cooperation, which then leads to self-assessed unit performance. The primary effect of supervisory behaviors is on workplace respect, which appears to enable workplace cooperation, which then yields unit performance.

Less obvious, perhaps, is that the model's simple linearity defines a critical path: Supervisory actions (at least those measured by the model) do not affect unit performance directly. Rather, performance depends on workplace cooperation that can only derive from a foundation of workplace respect, which is highly dependent on the key supervisory behaviors. (However, in a setting where cooperation as defined in this model is not essential for enterprise performance—where the summation of independent, individual efforts constitutes the work product—this model might be inapplicable.)

The Model's Simplicity May Lead to Underestimation of Its Significance

The model demonstrates that supervisors whose behaviors foster high workplace respect must rate highly across all four dimensions—ethical and emotional consistency, respectful communication, open-minded team playing, and willingness to accept responsibility and to act on it. Each of these behavioral qualities is a fundamental prerequisite to workplace respect, the critical path linking supervisory traits and workplace cooperation and—according to this model—the only pathway to unit performance. Simply stated, it is almost impossible for a unit to realize workplace respect, cooperation, and performance unless its supervision demonstrates all four sets of determinant behaviors. Strong performance along three dimensions cannot compensate for a supervisor's weakness in a fourth area. A commonsense view is that a supervisor's strengths can sometimes outweigh selective weaknesses but, as revealed by this model, not when it comes to the key behaviors that lead to cooperation-based unit performance.

Can High-Performance Teams Emerge without Supervision?

Anecdotal evidence and popular belief suggest that teams, provided with appropriate resources and empowered by the authority to solve problems as needed to pursue an understood mission, can develop effective patterns with little supervisory influence. This view is heralded as "the organization of the future" by proponents who extol its value in enterprises that must meet rapidly changing market demands through teamwork, collaboration, and information sharing. However, the Irvine model demonstrates the foundational role of supervision in enabling teamwork, collaboration, and information sharing, since the key supervisory behaviors are essential to foster workplace respect—the necessary precursor to these patterns of workplace cooperation.

Are These Supervisory Behaviors Innate or Learned?

Are the 35 key supervisory behaviors learned skills or personality traits? The evidence from UC Irvine is that these behaviors are not inborn, because supervisors (as a group) improved significantly when provided with data indicating how supervision was perceived with respect to the key behaviors by their employees in the immediate unit, in comparison to other units' supervisors, and in relation to organization-wide goals for each measured behavior.

Supervisors were assisted by a management consultant to improve in areas where they scored below that of other supervisors and the overall goal for a desired behavior. The excellent results—significant improvement overall, across all measured supervisory behaviors as well as all measures of workplace respect and cooperation—indicated that codification of performance expectations, measurement, feedback, and goal-setting had led to learning and improvement. (Whether a Hawthorne-like effect could explain such a significant and widespread measured improvement appears doubtful.) The conclusion is that these key supervisory behaviors—including the ones that seem more like traits than acquired skills—are learned.

Model Differs Sharply from Other Management Effectiveness Models

This model demonstrates that supervision can do little to influence directly workplace cooperation or outcomes. Rather, the main role of the effective supervisor is to excel in the 35 behaviors that lead to workplace respect—the foundation on which desired organizational patterns and, ultimately, performance critically depend. If you reread the behaviors, you will note that very few are accurately perceived from a top-down, supervisory vantage; all require bottom-up evaluation from subordinates. This points to the importance of a 360-degree performance evaluation process or a survey instrument centered (in either case) around the determinant supervisory behaviors. These behaviors can be improved upon through goal setting, measurement, and feedback (as has been the experience at UC Irvine).

The Value of a Behavioral Model

Managers need to base their actions on a valid model of what employees believe and value and how they can be motivated, especially when innovation or improvement are needed by the enterprise. Intuition and common sense do not consistently provide complete and reliable management insights. For example, without an empirical model, would it be obvious to a supervisor that expecting and rewarding the behaviors in the workplace cooperation cluster of patterns might prove futile unless the supervisor evidences behaviors and qualities that (first) foster workplace respect? Without the model, would it be apparent to the supervisor that teamwork is unlikely to develop without mutual respect in the workplace? These observations may seem intuitive and obvious after studying the model, but these causal links are weakly developed in some improvement models.

Similarly, would it be clear that respect for views of people from diverse backgrounds or support for equal opportunity are key supervisory behaviors that affect unit performance? These are often viewed as supplemental supervisory qualities which, although important, are not essential to enterprise performance. However, these factors' significance is understood when the model reveals the critical-path importance of workplace respect as the pivotal, intervening variable linking supervisory behaviors and workplace cooperation.

A validated model provides some assurance that the organization is not rewarding the wrong behaviors, placing incentives on the wrong values, or conveying the wrong expectations or conflicting messages. Whether intrinsic or explicit, every improvement protocol embodies a model of how people in a workplace lead, follow, solve problems, and communicate. Moreover, all improvement programs contain inherent values—about what forms of leading, following, solving problems, and communicating are expected, tolerated, rewarded, or praised.

The supervisor behavior factors in the model, the workplace respect variables, and the workplace cooperation patterns are worth measuring, adopting as performance goals and expectations, valuing in mission statements, reflecting in unit performance objectives, evaluating in individuals' performance appraisals, incorporating in workshops and training, and rewarding through formal and informal systems of recognition. These behavioral foundations balance and support (rather than supplant) the "technical" features of a management change model. This balance is important in a model to stimulate sustainable change. The most effective technical tools—process redesign techniques, design principles, customer satisfaction and performance measurement systems, and quality standards—become ineffectual unless they are balanced by behavioral elements centered around employee beliefs, values, rewards, incentives, and disincentives (of which many characterize the informal organization more than the formal organization).

The worth of a validated model stems from its likely effectiveness in stimulating improved enterprise performance as the values, expectations, and normative behaviors it embodies are fostered. Variables with little predictive value in the model can be essentially ignored, enabling limited resources to be concentrated on the factors that will most likely produce results. In a workplace with limited time and other resources to invest in improvement, especially given the imperative of uninterrupted production, the most efficient management change model is the leanest, simplest one. Moreover, extremely complicated management change models are likely to contain inconsistencies and incoherent, mixed messages.

Remaining Work

The Irvine model demonstrates a strong causal lineage originating with 35 key supervisory behaviors along four distinct dimensions which provide the foundation for workplace respect, workplace cooperation, and self-assessed unit performance. However, the model would be more compelling if workplace cooperation could be demonstrated to correlate with external/customer measurements of unit performance. This focus will comprise the next step in exploring the further development of this model.

Also worth knowing:

♦ Would the model emerge outside the context of the larger management change model—the Irvine Model for Sustaining Administrative Improvement? Said differently, although the supervisory effectiveness model discussed here emerged from the larger management change model, does it stand on its own?

♦ Would this same management effectiveness model emerge if the survey were administered in a nonuniversity, for-profit enterprise? That is, does the Irvine model reveal fundamental principles of management effectiveness, or is it an artifact of a particular organization or type of institution?

♦ Does the model omit (other) key supervisory behaviors? The Survey of Management and Organizational Patterns did not measure supervisors' behaviors in such areas as use of authority and strategy, or qualities such as charisma, influence, tenacity, competitive drive, or political astuteness. Whether these factors also affect cooperation and team-based performance remains to be tested in an expanded survey.

The model's robustness and significance can be evaluated only by testing it in different enterprises. The UC Irvine Model for Sustaining Administrative Improvement and the Survey of Management and Organizational Patterns can be accessed at http://www.abs.uci.edu.

IF YOU ADOPT (ALL OR PART OF) THIS MODEL

The Irvine management change model illustrates how organizational change in the critical areas of workplace respect and cooperation start from a foundation of distinct supervisory behaviors that can be codified as performance expectations. Do not attempt to implement this model without adopting these (or very similar) explicit supervisory and team performance standards, as well as measurement and reward systems to support new performance expectations.

Before implementing this (or any) behavioral model, examine the underlying and inherent values in order to determine whether they are valid in your organization or your envisioned organization. Every behavioral model contains embedded values (whether expressed or not) that will undermine implementation if they clash with mixed messages from other behavioral systems, such as the human resources system (as discussed earlier). Inherent values need to be made explicit and evaluated systematically for both validity and consistency.

It may not be necessary to adopt a management change model as comprehensive as the UC Irvine Model for Sustaining Administrative Improvement. This model's subset of value-based supervisory, cooperation, and respect expectations can be experienced consistently and coherently—as necessary for sustainable change—if integrated into performance objectives, performance evaluations, incentive programs, training workshops, measurement systems, recognition and reward systems, and stated goals for the enterprise. At its simplest, the supervisory effectiveness model explained above can be implemented by 1) measuring supervisory behaviors that foster respect in the workplace, 2) determining whether these behaviors lead to cooperation-based outcomes, and 3) if validated, providing data to supervisors and work groups to foster learning and performance improvement.

SUSTAINABLE IMPROVEMENT

Sustainable change requires a model that is:

◆ Balanced, with complementary behavioral and technical tools

◆ Empirically validated

◆ Consistent with (other) belief and value systems of both the formal and informal organization

◆ Internally coherent, with no conflicting elements that might trigger a retreat to status quo behaviors

♦ Capable of providing clear information about the behaviors that can be improved through measurement and feedback

Models that fall short of these fundamentals or which fail to engage and influence employee belief systems about what is expected, tolerated, rewarded, respected, and considered effective will not foster sustainable change.

Sustainable improvement in enterprise performance patterns requires consistency and coherence in value systems and in all related reward systems because, until new behaviors are embedded in shared values, they are vulnerable to status quo reversion. This is one reason why some enterprise improvement models have more lasting effects than others. The other reason is that many improvement programs—including ones that have the wrappings of sophistication—lack an underlying, empirically validated behavioral model that counterbalances their technical features and engages (not merely explains) the dynamic of values, expectations, rewards, disincentives, symbols, motivations, and beliefs that affect individual and team effectiveness.

APPENDIX

SURVEY OF MANAGEMENT AND ORGANIZATIONAL PATTERNS

Thank You!

Thank you for participating in this process. We are assessing our organization's strengths and its weaknesses. Your views and experiences are important to include in this survey.

Confidentiality

Your responses will remain anonymous, so please respond with complete honesty. Please respond to all questions for which you have an opinion. Completed surveys will be mailed directly to a processor (an external firm) where results will be summarized and the survey forms will be discarded. *Only summarized (averaged, not individual) responses will be reported.*

Your Comments

If this survey overlooks an issue that you think is important for evaluating the effectiveness of management or organizational patterns, please include your comments on the last page. These comments will be summarized by the processor in a way that protects their confidentiality. However, please do not include comments of a personal nature which cannot be summarized with the survey results.

How the Results Will Be Used

The goal behind this survey is to improve management practices and organizational effectiveness. Averaged responses will be summarized for each department and for the entire organization. Summary results will be provided to all employees by managers.

For the following questions please select one, most applicable response

1) While working with others in my department on a group task, I feel that:
   ❑ Everyone shares responsibility for the results
   ❑ Only a few people are responsible for the results
   ❑ Only the boss is responsible for the results

2) People who look for better ways of doing things are respected and rewarded in my department.
   ❑ Strongly agree   ❑ Agree somewhat
   ❑ Disagree somewhat   ❑ Strongly disagree

3) In my department, people experience a climate of mutual respect, at all job levels.
   ❑ Strongly agree   ❑ Agree somewhat
   ❑ Disagree somewhat   ❑ Strongly disagree

4) In my work group (those with whom I work most closely on a day-to-day basis) a suggestion about the way we do things:
   ❑ Is valued even if it's initially the wrong suggestion
   ❑ Is welcome but had better be right the first time
   ❑ Is not welcome

5) When work problems surface in my work group, my coworkers usually:
   ❑ Produce information and ideas that help solve the problem
   ❑ Say nothing; keep a low profile
   ❑ Produce information that shows why they were not at fault

6) I can provide honest, constructive criticism to my work group about the way it functions without being penalized.
   ❑ Strongly agree   ❑ Agree somewhat
   ❑ Disagree somewhat   ❑ Strongly disagree

7) I can share (work) problems without concern about appearing stupid to others in my work group.
   ❑ Strongly agree   ❑ Agree somewhat
   ❑ Disagree somewhat   ❑ Strongly disagree

8) In my work group, problems with the way we do our work are usually:

❑ Ignored   (or)   ❑ Faced and attended to

9) In my work group, interpersonal conflicts are:

❑ Ignored   (or)   ❑ Address and resolved

10) In my work group, differences of opinion about how to get the job done are:

❑ Discussed   (or)   ❑ Not discussed
❑ Resolved using facts (or)   ❑ Resolved using power

The following strengths and weaknesses pertain to your supervisor, the person to whom you directly report on a day-to-day basis:

11) My supervisor:

	Strongly Disagree	Disagree Somewhat	Agree Somewhat	Strongly Agree
Communicates what he/she expects me to accomplish	❑	❑	❑	❑
Works well with other managers	❑	❑	❑	❑
Supports equal opportunity	❑	❑	❑	❑
Models the behavior he/she expects from others	❑	❑	❑	❑
Accepts constructive criticism without becoming defensive	❑	❑	❑	❑
Communicates honestly with me	❑	❑	❑	❑
Keeps promises and commitments	❑	❑	❑	❑
Rewards the best performers	❑	❑	❑	❑
Seeks different views when solving problems	❑	❑	❑	❑
Values the experiences and perspectives of people from diverse backgrounds	❑	❑	❑	❑

Makes important decisions based on the organization's best interests	❑	❑	❑	❑
Acts in ways that build respect in him/her	❑	❑	❑	❑
Would act ethically even if it required personal sacrifice	❑	❑	❑	❑
Based his/her actions on a consistent set of principles	❑	❑	❑	❑
Has earned my complete trust	❑	❑	❑	❑
Takes steps to improve bad relationships	❑	❑	❑	❑
Trusts my judgment	❑	❑	❑	❑
Takes time to listen and understand my views	❑	❑	❑	❑
Finds "win-win" solutions	❑	❑	❑	❑
Helps me understand "the bigger picture"	❑	❑	❑	❑
Makes good decisions despite incomplete information	❑	❑	❑	❑
Admits mistakes and moves on	❑	❑	❑	❑
Does the most important things first	❑	❑	❑	❑
Shows respect when communicating	❑	❑	❑	❑
Separates vital tasks from less important ones	❑	❑	❑	❑
Cares about employees as individuals	❑	❑	❑	❑
Won't change direction if it means admitting a mistake	❑	❑	❑	❑
Is emotionally unpredictable	❑	❑	❑	❑
Blames others when things go wrong	❑	❑	❑	❑
Discourages my bringing up problems	❑	❑	❑	❑

Makes me feel stupid when we disagree	❏	❏	❏	❏
Makes excuses rather than accept responsibility	❏	❏	❏	❏
Gains advantage by holding back information	❏	❏	❏	❏
Loses his/her temper under pressure	❏	❏	❏	❏
Makes some people look good at others' expense	❏	❏	❏	❏

For the following questions please select one, most applicable response

12) Our customers rate my department's performance as:
   - ❏ Consistently outstanding
   - ❏ Usually very good
   - ❏ Good
   - ❏ Fair
   - ❏ Poor
   - ❏ Don't know

13) How effective is your department, in terms of quality and productivity, compared to its potential?
   - ❏ We perform at 90–100% of our full potential—consistently excellent
   - ❏ We perform at 70–90% of our potential—usually very good
   - ❏ We perform at 50–70% of our potential—average or somewhat better than average
   - ❏ We perform at less than 50% of our potential—below average

14) In your opinion, what is the main reason your department performs at less than 100% of its potential?

(© The Regents of the University of California. Survey used by permission.)

13

Managing Change in Higher Education: A Leader's Guide

D. Quinn Mills and Janet M. Pumo

A market analysis of higher education points to the mandate for change. In this Information Age, technology is not only changing back-office operations, it is fundamentally changing education. Successful leaders in all institutions know that sustained change requires organizational change. This chapter serves as a guide for leading higher education institutions through the turbulent times ahead.

FORCES FOR CHANGE

Several forces of change are influencing higher education in the Information Age:

* The technological revolution is creating capabilities and expectations for operational efficiency and student-centered services.

* The learning styles of students and their expectations for service have been influenced by their unprecedented exposure to technology before even arriving on campus.

◆ The globalization of higher education will demand the internationalization of our educational material and delivery systems.

◆ The affordability of higher education is threatened by rising costs.

Expectations for Operational Efficiency

The technological revolution is creating capabilities and expectations for operational efficiency and student-centered services. Technology is bringing change not only to how universities are administered, but to education itself. One of the most significant changes in technology is the expansion of global networks to provide access and connectivity. Institutions are investing heavily to participate in these networks, and users are embracing them with unprecedented speed.

A growing number of colleges are now offering courses, even entire programs, over the Internet. These courses provide convenience and potentially a more cost-effective form of education for students. Internet-delivered education and the associated services are proving popular with working adults and, surprisingly, with students on campuses who prefer the self-paced Internet courses over traditional classroom lectures.

Technology is changing expectations in several ways, such as:

◆ Students expect services to be integrated and customer-friendly.

◆ Students expect to take courses and access a variety of services without having to be away from home or work.

◆ Information can be accessed whenever and wherever the faculty, staff, or student wishes.

◆ Interactions with the institution are based on a student-centered, one-stop shopping model.

Student Exposure to Technology

The learning styles and expectations for service of students have been influenced by their unprecedented exposure to technology before even arriving on campus. Students are now seeking an education that will help them prepare for a future in the Information Age. Their learning styles have been shaped by their lifelong exposure to electronic media. Students seek institutions which provide the access and preparation critical to their development of which understanding and using information technology is a part.

Student services encompass dozens of activities that can affect student satisfaction, retention, and success. Students are behaving as consumers: They expect high-quality service and will seek out institutions with superior service and shun those with poor-quality student services. To remain competitive in the next decade, colleges and universities are increasingly selecting strategies that differentiate their institutions based on how well they create a student-centered environment.

Globalization of Higher Education

The globalization of higher education will demand the internationalization of our educational material and delivery systems. The United States now has only 19% of the world economy, compared to 70% immediately after World War II. Beyond increasing the international dimension of what we are teaching, we must focus on how best to serve a more global higher education market. As colleges and universities put offerings on the Internet, they become available to people anywhere in the world with the necessary technology and with the required language skills. This is both a challenge and an opportunity for institutions to internationalize and extend their brand image to a world-wide marketplace.

Economists now maintain that lack of education is a significant factor retarding economic growth in much of the world. Each additional year of education for the working population results in a full point of real (that is, adjusted for inflation) economic growth rate. Electronic delivery of high quality education will be very attractive to governments all over the world because it offers the possibility that a larger percentage of the population can access education, thereby increasing economic competitiveness.

Cost Escalation

The escalating costs of higher education threaten its affordability and accessibility for the average student. Price is an increasingly important factor in decision-making about colleges. In 1997 a record 33% of students cited financial assistance as a very important reason for choosing their college (Higher Education Research Institute, 1997).

The cost of higher education is rising rapidly. For the 1997–98 academic year, for example, the cost of higher education rose more than two times the rate of inflation and three times the growth rate of the average family income (The College Board, 1997). Tuition and fees per year at a four-year private college now average $18,119; at a two-year private college, $10,817; and at a four-year public college, $7,049. Costs at the top-tier colleges are higher, of course, often exceeding $30,000 per year.

> By 2008 students will pay an average of nearly $85,000 for four years at a public university, according to T. Rowe Price Associates Inc. . . . The crunch can already be seen in California. The state's higher education system faces an influx of at least 500,000 students over the next decade. Building facilities for this growth would require additional outlays of $5.2 billion. But . . . (it's not in the cards). Distance education via telecommunications holds promise, especially because today's grade-schoolers are more likely to attend college part-time while they hold down jobs. . . . Students will create a huge market for courses delivered directly to their homes or offices (Kaufman, 1997).

The Internet itself, used as an aid to traditional education—rather than an alternative delivery system—increases costs. "Even the expense of data [to colleges] has risen sharply. An online index of physics abstracts, for example, costs the University of Pennsylvania $50,400 a year; when the index was just a series of books, it cost $7,748" (Larsen, 1997).

For many state higher education systems, projected enrollments exceed the institutions' capacity to handle them through traditional teaching modes. College enrollments will expand by about 20%, from 15 million to 18 million, and university and college revenues from $175 billion to about $263 billion in today's dollars. Enrollments will rise about 20%, and tuition and fees about 20% above the rate of inflation (Winston, 1997). If anything, the growth in revenues may be larger since the Clinton administration has sponsored increased federal aid for higher education and many observers expect federal money to fund increased tuition.

THE MANDATE FOR INSTITUTIONAL CHANGE

It is clear that the changes in our economic environment, technological capabilities, and our students demand institutional change. How well institutions anticipate and address these changes will impact their ability to compete for the best faculty, students, and resources. And technology is becoming a key differentiator in higher education. Through technology new, nontraditional competitors have entered the higher education market. Many are characterized by strong philosophies of customer convenience, continuous quality improvement, and adaptation to learner needs. Organizations such as the University of Phoenix exemplify the viability of these principles in higher education. And the University of Phoenix's Online College, new cable company entrants, and business ventures such as Universal Learning, are examples of how technology is redefining who delivers advanced education today and tomorrow.

Like other sweeping social and economic changes in our history, the technology-enabled transformation of higher education will take decades to run its course.

This is no cause for a sigh of relief. It means the continuous demand for change will be with us for an extended period—and the pace will quicken. There are those institutions who will be at the forefront of the change curve and those who will lag. Economic history proves that the later you join the wave of change, the lower your returns. How do leaders affect their institutions' place on the change curve?

The role of leaders is critical to helping institutions continually absorb change. They must:

- ◆ Focus the changes
- ◆ Start early
- ◆ Actively manage changes through the entire transformation process

Focus the Changes

How quickly is higher education changing? Most campuses can point to "islands of innovation." In the change curve, these early adopters blaze new academic and administrative trails, using technology as the catalyst. Examples include the department that first offers courses via the Internet or the administrative office that redesigns their work flows and systems to better serve students.

These innovations result from significant investment by a few visionaries. However, as we move further along the technology-enabled change curve, more people join. The same structures and investments are no longer affordable. Trade-off decisions must be made to balance an institution's finite resources. The purpose of an organization's strategy is to help guide those trade-off decisions.

The same is true of an organization's capacity for change. It is a finite resource for which trade-off decisions are essential. A leader's job is to push as much change into an organization as possible without creating dysfunction. First, he or she must focus changes on the areas of greatest potential return. This is easier to do in the administrative realm where the goal is often efficiency and where progress is more easily measured. Chief financial officers and department heads are actively exploiting new technologies to prompt changes in how work is performed, campus-wide.

Unfortunately, what we are not seeing is a direct relationship between the administrative efficiencies and an increased investment in the academic applications of IT. When institutions are embarking upon wholesale replacements of their core administrative applications, to the tune of tens of millions of dollars each, and when they are streamlining their administrative business processes, these initiatives rarely promise to directly reallocate a portion of these savings to academic applications of technology.

Ironically, to date, institutions have invested the least in the areas where technology could help further distinguish institutions in the higher education marketplace. While there are exciting examples of innovation, pervasive changes in pedagogy are lagging. The desire and demand among students and faculty for change is climbing at unprecedented rates. Yet many institutions are stalled, unable to move past the "islands of innovation" phase and support the academic technology needs of a broader campus community. This is an area on which academic leaders need to focus.

This volume contains many examples of how administrative change can bring value to institutions. In general, there is less reluctance to pursue change in the administrative than the academic domain. One barrier in teaching and learning is the lack of clear, measurable objectives for technology in academia. We are more comfortable investing institutional dollars where we see a tangible financial return. Early adopter institutions invested in campus-wide academic technology with an eye on the future and an intuitive sense of the tangible, yet unmeasurable contribution to the institution's reputation. The focus of academic technology investments is not to exploit efficiency as much as it is to expand the educational scope, reach, and depth of an institution. If an institution waits until there is resultant data about the impact of technology on teaching and learning before it invests, it has assured itself a place at the tail end of the change curve.

How adaptive to change is your organizational culture? Where we really see the effects of a culture that is not adaptive to change is in the lack of programmatic change underway at so many institutions. The challenge is to maintain a content and delivery structure that matches the needs and capabilities of the Digital Age. To teach effectively with technology, even if the content isn't changing, you must change how you teach. The lesson learned from pioneering faculty is that we cannot simply bring the classroom to the desktop. We must fundamentally rethink the knowledge, assignments, discussions, and testing that are critical to each student's learning experience. Rethinking has been a recurring theme throughout the previous chapters— rethinking student services, research administration, human resources, etc. Change management disciplines are desperately needed to initiate and sustain programmatic renewal.

Start Early

For leading institutions, it is essential to be early on the change curve, although not necessarily first. With the advent of the Internet, being right and being first are less important. If you come up with the right answer first, it's on the Internet quickly. Execution becomes more important. While most organizations are effective at recognizing the need for change, envisioning the required changes and formalizing the decision to change are difficult. What they often lack is the ability to implement. This is where change management disciplines come into play.

Manage the Changes through the Entire Transformation Process

Change management has a weak image. Senior officers often view change management as tactical, peripheral, and discretionary. Change management consultants are viewed as the "hippies of the '90s." When implementing a major project, the change management component is often the first to be cut to save expenses. Yet change management disciplines are critical to increasing an institution's capacity to adapt to continual change. The next section of this chapter will focus on the role of senior management in managing change, from initiation to implementation.

Applying Change Management Principles in Higher Education

John Kotter, professor of leadership at the Harvard Business School, has analyzed the change programs of over 100 organizations (reengineering, right-sizing, restructuring, total quality management). His 1995 *Harvard Business Review* article and book *Leading Change: Why Transformation Efforts Fail* summarized the lessons learned and prescribed eight steps for transforming an organization.

1) Establish a sense of urgency

2) Form a powerful coalition

3) Create a vision

4) Communicate the vision

5) Empower others to act on the vision

6) Plan for and create short-term wins

7) Consolidate improvements and produce still more change

8) Institutionalize new approaches

Each of the steps in this change cycle has a unique dimension in higher education organizations. As we seek to capitalize on technological advances to revitalize our academic programs and administrative services, what forms of leadership are needed?

1) Establishing a sense of urgency

We are physically and psychologically programmed for equilibrium. The only changes we are comfortable with are the ones we initiate for ourselves. However, organizational change is not individually initiated: It is externally mandated by someone higher in the organization—and it is uncomfortable if you are really doing it. Therefore, we naturally resist organizational change. We attribute such proposed changes to a fad, a consultant's report, or to a particular leader whose tenure we are likely to outlive—and we wait. Intellectually, we require compelling reasons to change.

To break this initial barrier, leaders must open up, engaging campus members in an ongoing, candid dialogue about trends (competitors, student demographics, technological capabilities, economics, and sociopolitical shifts) and their potential impact on a given college or university. The purpose of these conversations is to monitor our present course and speed and to alert us to what is on the horizon.

A track record of honest and open communication builds organizational trust and sets the stage for the next step in the change process.

2) Forming a powerful coalition

Once an opportunity or threat that requires widespread change has been identified, we must assemble a group of people with enough power to lead the change effort. In our example of technology in teaching and learning, these individuals must be able to effect the required curricular, technological, and financial changes on campus. They are faculty, deans, senior academic officers, presidents, chancellors, budget officers, and chief information officers (CIOs). Their power and influence is critical to successful change. Among them, we must find the passionate few who are willing and able to work as a team for institutional change.

3) Creating a vision

At this point, we have established a sense of discontent with the status quo. We have assembled a group of change agents who are committed to building something better. We must now solicit and synthesize the best ideas from our stakeholders. Stakeholders are those constituencies who are directly influenced by the institution's success or failure; for example, the students, faculty, staff, community, trustees, legislators, alumni, and business leaders.

We must seek out the wants and needs of these stakeholders and articulate a desired state for our future academic programs and administrative services. This includes describing the strategies for achieving that vision, such as the role of information technology in teaching and learning, or viewing the student as the administrative customer. The vision itself is likely to come from the guiding coalition. However, the responsibility for initiating this effort most often lies with the senior academic officer or dean.

This vision should be easy to communicate and should appeal to the key stakeholders. It should help clarify the organization's direction. All the institutional changes that follow should support the vision. When organizations attempt change without an overarching vision, these change initiatives often seem like the "program de jour." A well-conceived vision helps guide future change initiatives and weed out counterproductive ones.

4) Communicating the vision

Communication that informs, inspires, and builds trust is an art. Managing change requires a great deal of artistic communication. Using every appropriate vehicle, it is the responsibility of campus leaders to discuss the vision and its implications. What new behaviors will be rewarded? What old behaviors will be discouraged? What role does each individual have in helping the institution achieve the desired state? How are the leaders themselves changing as part of this process?

The more these conversations are incorporated into the leaders' daily activities—faculty senate meetings, deans' sessions, or performance reviews—the more effectively the vision will be communicated. John Kotter found that most leaders under-communicate the vision by a factor of 10. In academia, we have the unique cultural phenomenon that leaders are afraid to communicate direction out of fear that no one will follow. In fact, these directive conversations are likely to incite outspoken resistance where there previously was none.

The most powerful communication vehicle that leaders have at their disposal is their own behavior. Antithetical actions by leaders are the fastest way to turn genuine change efforts into organizational farces. The campus community is quick to spot hypocrisies between what leaders say is important and what they fund, or what leaders say they value in faculty and staff and who they promote. The most successful leaders of change are those who personally model the way for others and "walk their talk." The second most successful leaders of change—there are none.

5)   *Empowering others to act on the vision*

To advance teaching and learning with technology, we must eliminate the obstacles that prevent faculty and students from exploiting these new capabilities. Recent educational surveys indicate that the primary obstacles to integrating technology into teaching and learning are the lack of faculty awareness about what is possible with technology and insufficient training and support, not faculty and student willingness. Often faculty do not know the success stories of their colleagues at the same institution. Each institution needs a forum where faculty can highlight their achievements with technology-enabled teaching and share lessons learned.

Faculty who have made successful inroads have invested substantial amounts of time. When the innovative use of technology in instruction is not a criterion for tenure or promotion, there is strong pressure for younger, tenure-track faculty to focus elsewhere. Leading institutions in this arena have restructured their technical support for faculty by teaming content experts (faculty) with curriculum designers and technology experts. In addition, they have made the needed investments in standard, reliable applications for classroom equipment.

Students' obstacles are fewer. Their chief concerns are 1) getting their computers up and running on the campus systems quickly before they fall behind, and 2) obtaining technical support in the residence halls. Monitors are present in student PC labs. However, most students are now arriving on campus with their own computers, and often more computer-enabled learning is occurring in the dorm room than in the lab. Most institutions don't have a mechanism to provide initial set-up assistance and ongoing, on-site technical support to students in the residence halls. Traditional help desks aren't staffed to handle calls from students and, whereas faculty and staff tend to call in during the day, students tend to call in at night when many help desks operate with only a skeleton crew or not at all.

Using student services as an example of an administrative segment, there are multiple obstacles to overcome as well. Some are conceptual. How should we define a student-centered environment that suits the needs of our population of students? Some are procedural, such as integrating student services functions so they appear seamless to the user. Others have to do with moving the adoption of changes from a select few in the administrative offices to a way of doing things that permeates the entire institution.

The role of the change leader is to understand what the key inhibitors are for a given set of stakeholders to adopt change and remove those inhibitors.

6) *Planning for and creating short-term wins*

When organizations undergo sweeping change, there is a period early on when performance actually decreases. We're busy learning the new administrative system or we are moving our existing course materials to an electronic format (rather than devising new course materials). The new introduction of technology can hamper short-term gains. The purpose of change management discipline is to minimize the depth and duration of that performance dip.

"Without planning short-term wins, too many people give up and may actively join the ranks of those people who have been resisting change" (Kotter, 1995). One way to plan wins is to establish incremental, achievable goals. In teaching and learning, for example, an institution might set up two types of faculty grants: individual grants for the specific purpose of fostering innovation in teaching and learning with technology and collaborative grants for spreading consistent academic technologies among multiple faculty within departments or across departments.

7) *Consolidating improvements and producing still more change*

A common mistake we make in change programs is to declare victory too soon. New approaches—whether in teaching and learning or research administration or human resources—are oftentimes tentative and incremental; they can take several years to become part of an institution's culture. Instead of declaring victory, the short-term wins are best used to gain the credibility needed to take on other, more difficult changes. These changes may include revisiting the hiring, promotion, tenure, or performance evaluation practices of the institution. Such policies will have a profound impact on the continued momentum of change within an organization.

8) *Institutionalizing new approaches*

The purpose of this final step is twofold: 1) to articulate the connection between the resulting changes in behavior and the institution's success and 2) to develop a means to root those desired changes in the culture of the institution. Periodic quantitative and qualitative surveys of faculty, students, and alumni will help determine whether the changes are occurring as desired. The second component ensures that the next generation of leaders at the institution personifies the new approaches. Succession planning is key. One poor selection of a senior officer can derail an institution for years. To help ensure a good successor, educate the selection committee about the transformation process and ensure that the qualities of a strong change leader are requisite to being awarded the position.

CONCLUSION

The market for higher education in the United States is already large and will expand significantly. "America has 14.5 million [college] students. . . . Its universities earn, on one estimate, $175 billion a year, making them twice as big a 'business' as airlines" (*The Economist*, 1996). College enrollments will expand by some 20%, college revenues by some 50% on an inflation-adjusted basis, and business spending on education and training by some 35%. Those colleges and universities which embrace technology to cope with growing domestic and global markets will contribute to further expanding those markets.

Technology is changing the way in which institutions distinguish themselves in the education marketplace. It will not displace the current education system. Technology-enabled education will complement the learning styles of an increasingly technology-savvy student base and better meet the needs of these graduates' employers. And technology is changing the rules by which institutions compete for students, faculty, and staff against nontraditional entrants into the education marketplace.

To foster a campus culture that can adopt new technology-enabled education practices, redesign student-centered services, and rethink administration, leaders must apply fundamental change management techniques. Their leadership will build the campuses with great vision, passion, resources, and focus.

REFERENCES

The College Board. (1997, September). *Trends in student aid.* New York, NY: The College Board.

The Economist. (1996, October). *The Economist Review,* 5.

Higher Education Research Institute. (1997, January 1). *Academic and political engagement among nation's college freshman is at all-time low, UCLA Study Finds.* Washington, DC: Higher Education Research Institute.

Kaufman, J. (1997, February 4). Generation Y. *Wall Street Journal,* 1 ff.

Kotter, J. P. (1995, March-April). Leading change: Why transformation efforts fail. *Harvard Business Review.*

Kotter, J. P. (1996). *Leading change.* Boston, MA: Harvard Business School Press.

Larsen, E. (1997, March 17). Why colleges cost too much. *Time,* 46–55.

Winston, G. (1997, May 1). Long lines about the best colleges are likely to get longer. *The New York Times,* D2.

14

Renewal as an Institutional Imperative

Richard N. Katz and Diana G. Oblinger

I t is clear that the shift to a so-called knowledge or information economy is well underway. Networks are linking disparate sectors of the
world's economy, and the capacity to create knowledge is supplanting
labor, land, and capital as the dominant source of wealth. In a knowledge economy it is axiomatic that education is a precursor to prosperity. *Fortune* magazine's Richard Tomlinson reports that "in the new
China, even unskilled jobs like being a janitor now require a high
school education" (Tomlinson, 1998).

It is reasonable to expect that a global society and economy that is
powered by knowledge and fueled by education might establish the
preconditions for a renaissance in US colleges and universities which
have long enjoyed global preeminence in delivering postsecondary
education. Certainly, the 1990s witnessed a new and exciting dialogue
among collegiate leaders and educators about the nature of teaching
and learning, the role of the campus in education, the pedagogical
merits of asynchronous learning, and so forth. The new possibilities
enabled by the network, such as the potential to link individuals and
organizations in virtual global environments, are stimulating new
thinking about the art and science of teaching.

While the heightened importance of education is likely to bode well for educators, it is not yet clear how much of this social and economic premium will accrue to their institutions. The new opportunities presented by information technologies are attracting the interest of new educational providers. Particularly in the area of skill development, for-profit enterprises have moved quickly and decisively to educate adults in software development, network administration, and related areas. In other cases, new institutions such as the University of Phoenix are emerging to occupy profitable niches in the degree-granting segment of postsecondary education. In fact, authors such as Davis and Botkin (1994) speculate that tomorrow's corporations will provide significant elements of the educational mission delivered by today's colleges and universities.

The ability of colleges and universities to seize the opportunity to retain preeminence in preparing individuals for citizenship and economic prosperity in the Knowledge Age will depend on those institutions' abilities to renew themselves. William Massy reminds us that colleges and universities have long demonstrated this capacity. Of the 66 institutions that existed continuously since the 1530 founding of the Lutheran Church, 62 are universities (Massy, 1997). The enduring relevance and viability of colleges and universities, in the face of war, revolution, economic, and political upheaval testifies to both the enduring value of structured instruction and to these institutions' adaptive abilities. The important question facing our educational leaders is whether or not the possibilities presented by global networking and technical integration represent changes in educational tools, or if they represent fundamental changes in the very nature of how teaching and learning might be conducted. Either interpretation of this question presents a challenge of renewal. Success in surmounting these challenges, however, will depend on institutional interventions of differing natures and intensity and on distinct time scales.

In some ways, the durability of colleges and universities as institutions has derived from their political and economic isolation. In political terms, democratic societies have long accepted the notion that scholars' quests for truth depends, in part, on a lack of political intrusion into scholarship and instruction. The ivory tower metaphor is an apt one insofar as it signifies the insulation of the academy from the political trends and pressures of the day. Similarly, public universities have been insulated from the market and have designed academic programs less from an objective of imbuing students with marketable skills than from the objective of developing those critical thinking abilities that prepare students for lifelong participation in democratic societies and for economic prosperity.

This Jeffersonian ideal of a college education is increasingly under tension from the market realities and time pressures of the networked society. If the premise of the Knowledge Age is that everyone (and everything) is connected to everyone—all of the time—institutions of higher learning cannot maintain political and economic distance from the societies they serve or the economies in which they operate. As a result, colleges and universities are challenged increasingly to deliver curricula that respond to market needs, to shift priorities away from research and toward instruction, and to account with increasing specificity for their effectiveness as educators and their efficiency as resource stewards. In the networked world, time is of the essence. In such environments, corporate leaders faced with the need to invest billions of dollars on products with life cycles measured in months (e.g., semiconductors) cannot long tolerate skill deficiencies in the work force. Such leaders will use networks to find talent globally and will become increasingly insensitive to either the national origin or the academic credentials of the skilled individuals they seek. Individuals seeking education in such a context will, of necessity, view the collegiate opportunity through the lens of competitiveness in the job market. The question, therefore, is not whether existing colleges and universities are able to renew themselves to maintain relevance and appeal. Rather, the question is whether existing colleges and universities can renew themselves in time.

Successfully renewing today's colleges and universities will depend on rapid, concerted, and planned action along many fronts. This volume deals expressly with the administrative dimension of the higher education enterprise; the environment, processes, and tools that make it possible for educators to deliver instruction, for students to learn, and for researchers to produce meaningful scholarship. The insights reflected by this volume's contributors suggest both a legacy of and need for change in a number of arenas.

RENEWING INSTITUTIONAL LEADERSHIP AND GOVERNANCE

Colleges and universities have been described as "amiable, anarchic, self-correcting collectives of scholars with a small contingent of dignified caretakers at the unavoidable business edge" (Keller, 1983). Whether or not such a characterization was ever in fact true, it is most certainly not true today. The modern university is more akin to Lee and Bowen's concept of a "multiversity" (Lee & Bowen, 1975), offering a range of educational, social, logistical, theatrical, medical, security, and other services to tens of thousands of students, parents, alumni, and others. The leaders of such institutions manage idiosyncratic and highly specialized physical plants to support scientific research and, in many cases, multibillion dollar operating budgets and endowments. The leadership of such enterprises demands significantly more than dignified care taking. Smaller institutions, while less complex, may face a condition of near-term oversupply and are often engaged in tuition discounting that might be characterized as price wars in other sectors. The leaders of such institutions must now be fluent in the language of marketing, pricing, customer service, and competition (Selingo, 1998). The issues raised by this changing context are numerous.

For example, can universities continue to depend on their institutional leaders to fill the increasingly complex roles demanded of them? The empirical and anecdotal evidence is disheartening. In general, the term of office of today's college and university presidents is believed to range from three to seven years. If one precondition for sustainable institutional change is the long-term presence of an engaged and committed leader, then higher education's dominant leadership development model creates risk. (According to *The Chronicle of Higher Education 1998–1999 Almanac Issue*, in 1995 26.5% of college and university presidents had served in their current positions for a period of two years or less.)

Strong and sustained leadership is particularly critical in colleges and universities due to the political nature of governance at these institutions. Professor Michael Finlayson's cautionary tale in this volume reminds us that changing administrative culture and practice does not happen until or unless all the leaders embrace both the objectives of the proposed change and the processes involved in achieving the desired change. If lessons are to be drawn from industry, existing colleges and universities are faced with a unique and challenging circumstance. In industry, decision-making authority is frequently clear and highly centralized, while processes and supporting systems are highly decentralized. On most campuses, political authority is shared among central administrators, deans, unions, and faculty, while many processes and their supporting systems remain centralized. College and university governance is effective in environments that are insulated from market and political pressures. In such environments, institutional decisions are made consensually, short-term objectives are subordinated to the perceived long-term institutional good, and individuals are empowered to seek the truth without interference. In such environments, university leaders "discover preferences through action more often than [they] act on the basis of preference" (Cohen & March, 1974). In many ways, these organizational anomalies and their effects on institutional leadership account for both the stability and the academic excellence of these institutions. In today's context of interconnectedness and of dwindling political and economic insulation, these aspects of governance and culture prevent change.

If the dominant methodology of successful change management is goal setting, a political system of governance that drives goals underground hinders change. If an organization is optimized for insulation from market or political pressures, the result, in a networked society, is likely a failure to adopt a service culture or to recognize a vulnerability to new—and less insulated—competitors. John Gardner described this challenge well when he concluded: "We have now proven that a university community can make life unlivable for a president. . . . We can fight so savagely that he is clawed to ribbons in the process" (Gardner, Atwell, & Berdahl, 1985).

The contributors to this volume are breaking with tradition. In a courageous break with the constraints of leading in political environments, David Roselle (Chapter 1) describes a program of campus change initiatives that are derived from an explicit and clear set of institutional goals. At the core of the University of Delaware's program is the goal of creating a living and learning environment that places students in the center of the campus service system. Similarly, Robert Kvavik and Michael Handberg (Chapter 7) describe fundamental changes at the University of Minnesota in which centralized and producer-oriented services are yielding to "decentralized and learner-oriented services, including numerous opportunities for self-help as well as access to information and services on the part of students and faculty with concomitant greater local authority and responsibility." In effect, the renewal of these institutions is demanding an engaged leadership, explicit goal setting, as well as a responsive and service-oriented culture.

RENEWING INSTITUTIONAL CULTURE, ORGANIZATION, AND HUMAN RESOURCES

In addition to renewing institutional approaches to leadership and governance, the contributors to this volume are unanimous in describing a powerful shift to a service-oriented institutional culture. Michael Finlayson (Chapter 2) describes the rethinking of the University of Toronto's administrative work as emanating from President Prichard's desire to make Toronto's administrative activities, structures, and practices "directly responsive" to the academic mission of the university. James McKee, Sharon Kiser, and Russ Lea (Chapter 8) describe the transformation of university research administration in ways that emphasize service to researchers by reducing bureaucracy and reorganizing to distribute authority and accountability to the unit level.

The cultural shift from an administrative culture that was optimized for accuracy (in a low-technology context) to one that is optimized for service is central to the renewal of university administration. It is also described by those leaders in this volume as perhaps the most difficult area of institutional renewal. UC Irvine's Wendell Brase describes a behavioral approach designed to effect cultural change directly (Chapter 12). Elements of the award-winning approach at UC Irvine included the implementation of teamwork principles, effectiveness principles, and simplification goals and principles. These goals and principles, according to Brase, were "intentionally crafted to alter values and status quo behaviors that have become comfortable." To effect cultural change in entrenched bureaucracies, Brase and fellow contributor Thomas Connolly (Chapter 9) describe a number of changes to the human resources systems and practices that either foster or reinforce behaviors that are compatible with the desired shift to a service-oriented administrative culture. Organizational, cultural, and human resource interventions are woven throughout this volume and include:

◆ Identifying new goals, norms, and work force behaviors

◆ Creating new organizational forms, including cross-disciplinary teams, centers, consortia, and others

◆ Delayering administrative organizations to increase spans of managerial control, broaden job responsibilities, and eliminate the incentives for individuals to build administrative fiefdoms

◆ Outsourcing

◆ Creating programs that facilitate the redeployment of individuals whose jobs may be altered or lost

◆ Implementing new outcome-based performance measurement systems and rewards for the desired behavioral outcomes such as customer service and teamwork

In virtually all cases, the contributors to this volume describe a variety of strategies that they have employed to reinforce their roles as agents of continuous transformation. This is quite a renewal-oriented view of the university administrator. Increasingly, the term "partner" is used to characterize a multitude of relationships, including those between administrators and faculty, between institutions and their governmental sponsors, and between campuses and corporations.

RENEWING INFORMATION TECHNOLOGIES, RESOURCES, AND SERVICES

If the renewal of leadership and governance is the precondition for changing colleges and universities, and changing institutional norms and values is the dominant challenge facing administrators, the renewal of campus information technologies and resources as well as the services that underlie these technologies is the driver and enabler of institutional transformation. The network—as the newly dominant means of facilitating institutional communication—is making it possible to alter organizational structures and to mediate new collaborative organizational forms. Increasingly, college and university leaders are able to communicate throughout and beyond the campus and can ensure that important institutional goals are aligned and communicated in a consistent fashion across the enterprise.

Networks and the common user interface of the World Wide Web are making it possible for college and university service providers to rethink and reorganize their service delivery strategies and approaches. Thomas Connolly, for example (Chapter 9), describes employment practices that include:

♦ Electronic job postings via the web

♦ Online applications forms and résumé builders

♦ Résumé scanning and online applicant tracking

♦ Online testing, etc.

The logic of network-enabling campus services is described with great variety and richness by this volume's contributors. James McKee, Sharon Kiser, and Russ Lea describe the application of web and networking technologies to the processes of sourcing research sponsors, proposal writing, reporting on research findings, and commercializing new knowledge through patents, copyrights, and licenses (Chapter 8). Robert Kvavik and Michael Handberg of the University of Minnesota (Chapter 7) and David Roselle of the University of Delaware (Chapter 1) describe how information technology and networks are being deployed at their institutions to alter the primary models of delivering key student services to ones that feature automated transactions, student self-help, ease of customer use, and one-stop shopping.

Essayist Martin Clague introduces the reader to electronic commerce in the higher education context and suggests that networks which convey $2 billion of transactions today may carry as much as $1 trillion of transactions by 2010 (Chapter 3). He describes a future of higher education in which college and university applicants will review descriptive materials over networks, will apply for admission and financial aid over the network, will select courses from electronic catalogs, and will enroll, register, and pay for their education over networks. Of course, in this highly networked future, many courses will be delivered over networks, and the vast holdings of college and university libraries will be accessed over networks. The efforts of many of the authors of this volume signify the creation of the foundational building blocks for creating new links between universities and the various stakeholders they serve.

Polley Ann McClure, John Smith, and Teresa Lockard remind us that the ever more sophisticated information technology environments that enable these kinds of institutional transformations depend on increasingly sophisticated networks of specialists who provide training, maintenance, and support for the myriad users of technology on campus (Chapter 4). These authors describe a shift from the centralized tools, techniques, and approaches that enabled campus mainframe computing to distribute models of support that will be required in highly networked and organizationally distributed environments. McClure and her colleagues advise us about the limits inherent in efforts to scale technical support in complex and heterogeneous environments. They describe a variety of strategies designed to make it possible for institutions to focus on their primary missions of learning, research, and outreach rather than wasting resources "struggling with computers, applications and networks." These strategies include:

♦ Coupling of institutional infrastructure and standards to user priorities

♦ Providing a reliable and robust infrastructure that guarantees a level of functionality

♦ Managing a distributed environment in a way that ensures all users' needs are met

McClure, Smith, and Lockard describe the environments (cultural, political, technical) that influence the type of support models that institutions should consider, the organizational and communications strategies that institutions need to develop and deploy, and an architecture for defining responsibility and authority across a support spectrum ranging from highly centralized to highly distributed.

RENEW THE COMPACT

One benefit of higher education's historical isolation has been our enjoyment of a modest insulation from broader political processes and pressures. In the days before the Morrill Act, the research university,

STAKEHOLDER	GOALS
Governors and Legislators	• Increased access • Greater fiscal efficiency
Parents	• Affordability • Jobs after graduation
Students	• Affordability • Convenience and comfort • Employability after graduation
Patients	• Life-saving innovations • Affordability • Care for the medically indigent
Federal Government	• World-class research • Inexpensive research infrastructure

FIGURE 14.1   Constituents' Goals

and the GI Bill with its mass education, the compact between the academy and its constituents was more straightforward. The inherent compact, in simpler times, implied that if elite parents sent their sons to our institutions, these men would be returned to their families prepared for citizenship in a pluralistic society. The federalization of research and financial aid, the evolution of the multiversity and the remarkable opening of the postsecondary educational enterprise to large segments of an increasingly multicultural society have altered our assumptions about the inherent compact between educational institutions and their stakeholders in fundamental ways. The changing nature of the relationship between colleges and universities and their stakeholders plays out in frequent and cacophonous calls for increased accountability. This cacophony reflects the diverse goals of constituents served by the modern college and university enterprise.

These examples are polarized to illustrate the point that higher education is increasingly pressed to achieve a number of implied and, often contradictory, stakeholder goals. To the extent that stakeholder goals are in conflict or to the extent that these goals are pursued through a variety of reporting requirements or other regulatory constraints, college and university leaders are constrained from making some of the very changes that are central to their renewal.

Many colleges and universities have recognized that the accretion of rules and regulations has fueled the growth of staff, eroding both efficiency and service. Contributor Kristine Hafner describes the efforts of the University of California (Chapter 11) to develop and implement a new approach to institutional accountability that would "demonstrate accountability by delivering consistently high degrees of productivity and service quality for fixed or decreasing cost to the university." This approach required a shift in the emphasis of this university's internal control systems from procedural controls (rules, regulations, policies) to controls that would rely on measurement and other diagnostic means (goal setting, performance evaluation, assessment). Working with IBM, this university has worked to implement an approach to managing institutional performance known as the balanced scorecard (Kaplan & Norton, 1992).

CONCLUSION

It is clear that colleges and universities are remarkable and unusual organizations. It is also clear that the durability and sustainability of these institutions derives, in part, from the ability of these institutions to adapt to changing conditions. These institutions have demonstrated a remarkable ability to serve their societies in the face of widespread social, political, and technological change.

It is most tempting (and probably correct) to conclude that most colleges and universities will survive. Many, in fact, will prosper. The dawn of the Knowledge Age places a premium on education and, in fact, on higher education and will ensure prosperity for many. It is also heartening to conclude that the destinies of our colleges and universities are in the hands of remarkably able stewards. The leaders of this enterprise, who are represented in this volume, have been quick to identify theirs as a transformation mission and to adapt changing technology and a changing work force to the goals of enhanced service, productivity, and accountability.

It is also true that colleges and universities are at risk. Change, adaptation, and renewal depend today—more than ever—on speed. Speed of action, in turn, depends on a committed leadership and on a system of governance and an institutional culture that not only accepts change, but fosters it. It is clear from the authors of this text that change in higher education will not be paced by either technology or the market, but by the internal campus processes for consensus-building on which such change depends. Leadership, governance, and culture—not infrastructure, opportunity, or threat—will determine which colleges and universities will adapt successfully to a changing environment.

Perhaps the only just conclusions are that 1) colleges and universities must change, and 2) change is very hard. If there are common threads throughout this volume, they are the threads of hard work, communication, and pragmatism. Our authors tend to eschew the language and rhetoric of change and the jargon of reengineering in favor of adapting current thinking from industry to the culture and climate of the academy. As Michael Finlayson puts it, "When a system threatens to drive processes and policies, beware!" Unless the gap between theory and practice is aired and discussed and rethought, if necessary, there will always be suspicion in the field that the central administration is up to "no good."

The learning revolution is now underway and is creating the opportunity for faculty to join their administrative colleagues in a collaborative discussion about renewing the higher education enterprise. This new opportunity provides the greatest basis for ongoing hope that colleges and universities will once again address the challenge of change and renew themselves for continued relevancy, viability, and leadership in the time to come.

REFERENCES

Cohen, M. D., & March, J. G. (1974). *Leadership and ambiguity: The American college president.* New York, NY: McGraw-Hill.

The Chronicle of Higher Education 1998–1999 Almanac Issue. (1998, August 28). *Chronicle of Higher Education, XLV* (1).

Davis, S., & Botkin, J. (1994). *The monster under the bed: How business is mastering the opportunity of knowledge for profit.* New York, NY: Simon & Schuster.

Gardner, J. W., Atwell, R. H., & Berdahl, R. O. (1985). *Cooperation and conflict: The public and private sectors in higher education.* Washington, DC: Association of Governing Boards of Universities and Colleges.

Kaplan, R. S., & Norton, D. P. (1992, January-February). The Balanced Scorecard: Measures that drive performance. *Harvard Business Review.*

Keller, G. (1983). *Academic strategy: The management revolution in higher education.* Baltimore, MD: Johns Hopkins University Press.

Kerr, C., & Gade, M. L. (1986). *The many lives of academic presidents: Place, time, and character.* Washington, DC: Association of Governing Boards.

Lee, E. C., & Bowen, F. M. (1975). *Managing multicampus systems: Effective administration in an unsteady state.* San Francisco, CA: Jossey-Bass.

Massy, W. F. (1997). Life on the wired campus: How information technology will shape institutional futures. In D. G. Oblinger & S. C. Rush (Eds.), *The learning revolution: The challenge of information technology in the academy.* Bolton, MA: Anker.

Selingo, J. (1998, October 23). University of Phoenix picks New Jersey for its first foray in eastern US. *Chronicle of Higher Education, XLV* (9), A28.

Tomlinson, R. (1998, July 6). The China that Clinton won't see. *Fortune,* 132.

REFERENCES

Access America. (1997). *National performance review.* (US) PRVP 42.2:AC 2. [0556-C]. Government Information Technology Services Board. [http://gits.gov/htm/access.htm.]

Alspaugh, G., & Voss, B. (1998, April 14). Correspondence.

Bakos, Y. J., & Brynjolfsson, E. (1993, Fall). Information technology, incentives, and the optimal number of suppliers. *Journal of Management Information Systems, 10* (2), 37–53.

Barbett, S., & Korb, R. A. (1997, July). *Current funds revenues and expenditures of institutions of higher education: Fiscal years 1987 through 1995.* Washington, DC: US Department of Education, National Center for Education Statistics.

Battin, P., & Hawkins, B. L. (1998). *The mirage of continuity: Reconfiguring academic information resources in the 21st century.* Washington, DC: Council on Library and Information Resources and the Association of American Universities.

Benjamin, R., & Carroll, S. J. (1996). The implication of the changed environment for governance in higher education. In W. Tierney (Ed.), *The responsive university: Restructuring for performance,* 92–119. Baltimore, MD: Johns Hopkins University Press.

Bensaou, M., & Venkatraman, N. (1995). Configurations of interorganizational relationships: A comparison between US and Japanese automakers. *Management Science, 41* (9), 1471–1492.

Caspa, H. (1997, Winter). The price of higher education. *NCURA Research Management Review, 9* (2), 29–32.

The Chronicle of Higher Education 1998–1999 Almanac Issue. (1998, August 28). *Chronicle of Higher Education, XLV* (1).

Cohen, M. D., & March, J. G. (1974). *Leadership and ambiguity: The American college president.* New York, NY: McGraw-Hill.

315

The College Board. (1997, September). *Trends in student aid.* New York, NY: The College Board.

Colleges of the Fenway. (1996, March). *Principles of collaboration.* Boston, MA: Colleges of the Fenway.

Committee on Science, Engineering, and Public Policy (CSEPP). (1993). *Science, technology, and the federal government: National goals for a new era.* Washington, DC: National Academy of Sciences.

Connolly, T. R. (1995). *Human resources capabilities change management plan.* Unpublished, p. 8.

Connolly, T. R. (1997, June). Transforming human resources. *Management Review,* 10–16.

Connolly, T. R., & Mastranunzio, J. (1995). *Global challenges require new HR capabilities.* Unpublished.

Davenport, T. H., De Long, D. W., & Beers, M. C. (1998, Winter). Successful knowledge management projects. *Sloan Management Review,* 43–57.

Davenport, T. H., Jarvenpaa, S. L., & Beers, M. C. (1996, Summer). Managing and improving knowledge work processes. *Sloan Management Review, 38,* 53–65.

Davis, S., & Botkin, J. (1994). *The monster under the bed: How business is mastering the opportunity of knowledge for profit.* New York, NY: Simon & Schuster.

Denton, J., & Hunter, F. A. (1997, Spring). The multiple effects of influencing external funding productivity. *NCURA Research Management Review, 9* (1), 37–50.

Dolence, M. G., & Norris, D. M. (1995). *Transforming higher education: A vision for learning in the 21st century.* Ann Arbor, MI: Society for College and University Planning.

Drucker, P. (1995). *Managing in a time of great change.* Dutton, NY: Truman Talley Books.

Dyer, J. H. (1996). Does governance matter? Keiretsu alliances and asset specificity as sources of Japanese competitive advantage. *Organization Science, 7* (6), 649–666.

The Economist. (1996, October). *The Economist Review,* 5.

Eleey, M. (1993, Fall). Managing to change: The Wharton School's distributed staff model for computing support. *Cause/Effect, 16* (3), 53–55.

Gambetta, D. (1994). *Trust: Making and breaking cooperative relations.* London, England: Basil Blackwell.

Gardner, J. W. (1963). *Self-renewal: The individual and the innovative society.* New York, NY: Harper & Row.

Gardner, J. W., Atwell, R. H., & Berdahl, R. O. (1985). *Cooperation and conflict: The public and private sectors in higher education.* Washington, DC: Association of Governing Boards of Universities and Colleges.

Glazer, R. (1990). Marketing in an information intensive environment: Strategic implications of knowledge as an asset. *Marketing Sciences Institute,* Working Paper.

Gleason, B. W. (1997, December 8). *Campus of the future draft reports.* Boston College. Unpublished.

Gore, A. (1997). Introduction. In *Access America.* (1997). *National performance review.* (US) PRVP 42.2:AC 2. [0556-C]. Washington, DC: Government Information Technology Services Board. [http://gits.gov/htm/intro.htm.]

Government-University-Industry Research Roundtable (GUIRR). (1986). *New alliances and partnerships in American science and engineering.* Washington, DC: National Academy Press.

Government-University-Industry Research Roundtable (GUIRR). (1994). *Stresses on research and education at colleges and universities: Institutional and sponsoring agency responses.* Washington, DC: National Academy Press.

Grant, G. E. (1997, Spring) Is this your research administration? *SRA Journal, 28* (3&4), 35–37.

Gunston, D. H., & Keniston, K. (Eds.). (1994). *The fragile contract: University science and the federal government.* Cambridge, MA: MIT Press.

Hammer, M., & Champy, J. (1993). *Reengineering the corporation: A manifesto for business revolution.* New York, NY: HarperCollins.

Henderson, J. C. (1990, Winter). Plugging into strategic partnerships: The IS-line connection. *Sloan Management Review.*

Henderson, R. M., & Clark, K. B. (1990). Architectural innovation: The reconfiguration of existing product technologies and the failure of established firms. *Administrative Science Quarterly, 35,* 9–30.

Higher Education Research Institute. (1997, January 1). *Academic and political engagement among nation's college freshman is at all-time low, UCLA Study Finds.* Washington, DC: Higher Education Research Institute.

Horowitz, F. D. (1997, Winter). For want of a crystal ball. *NCURA Research Management Review, 9* (2), 33–39.

Jonas, S., Katz, R. N., Martinson, L., Plympton, M. F., Relyea, S. W., Rennie, E. D., Rudy, J. A., & Walsh, J. F. (1997). *Campus financial systems for the future.* Washington, DC: National Association of College and University Business Officers and CAUSE. [http://www.cause.org/pub/fis/ch1/1b.html.]

Kaganoff, T. (1998). *Collaboration technology and outsourcing initiatives in higher education: A literature review.* Rand Education report prepared for Foundation for Independent Higher Education.

Kaplan, R. S., & Norton, D. P. (1992, January-February). The balanced scorecard: Measures that drive performance. *Harvard Business Review.*

Kaplan, R. S., & Norton, D. P. (1993, September/October). Putting the balanced scorecard to work. *Harvard Business Review.*

Kaplan, R. S., & Norton, D. P. (1996, January/February). Using the balanced scorecard as a strategic management system. *Harvard Business Review.*

Kaufman, J. (1997, February 4). Generation Y. *Wall Street Journal,* 1 ff.

Kava, P. (1998, March 11–13). Presentation handouts at the ACM SIGUCCS Computer Services Management Symposium 25.

Keller, G. (1983). *Academic strategy: The management revolution in higher education.* Baltimore, MD: Johns Hopkins University Press.

Kerr, C., & Gade, M. L. (1986). *The many lives of academic presidents: Place, time, and character.* Washington, DC: Association of Governing Boards.

Kogut, B., & Zander, U. (1992, August). Knowledge of the firm, combinative capabilities, and the replication of technology. *Organization Science, 3* (3), 383–397.

Kotter, J. P. (1995, March-April). Leading change: Why transformation efforts fail. *Harvard Business Review.*

Kotter, J. P. (1996). *Leading change.* Boston, MA: Harvard Business School Press.

Lane, N. (1996). *Science and engineering indicators.* NSF report. Washington, DC: National Science Foundation. [http://www.nsf.gov/sbe/srs/seind96/ovquotes.htm.]

Langenberg, D. N. (1997, Winter). The past as prologue: What the future holds for research universities. *NCURA Research Management Review, 9* (2), 41–46.

Larsen, E. (1997, March 17). Why colleges cost too much. *Time,* 46–55.

Lasper, G. (1994, October 18). *Statement on resolution of outstanding disputes between Stanford and the government on indirect cost issues.* Palo Alto, CA: Stanford University.

Lee, E. C., & Bowen, F. M. (1975). *Managing multicampus systems: Effective administration in an unsteady state.* San Francisco, CA: Jossey-Bass.

Massy, W. F. (1997). Life on the wired campus: How information technology will shape institutional futures. In D. G. Oblinger & S. C. Rush (Eds.), *The learning revolution: The challenge of information technology in the academy.* Bolton, MA: Anker.

McClure, P. A., Smith, J. W., & Sitko, T. D. (1997). The crisis in information technology support: Has our current model reached its limit? *CAUSE Professional Paper Series, 16.*

Monteverde, K. (1995). Technical dialog as an incentive for vertical integration in the semiconductor industry. *Management Science, 41* (10), 1624–1638.

Monteverde, K., & Teece, D. J. (1982). Appropriable rents and quasi-vertical integration. *Journal of Law and Economics, 25,* 321–328.

Moore, G. A. (1991). *Crossing the chasm: Marketing and selling high-tech products to mainstream customers.* New York, NY: Harper Business Press.

National Academy of Sciences, Committee on Science, Engineering, and Public Policy. (1996). *An assessment of the National Science Foundation's science and technology centers program.* Washington, DC: National Academy of Sciences.

National Institutes of Health. (1997, May). *NIH era and reinvention status report.* Washington, DC: National Institutes of Health. [http://www.nih.gov/grants/reinvention/statusreport0597.htm#I.]

National Science Foundation. (1996). *1996 research and development indicators.* Washington, DC: National Science Foundation.

Nonaka, I., & Takeuchi, H. (1995). *The knowledge creating company: How Japanese companies create the dynamics of innovation.* New York, NY: Oxford University Press.

Pirrong, S. (1993). Contracting practices in bulk shipping markets: A transactions cost explanation. *Journal of Law and Economics, 36,* 937–976.

Powell, W. W. (1990). Neither market nor hierarchy: Networks forms of organization. In L. L. Cummings and B. Staw (Eds.), *Research in organization behavior.* Greenwich, CT: JAI Press, 295–336b.

Quinn, J. B. (1992). *Intelligent enterprise.* New York, NY: Free Press.

Relyea, S. W. (1998, June). From gutter balls to strikes: UCSD's balanced scorecard program. *NACUBO Business Officer.*

Rosovsky, H. (1990). *The university: An owner's manual.* New York, NY: Norton.

Rush, S. (1994). Benchmarking: How good is good? *Measuring institutional performance in higher education*. Princeton, NJ: Peterson's Guides.

Selingo, J. (1998, October 23). University of Phoenix picks New Jersey for its first foray in eastern US. *Chronicle of Higher Education, XLV* (9), A28.

Smith, J. W. (1990, September). *The interaction of technology, economics, and culture as a basis for understanding academic computing support needs*. ACM SIGUCCS User Services Conference 18.

Smith, J. W. (1994, October). *User's guide for shadowy crystal ball: Practical tips and techniques for planning the future*. ACM SIGUCCS User Services Conference 22.

Smith, J. W. (1997, December 5). *A whole-product approach to standards*. CAUSE annual conference.

Tomlinson, R. (1998, July 6). The China that Clinton won't see. *Fortune*, 132.

Ulrich, D. (1998, January/February). A new mandate for human resources. *Harvard University Business Review, 76* (1), 124–134.

University of California Office of the President. (1996). *UC means business: The economic impact of the University of California*. Oakland, CA: University of California Regents.

University of Virginia. (1997). *Data digest*. Charlottesville, VA: University of Virginia.

Venkatraman, N. (Spring 1997). Beyond outsourcing: Managing IT resources as a value center. *Sloan Management Review, 38*, 51–64.

Venkatraman, N., & Zaheer, A. (1994). Electronic integration and strategic advantage: A quasi-experimental study in the insurance industry. *Information Systems Research, 1* (4).

Waugaman, P. (1998, April 6). *Down the slippery slope: When faculty get involved in technology commercialization*. Technology Transfer and Management, Inc. Biloxi, MS: SRA Southern Section Meeting.

Werner, J. (1997, October 7). *Ben Franklin Partnership Program: Leveraging state and federal research and technology incentive programs.* Presentation to the Society of Research Administrators. Atlanta, GA.

Williamson, O. (1979). Transaction cost economics: The governance of contractual relations. *Journal of Law and Economics, 22,* 233.

Williamson, O. (1994). Transaction cost economics and organization theory. In N. J. Smelser & R. Swedberg (Eds.), *The handbook of economic sociology* (1st. ed.), 77–107. Princeton, NJ: Princeton University Press.

Winston, G. (1997, May 1). Long lines about the best colleges are likely to get longer. *The New York Times,* D2.

Woodrow, R. J. (1998). *Management for research in US universities.* Washington, DC: NACUBO.

INDEX

Ace Hardware, 57
Activmedia, 59
Administration project, 20-41
  and the Administrative
    Management System (AMS), 38
  and financial information systems
    (FIS), 30-31, 33
  Human Resources Information
    System (HRIS), 20, 31, 33
Administrative Management System
    (AMS), 38
  four modules of, 40
Advance Technology Program (ATP),
    168
Advisor, vs. partner, 197
Agora, 218-242
  features of, 225-233
  journey, 240-242
  just-in-time-information, 233-240
  origins of, 219-224
  process flow, 226
  sample checklist, 232
AIDS Treatment News, 55
Albright, R., 15
Alspaugh, G., 84, 86, 98, 315
American National Standards Institute
    (ANSI), 184
  electronic data interchange stan-
    dard, 184, 185
Amgen, 170
Andrews, D., 13
ARAMARK, 108
Arce, G. R., 15
Arpanet, 6
Asset-specific relationships, 102
Atwell, R. H., 306, 313, 317

BAAN, 110
Bakken, M., 137

Bakos, Y. J., 100, 123, 315
Barbett, S., 188, 315
Bason, C., 14
Battin, P., 315
Beers, M. C., 102, 123, 316
Benefits, and human resources, 215
Ben Franklin Program, 171
Benjamin, R., 99, 123, 315
Bensaou, M., 123, 315
Berdahl, R. O., 306, 313, 317
The Boston Business Journal, 126
Boston College, 212, 218-242
Botkin, J., 303, 313, 316
Bowen, F. M., 305, 314, 319
Brase, W. C., 265, 307
Brockmann, J. R., 13, 18
Brookstone, 49, 50
Brynjolfsson, E., 100, 123, 315
Brynteson, S., 8
Burroughs, 5, 6
Business Communication Quarterly, 13
Business Index ASAP, 8

California, Davis, University of (UCD),
    87-90, 96, 97, 257
  technical support program, 88-90
California, Irvine, University of, 307
  Center for Statistical Consulting,
    272
  Model for Sustaining
    Administrative Improvement,
    267-271, 280,   281
California, San Diego, University of
    (UCSD), 214, 257, 258
California, University of (UC), 21, 170,
    190, 245-264, 311
  creating a performance measure-
    ment culture, 256-257
  the future, 248-253

performance architecture, 246-248
and performance management, 259-264
using the balanced scorecard, 257-259
vision and departmental strategy, 255-256
vision and strategy, 253-255
California at Los Angeles, University of (UCLA), 22, 177
California State University (CSU), 112
California Virtual University, 59-61
Cal Tech, 260
Campus of the future; *See* Agora
Carper, T. R., 14-15
Carroll, S. J., 99, 123, 315
Caspa, H., 188, 315
CAUSE Award for Best Practices in Higher Education Information Resources, 12, 267
CAUSE Award for Excellence in Campus Networking, 5, 6
Centralized model of support, 63
Cerf, V., 15
Certified Research Administrator, 186
Champy, J., 189, 318
The Changing Times, 37
Cheever, D., 137
Chicago, University of, 216
Chiron Corporation, 170
The Chronicle of Higher Education, 126
The Chronicle of Higher Education 1998-1999 Almanac Issue, 305
Clague, M. C., 45, 309
Claremont Colleges, 133
Clark, K. B., 102, 118, 124, 318
Cohen, M. D., 306, 313, 315
The College Board, 291
The Colleges of the Fenway, 126-138
administrative collaboration, 134-137
collaboration principles, 128-133
presidential leadership, 137-138
two year collaboration results, 133-134
Columbia University, 213

Committee on Science, Engineering, and Public Policy (CSEPP), 162, 168, 173, 188
Compensation, and human resources, 215
Computer Architecture and Parallel Systems Laboratory (CAPSL), 15
Computer Select, 86
Connolly, T. R., 191, 196, 198, 201, 205, 211, 307, 309, 316
Consolidated Omnibus Budget Reconciliation Act (COBRA), 215
Consumer Reports, 53
Cornell University, 162, 212, 215, 216
Cross-campus reengineering, 161-162

Davenport, T. H., 102, 123, 316
Davies, B., 21, 22, 23, 30, 31, 32, 33, 37, 41
Davis, S., 303, 313, 316
Davis Educational Foundation, 131, 134
Decentralized model of support, 64
Dedicated asset specificity, 102
Delaware, University of, 3-19, 309
CAUSE Award for Best Practices in Higher Education Information Resources, 12
CAUSE Award for Excellence in Campus Networking, 5
Hugh R. Sharp campus, 5
living and learning environment, 11-16
Newark campus, 5
"one-stop shopping", 10-11
the paperless campus, 7-9
Responsible Computing Awareness Program, 12
technology installation, 5-7
DELCAT, 8
De Long, D. W., 123, 316
de Lorenzo, D. M., 5
Denton, J., 188, 316
Diehl, L., 11
DiMartile, J. V., 10
Dimond, J., 41
Distributed Computing Support, 62-98
design considerations, 74-83

environmental considerations, 67-71
program examples, 83-96
reasons for, 64-66
responsibility and authority, 73-74
support topology, 71-73
Distributed model of support, 64
Distributed Support Assistant Program, 85
Distributed Support Assistants; *See* DSAs
Dolence, M. G., 141, 142, 154, 316
Drucker, P., 194, 211, 316
DSAs, 85
Duke University, 212, 215
Dyer, J. H., 124, 316

e-Business, 45-61
launching a web-based business, 58-59
and technology, 46-47
vs. e-commerce, 47-58
The Economist, 300
EDUCAUSE, 199
Eisner, Sister Janet, 126
Electronic Commerce Committee, 184
Electronic Community Citizenship Examination (ECCE), 12
Electronic Research Administration (ERA), 182-185, 183
Eleey, M., 96, 98, 317
Emmanuel College, 126, 127
Employee data, and human resources, 216
Employee relations, and human resources, 212
England, M., 40, 41
Expertise dominant relationships (ExpD), 103, 104, 116-118
and higher education, 107-108
and information technology, 108-109
and retail, 107
and trust, 120
Expertise specificity, 103
Extranets, 57

The Farmers' Almanac, 261

Federal Demonstration Project (FDP), 165, 166
Fidelity Corporation, 134
Finlayson, A., 41
Finlayson, M., 20, 33, 305, 307
Five Colleges, Inc., 133
Fleming, W. J., 218
Fortune, 302
Foster, S. J., 6, 15
Fujitsu Limited, 112

Gade, M. L., 314, 319
Gambetta, D., 119, 124, 317
Gao, G. R., 15
Gardner, J. W., 306, 313, 317
Genentech, 170
Glazer, J. H., 102
Glazer, R., 124, 317
Gleason, B. W., 218, 219, 242, 317
Gore, A., 15, 188, 317
Government Performance and Results Act, 183
Government-University-Industry Research Roundtable (GUIRR), 157, 160, 173, 189
New Alliances report, 170
Grant, G. E., 189, 317
Grant Application and Management System (GAMS), 180-181
Grim, D. J., 6
GTE Corporation, 112
Gunston, D. H., 157, 162, 163, 164, 189, 317

Hafner, K. A., 245, 311
Hammer, M., 189, 318
Handberg, M. N., 139, 306, 309
Handley, C., 36
Haphazard model of support, 64, 66
Harvard Business Review, 249, 295
Harvard Business School, 295
Harvard University, 213, 215, 216, 217
Hawkins, B. L., 315
Henderson, J. C., 99, 124, 318
Henderson, R. M., 102, 118, 124, 318
Hierarchy governance structure, 101
Higher education, 288-300
forces for change, 288-291

mandate for institutional change, 292-
  300
Higher Education Research Institute,
  291
Hofstetter, F. T., 17
Hollowell, D., 5, 7
Horowitz, F. D., 189, 318
Hughes Space and Communications,
  112
Human resources, 191-211
  best practices, 199-201, 212-217
  changing roles, 201-205
  evolution of, 196-199
  functions in partnership model, 204
  implementation, 207-209
  information technology (HRIT),
    205, 206
  or vision, 205-207
  process, 200
Human Resources Information System
  (HRIS), 20, 31, 33
Hunter, F. A., 188, 316
Hybrid governance structure, 101

IAC Expanded Academic Index
  ASAP, 8
IBM, 5, 112, 136, 137, 149-150, 248, 312
Illinois, University of, 212, 214
INCONGRESS, 55
Indiana University, 84-87, 96, 97
  distributed support program, 84-86
Information technology (IT), 62, 100,
  101
  and collaborative environments,
    135-137
  and expertise dominant relation-
    ships, 108-109
  and human resources, 205, 206
  and market exchange relationships,
    106-107
  and process dominant relation-
    ships, 110
  and relationships, 120-122
  and strategic relationships, 112-113
Institute for Transforming
  Undergraduate Education
  (ITUE), 17
Internet, 6, 45, 223, 291, 294

Internet-based business, 46
  delivering distance education, 56
  distributing information, 54-56
  extending market reach, 53-54
  managing business partners, 57
  promoting brand awareness, 52-53
  selling goods and services, 48-50
Intranet principles, 222-224
ISO 9000 standards, 105
Itelliquest, 59

Jacobson, C. W., 10
Jarvenpaa, S. L., 102, 123
John Deere, 105
Johns Hopkins University, 216
Jonas, S., 189, 318
JVC, 171

Kaganoff, T., 99, 124, 318
Kaplan, R., 248, 249, 250
Kaplan, R. S., 264, 312, 314, 318
Katz, R. N., 189, 318
Kaufman, J., 291, 301, 318
Kava, P., 89, 98, 318
Keller, G., 305, 314, 319
Kelly, N., 34-37
Keniston, K., 157, 162, 163, 164, 189,
  317
Kerr, C., 314, 319
Kiser, S. L., 155, 307, 309
Kogut, B., 105, 124, 319
Korb, R. A., 188, 315
Kotter, J. P., 295, 301, 319
Kozmo.com, Inc., 58
KPMG Peat Marwick, 34
Kruger, K., 13
Kvavik, R. B., 139, 306, 309

Land, E., 207
Land's End, 49
Lane, N., 187, 189, 319
Langenberg, D. N., 189, 319
Larsen, E., 291, 301, 319
Lasper, G., 164, 189, 319
Lea, Russ, 155, 307, 309
*Leading Change: Why Transformation
  Efforts Fail*, 295
Lee, E. C., 305, 314, 319

Levi Strauss & Co., 53
Lockard, T. W., 62, 310
Lynch, T. G., 18
Lyons Studio, 13

Management and organizational patterns, survey of, 283-287
Management framework, integrated elements, 194
March, J. G., 306, 313, 315
Market exchange relationships (Mkt), 103, 104
  and higher education, 106
  and information technology (IT), 106-107
  and retail, 104-106
Market governance structure, 101
Martinson, L., 189, 318
Massachusetts College of Pharmacy and Allied Health Sciences, 126-138
Massachusetts Institute of Technology (MIT), 212, 213, 214, 215, 216, 217
Massy, W. F., 303, 314, 319
Mastranunzio, J., 201, 211, 316
McClure, P. ., 62, 83, 98, 310, 319
McKee, James P., 155, 307, 309
McKinsey and Company, 23, 32
Medical, Academic, and Scientific Community Organization (MASCO), 133, 134
Menino, T., 126-127
Mercedes-Benz, 171
Miami, University of, 213, 214, 215, 216
Michigan, University of, 198, 212
Microsoft, 112
Microsoft TechNet, 86
Mills, D. Q., 288
Mills, D. L., 15
Minnesota, University of, 112, 139, 142-150, 164, 215, 216, 306, 309
  developing new vision, 144-150
  partnering for success, 149-150
  Models of support, 63-64, 66
Monahan, C., 137
Money, 9
Monterrey Tech System, 56

Monteverde, K., 102, 124, 320
Moore, G. A., 69, 74, 98, 320
Morrill Act, 310
Morris, C., 11
Murray, G., 41

National Academy of Sciences, 173
National Association of College & University Business Officers, 267
National Council of University Research Administrators (NCURA), 186
National Council on Programs in Technical and Scientific Communication, 13
National Institute of Health (NIH), 159, 163, 166, 183, 184, 185, 189, 190
National Science Foundation, 17, 157, 159, 161, 167, 168, 169, 173, 182, 83, 184
  FASTLANE project, 165, 185
  Presidential Early Career Award for Scientists and Engineers, 14
National Textile Center (NTC), 174, 175
New York University, 164
Nichols, R., 13
Nonaka, I., 102, 124, 320
Norris, D. M., 141, 142, 154, 316
North Carolina State University (NCSU), 162, 171, 174, 180, 181
Northern Arizona, University of, 215
Northwestern University, 212, 215, 216
Norton, D. P., 248, 249, 250, 264, 312, 314, 318
Notre Dame de Namur, Sisters of, 127
Novell Support Connection, 86
Nua, Ltd., 59

Office Depot, 57
Oganizational structure, in human resources, 216-217
Ohio State University, 162, 215, 216
1-800-Batteries, 52
Ontario Institute for Studies in Education, 36
Oracle, 183, 199

Partner, vs. advisor, 197
Partnership for Performance, 245-264
Partnership model, 202
  human resource functions in, 204
Partners in Computing Support (PICS)
    program, 84-85, 86, 87
Patent Amendment Act of 1980, 168
Payroll, and human resources, 215-216
Pennsylvania, University of, 180, 214,
    215, 216, 291
Pennsylvania State University, 212,
    213, 214, 215, 216
PeopleSoft, 110, 183, 199
Performance assessment, and human
    resources, 214
Performance contract, 108, 120, 121
Phoenix, University of, 303
  Online College, 292
Physical asset specificity, 101
Pinholster, G., 3
Pirrong, S., 102, 124, 320
Plympton, M. F., 189, 318
Polaroid, 207
Powell, W. W., 101, 124, 320
Pricewaterhouse Coopers, 144
Prichard, R., 21, 22, 39, 307
Princeton University, 215, 216, 217
Pritchard, M. V., 17
Process dominant relationships
    (ProcD), 103, 104, 113, 116-118
  and higher education, 110
  and information technology, 110
  and retail, 109-110
  and trust, 120
Process improvement, 265-282
  Irvine Management Change Model,
    267-271
  naive side of, 265-267
  Supervisory Effectiveness Model,
    272-281
  sustainable improvement, 281-282
  teamwork and cooperation,
    271-272
Process specificity, 103
Proctor and Gamble, 119
Provider/consumer relationships
  attributes of, 113-115
  management processes in, 114

  managing a portfolio, 115-122
  theoretical perspectives on, 101-113
Pumo, J. M., 288
Purchase order with check (POWC)
    program, 7
Purchasing card, 8
Purdue University, 84

Quinn, J. B., 103, 125, 320

Reedy, C., 16
Relationship-specific assets, 101
Relyea, S. W., 189, 259, 264, 318, 320
Renewal, 302-313
  of the compact, 310-312
  culture, organization, and human
    resources, 307-308
  information technologies, resources,
    and services, 308-310
  institutional leadership and gover-
    nance, 305-307
Rennie, E. D., 189, 318
Research administration, 155-188
  defined, 156
  electronic research administration,
    182-185
  in nonacademic hybrid organiza-
    tions, 172-181
  profession of generalists,
    186-187
  transformation, 166-172
  understanding, 156-158
  and university competitive goals,
    159-166
Research Administrators Certification
    Council, 186
Research Process Managers (RPMs),
    179, 180
Roselle, D. P., 3, 306, 309
Rosovsky, H., 210, 211, 320
Royal Bank of Canada, 33
Rudy, J. A., 189, 318
Rush, S., 247, 264, 321
Rylee, C., 9

Salaway, G., 22
Saniga, E., 14
SAP, 110

Science and Technology Centers
(STCs), 173
SCT, 183
Selection and hiring, and human
resources, 212-213
Selingo, J., 305, 314, 321
Service function responsibilities, 203
Seton Hall University, 214
Simmons College, 126-138
Site specificity, and assets, 101-102
Sitko, T. D., 83, 98, 319
Small Business Innovation
Development Act, 170
Small Business Innovation Research
(SBIR) Program, 170, 171
Smith, J. W., 62, 68, 76, 83, 98, 310, 319,
321
Society for Technical Communication,
13
Society of Research Administrators
(SRA), 186
Southern California, University of
(USC), 260
Special relationship, 120, 121-122
Stanford University, 164, 212, 215, 216,
260
Strategic alliance; *See* Strategic rela-
tionships (Strat)
Strategic relationships (Strat), 103, 104,
110, 118-119
and higher education, 111
and information technology, 112-113
and retail, 111
and trust, 120
Student services, 139-154
and change, 140-142
transformation at the University of
Minnesota, 142-150
transformation impace, 150
transforming, 140
vision implementation, 150-153
Subramani, M. R., 99

T. Rowe Price Associates Inc., 291
Takeuchi, H., 102, 124, 320
TCP/IP, 46
Technical Support Coordinators; *See*
TSCs

Technological transformation, 3-19
installation, 5-7
learning experiences, 16-18
living and learning improvement,
11-16
the paperless campus, 7-9
and student learning, 10-11
Technology-enabled processes, and
process-centered design, 195
Technology Reinvestment Project
(TRP), 168
Teece, D. J., 124, 320
Temporal asset specificity, 102
Texas, University of, 213
Thomas Jefferson University, 164
360 degree feedback, and human
resources, 214-215
Tomlinson, R., 302, 314, 321
Toronto, University of, 20-41, 307
Training, and human resources, 213-
214
Transactional exchange, 104, 120-121
Transactional trust, 119
Transaction cost economics
(TCE), 101
Trust, in relationships, 119-120
TSCs, 88-90

U-Discover, 8
Ulrich, D., 198, 211, 321
Unisys, 5
United States Department of Energy,
248, 257
United States Department of the
Treasury, 165
United States Internal Revenue Service
(IRS), 264
USA Today, 267
US Electronic Grant Project, 165, 185
US Office of Naval Research, 14
Universal Learning, 292
Universities of Cambridge and Oxford,
133
The University: An Owner's Manual
(Rosovsky), 210
University Information Technology
Services (UITS), 84, 85
US News and World Report, 9

Value creation and appropriation, 115-
    119
van der Weide, D. W., 14
Van Domelen, J., 137
Venkatraman, N., 102, 103, 123, 125,
    315, 321
Vermont, University of, 214, 216
Virginia Polytechnic Institute and State
    University, 180
Virginia, University of (UVA), 90-94,
    96, 97, 161
    Departmental Computing Support
        program, 91-94
Voss, B., 84, 86, 98, 315

Wal-Mart, 119
Walsh, J. F., 189, 318
Walueff, G. S., 7
Watson, G. H., 4, 5, 17
Waugaman, P., 161, 190, 321
Wentworth Institute of Technology,
    126-138

Werner, J., 171, 190, 322
Wesleyan University, 216
Wharton School, University of
    Pennsylvania, 94-96, 97
    distributed program structure, 95-
        96
Wheelock College, 126-138
White, H. B., II, 16
Williamson, O., 101, 102, 125, 322
Windley, T., 10
Winston, G., 291, 301, 322
Wolferman's, 54
Woodrow, R. J., 190, 322
World Wide Web (WWW), 46, 185, 309

Yahoo! Internet Life, 5

Zaheer, A., 102, 125, 321
Zander, U., 105, 124, 319